Power and the People

Power and the People

A History of British Energy

Arthur Downing

VERSO
London • New York

First published by Verso 2026

The manufacturer's authorized representative in the EU
for product safety (GPSR) is LOGOS EUROPE, 9 rue
Nicolas Poussin, 17000, La Rochelle, France
contact@logoseurope.eu

1 3 5 7 9 10 8 6 4 2

Verso
UK: 6 Meard Street, London W1F 0EG
US: 207 East 32nd Street, New York, NY 10016
versobooks.com

Verso is the imprint of New Left Books

ISBN-13: 978-1-83674-100-8
ISBN-13: 978-1-83674-102-2 (UK EBK)
ISBN-13: 978-1-83674-103-9 (US EBK)

British Library Cataloguing in Publication Data
A catalogue record for this book is available from the British Library

Library of Congress Cataloging-in-Publication Data
A catalog record for this book is available from the Library of Congress

Typeset in Sabon by Biblichor Ltd, Scotland
Printed and bound by CPI Group (UK) Ltd, Croydon CR0 4YY

For Rachel, Eden and Ada

Contents

We may never, this side of death, drive the invader out of our territory, but we must be in the Resistance . . . And this, so far as I can yet see, must be begun again every day. Our morning prayer should be that in the Imitation: Da hodie perfecte incipere – *grant me to make an unflawed beginning today, for I have done nothing yet.*

– C. S. Lewis, 'A Slip of the Tongue',
The Weight of Glory, 1956

There comes a time in the history of a nation when he who tinkers is lost.

– William Jowett, paymaster general, 1942

The Central Electricity Generating Board is owned by the people of England and Wales, and they have to supply our capital requirements.

– Christopher Hinton, chairman of the Central
Electricity Generating Board, 1960

Acknowledgements

I decided I wanted to write a book about the history of energy in Britain after a tour around a National Grid substation in St John's Wood a few years ago. My guide on that trip was James Watson, a man with an encyclopaedic knowledge of the electricity system and its history. I have come to realise that James is the model of an engineer-as-steward, both of the physical infrastructure built by past generations and of their stories. I am grateful to James for sharing his thoughts and research over the years.

Grace Blakeley, Brett Christophers, Cecilia Heyes, James Meek and Luke Sherlock offered me much-needed advice and help as I tried to get this book off the ground. I am indebted to many colleagues, past and present, who have patiently engaged with me about my ideas: Maurice Berns, Clementine Cowton, Max Forshaw, Andy Hackett, Tim Heal, Martin Hoegel, Hamish Lazell and Jake Tudge. A special thank you to Jack Richardson, Bas Sudmeijer and Nako Thompson for reading drafts of various chapters.

I am also grateful to the small army of energy-history enthusiasts in the industry who have shared stories and materials with me. There are too many to list in full, but in particular: Tony Ballance, Adam Bell, Kingsmill Bond, Robert Boswall, Tony Curzon Price, Joe Perkins, Nick Speechley and Russell Thomas.

I feel extremely lucky to have met Mathew Lawrence early in the writing process. He introduced me to a community of like-minded thinkers and activists: Donal Brown, Gareth Fearn, Stephen Hall, Chris Hayes, Sandeep Vaheesan.

I am not an academic, but I have found the world of academia to be extremely open and welcoming. Many scholars responded to my random emails and shared insights, read drafts and invited me to seminars: Elizabeth Chatterjee, Marianna Dudley, Roger Fouquet, Jean-Baptiste Fressoz, Ewan Gibbs, Leslie Hannah, Katrina Navickas, Jim Tomlinson, John Vickers, Séveric Yersin. Kate Bayliss, Gwyn Bevan and Abby Innes helped me to understand how my research fit into broader debates about the crisis in Britain's political economy.

I am particularly grateful to Martin Chick, David Edgerton, Dieter Helm and Avner Offer for providing detailed comments on the entire manuscript.

Thank you to Leo Hollis at Verso for guiding me through the process.

Thank you to my parents, Sylvia and Mick, who read every word. Your eye for detail, sense of humour and unwavering support have made writing a joy. I love you. Any faults or errors in this book of course remain mine alone.

Finally, and most importantly, I want to thank my family. This book would not have been possible without the intellect, patience and love of my wife, Rachel. You selflessly gave me the time and space to write and for that I am eternally grateful. At numerous critical moments in the process, you helped turn my wandering thoughts into something coherent. This book is dedicated to you and our children, Eden and Ada, in the hope it can play a small role in building a new energy system that truly serves future generations of British citizens.

Abbreviations

AC	alternating current
AGR	Advanced Gas-Cooled Reactor
BEA	British Electricity Authority
BECCS	bioenergy with carbon capture and storage
CapEx	capital expenditure
CCC	Climate Change Committee
CCGT	combined-cycle gas turbine
CCS	carbon capture and storage
CEB	Central Electricity Board
CEGB	Central Electricity Generating Board
CfD	contract for difference
CMA	Competition and Markets Authority
DC	direct current
DESNZ	Department for Energy Security and Net Zero
EDF	Électricité de France
EMR	Electricity Market Reform
EPR	European pressurised water reactor
FES	Future Energy Scenarios
GLCC	Gas Light and Coke Company
GOAL	Generator Ordering and Loading (CEGB power-station dispatch model)
GW	gigawatt
GWh	gigawatt hour
IAM	integrated assessment model
IEA	Institute of Economic Affairs
IPCC	Intergovernmental Panel on Climate Change
IPPR	Institute for Public Policy Research

kWh	kilowatt hour
LCOE	levelised cost of electricity
LNG	liquified natural gas
MMC	Monopolies and Mergers Commission
MW	megawatt
MWh	megawatt hour
NESCo	North Eastern Electric Supply Company
NESO	National Energy System Operator
NETA	New Electricity Trading Arrangements
NSHEB	North of Scotland Hydro-Electric Board
Offer	Office of Electricity Regulation
Ofgas	Office of Gas Supply
Ofgem	Office of Gas and Electricity Markets
PWR	pressurised water reactor
REC	regional electricity company
REMA	Review of Electricity Market Arrangements
RESP	regional energy strategic planner
RIIO	Revenue = Incentives + Innovation + Outputs
RPI-X	retail price index minus an X factor
SSE	Scottish and Southern Energy
TFP	total factor productivity
TWh	terawatt hour

Introduction

Every day the climate crisis intensifies, with storms and temperature anomalies relentlessly announcing that humanity is failing to limit greenhouse gas emissions. Global average temperatures have surpassed 1.5 degrees Celsius above pre-industrial levels. We are on track for 2.0 degrees – or much worse.

What is civilisation's strategy for preventing a catastrophic climate crisis? It is, in short, to revolutionise the energy system. The political economist Brett Christophers neatly summed it up as a 'double bet' on electricity: electrify all demand and decarbonise all electricity generation.[1] The simplicity of the phrase obscures the scale and complexity of the undertaking. We must build a colossal amount of infrastructure. Citizens and consumers must change how they use energy, from how they heat their homes to how they fuel their cars. The way we orchestrate the electricity system to keep supply and demand in perfect balance will also have to change, given that we will become more reliant on intermittent renewables. In parallel, we must shut down the entire existing fossil fuel industry, and in the process write off trillions of dollars of assets.

In 1941 the great French historian Marc Bloch gave his approval to a statement by the French poet and philosopher Paul Valéry, that the electricity system had 'more meaning and greater possibility of shaping our immediate future than all the political events combined'.[2] These words are truer now than ever before. It is no exaggeration to say that societies are entrusting the future of the human species to this system.

Today, many countries around the world have electricity systems that are modelled on Britain's. In the 1980s, just as the reality of climate change was becoming apparent, Britain was busy incubating a new way of organising energy. Over just a few years the electricity and gas industries were broken up and transferred from public to private ownership. New markets and commercial mechanisms were created. The British model of privatisation was then exported around the world. International organisations like the World Bank told governments that this was the ideal to which they should aspire. By 1996 British politicians would boast that in fifteen years privatisation had gone from 'revolutionary new approach . . . to being accepted worldwide as economic orthodoxy'.[3]

Fast-forward to today and the British energy system is in dire straits, having fared particularly badly in the global energy crisis of the early 2020s. In 2021 energy markets began to tighten due to a rapid economic rebound following the pandemic. The situation intensified after Russia's invasion of the Ukraine in February 2022 reduced the supply of gas. In Europe, gas prices rose 1,000 per cent and electricity prices 1,500 per cent between January 2021 and August 2022.

It is often said that you get to know who someone really is in a crisis. The energy crisis exposed Britain's electricity and gas industries for what they are: fragile, fragmented, comically complicated and hopelessly dependent on imported fossil fuels. Markets, private sector companies and financiers are in control, and the state and citizens are at the periphery. The events in Whitehall could have been an episode of the comedy shows *The Thick of It* or *Veep*. Ministers and civil servants turned to each of the big energy companies and asked if they had a plan. Most answered, 'It's not our responsibility.' One summarised the problem perfectly: 'The underlying market arrangements in the UK are predicated on the basis that the market will provide.'[4]

As the crisis deepened, officials in Whitehall became increasingly alarmed. It became apparent that citizens would suffer. The government tried to directly buy gas itself but found the complexity of the market an insurmountable hurdle. In the end, the state threw money at the problem. Energy suppliers were told to pay whatever was necessary, consumer bills were capped and the state picked up the shortfall. The combined support measures cost the taxpayer at least £40 billion. Most of that money went to oil and gas companies, and 50 per cent of the profits generated over the course of the crisis went to the wealthiest 1 per cent.[5] In its wake there were the usual recriminations and calls for fundamental reform. As had been the case for a decade, complexity scuppered these initiatives.

The term 'crisis' is bandied around so much today that it is easy to become numb to it. Turn on a British news channel and you will be presented with a long list of areas of life to which the word 'crisis' has been affixed – the cost of living, social care, healthcare, housing, migration, education, water, the climate. The term is particularly fitting, though, for energy. A crisis is more than just bad things happening. It is a critical juncture where decisions need to be taken about the future because inaction will only make things worse. Will Britain remain wedded to privatisation? Or does the scale of the climate crisis necessitate a different kind of energy system?

This book is a history of the origins of the present crisis. It focuses on two pivotal and intertwined industries, electricity and gas (or networked energy), in Britain. The argument is simple: patterns of ownership explain how these industries were built and then broken. Between 1926 and 1979 state-owned enterprises built infrastructure at a massive scale and breakneck speed. These were years of the technologically sublime: electricity networks, coal-fired power stations, nuclear and hydroelectric plants, power stations inside mountains, liquified natural gas facilities, gas transportation networks. The system builders developed mega infrastructure faster and cheaper than Britain's private sector companies can today. This frenzied construction bonanza changed the landscape of Britain and the fabric of everyday life for citizens. Millions of appliances in millions of homes were replaced by the state. If we are looking for guidance for how to transform the energy system today, the story of the nationalised era must be rescued from the enormous condescension of posterity.

In the 1980s and 1990s, the electricity and gas industries were broken apart and sold off to the private sector. Private ownership shifted the focus from asset building to asset sweating. Privatisation worked for a short time, but then the model started to break down. Climate change introduced a new problem. In response, the privatised system was gradually adapted and over decades became the complex and contradictory system that is crumbling today.

To give you a sense of how superb Britain used to be at building energy infrastructure, consider the case of the electricity networks. Between 1929 and 1934 the state-owned Central Electricity Board built the first National Grid. It was an electricity network of just over 3,000 miles in length with 297 substations. It was built at a rate of around 500 miles a year. It cost just £26.7 million, or £1.9 billion in 2024 prices. In the 1950s and 1960s, the state-owned Central Electricity Generating Board (CEGB) built the 'supergrid'. It was shorter than the first grid, 1,150 miles in length, but double the voltage. It took less than a decade to approve, design and construct: the CEGB built at a speed faster than even China today. The supergrid cost just £52 million, or £2.0 billion in 2024 prices. Today, Britain's three private sector electricity transmission companies are currently undertaking what they term the 'Great Grid Upgrade'. Between 2025 and 2035 it is hoped they will construct just 620 miles of onshore high-voltage grid at a cost of nearly £20 billion, meaning that these companies cost around fifty times more per mile than the state-owned Central Electricity Board of nearly a century ago, while the latter was eight times faster.

What is the energy system? In one sense, it is a physical thing made up of objects. Most books about energy or climate change use this lens, focusing on technologies and commodities. The cast of characters includes pylons, pipes, solar panels, electric cars, batteries, oil, gas and electrons. This gives the strange impression that the energy system is a set of relationships between inanimate objects, when in fact it is a set of social relationships between people, organisations, companies and the state. It is impossible to understand energy today without understanding the companies that control the means of making, moving and selling energy. The actions of these companies are heavily influenced by rules and regulations defined by the state. Energy is therefore a political industry. This book is primarily about the political economy of energy: the techno-economic system (technology, firms and markets) and its governance by political and regulatory systems (laws, policies, institutions).

Energy is history. The plant and equipment that comprise the system live very long lives. Each generation builds a layer of infrastructure upon the one built by the last. Many gas-fired power stations constructed in the 1990s were built on sites of older coal-fired plant. Choices made far back in time shape the choices available to us today. This is why the energy system is often described as having a 'path dependency'. Energy is a marvellous example of Marx's observation that the 'tradition of all dead generations weighs like a nightmare on the brains of the living'. History also helps us see that there is nothing inevitable or 'natural' about how we run the energy system today; it is the product of choices made by people in the recent past.

Many histories of energy rely on the concept of an 'energy transition'.[6] This is the theory that human societies have periodically shifted from using one type of technology or fuel to another. The past is often carved up into 'ages' – the ages of steam, coal, oil, electricity, nuclear.[7] Transitions are conceptualised using S-curves, where the diffusion of a technology or fuel is modelled as following a logistic function (slow at first, then rapid, then plateauing). The assumption is that technologies are in competition, and the economically superior ones eventually displace others. This conceptualisation of history dominates the energy industry and the upper echelons of climate politics. In 2022 the Intergovernmental Panel on Climate Change report used a set of intersecting S-curves to explain how renewables will replace fossil fuels.

The concept of an energy transition is flawed when applied to the past. The typical 'ages' fall apart on inspection. The age of steam is deemed to be synonymous with the Industrial Revolution, but the first mechanised cotton mills were water-powered. Coal was a feedstock for steam, electricity and gas throughout the twentieth century. The discovery of oil and gas in the North Sea had as profound an impact on electricity in the 1990s as oil did on motor transportation in the 1950s and 1960s. The notion that technologies rise and fall obscures that at any point in time the energy system is a jumble of new and old technology. Engineering is as much about stewardship of assets – tinkering, maintaining, augmenting – as it is invention. Even invention is a process of 'combinatory evolution', where old things are combined to create new things. Consequently, technology develops both extremely fast and very slow; it is easy to create a new technology, historical circumstances play a pivotal role in what gets picked up, and once selected it is very difficult to dislodge.[8]

Energy transitions have occurred (depending on your definition), but they are rare and protracted, the average duration being around a century. Technologies and fuels are often entangled in interdependent relationships as much as they are in competition. The notion that 'we have been through energy transitions before' is comforting. It makes the present transition seem inevitable. The downside of the story is that it produces political procrastination and shies away from confronting the magnitude of what societies are attempting today: the first all-encompassing rapid energy transition in human history.[9]

This book offers a different type of energy history, focused on the interaction of political agency and technological change. The development of the electricity and gas industries in Britain over the last 200 years is a story of punctuated equilibrium: decades when industrial structure and state policy were stable, punctuated by short periods of radical overhaul. State-directed resets were a response to pent up technological and economic forces. In a Marxist framework, such moments of disruption occur when the forces of production change faster than the social relations of production. In more conventional economic writing, resets were what one influential thinker on 'technological revolutions' has termed 'institutional re-compositions'.[10]

The relationship went both ways. State intervention unleashed new dynamics and allowed technologies to flourish in novel and unexpected ways. Resets to political economy shaped what technologies and fuels were invented and used. To borrow a term from Joseph Schumpeter, these were gales of creative destruction, blown by the state.[11] The impact of these resets is visible in long-run trends in investment, consumption, the price of energy and the price of energy services (lighting, transport, heating). When our present predicament is viewed from this perspective, it seems likely that we must change the institutions and policies that govern the energy system to ensure the first rapid energy transition.

The historical argument

The last 200 years of Britain's energy history can be grouped into four phases: localised, rationalised, nationalised and privatised energy.[12] These phases are quite different to those typically used in energy history and emphasise that the political economy was just as malleable as technology.

The period from 1810 to 1920 was a phase of localised energy. Over the nineteenth century, hundreds of gas and electricity firms sprang up all over the country. Building the infrastructure was a speculative venture that involved significant risk. The technology was immature, the upfront costs were enormous and there was uncertainty over long-term demand. Firms were vertically integrated monopolies operating within a particular area, although some competition was allowed. Vertical integration made sense because engineers and entrepreneurs needed to synchronise all the parts of the system, addressing bottlenecks as technology evolved. Allowing many local firms to operate also made sense, because it increased variation and experimentation, which led to technological improvements. The central state's role was restricted to light-touch regulation, which ended up being ineffective. From the late 1860s, privately held firms were increasingly criticised for high prices, excessive profits and poor service.

In response to the failures of the private sector, the local municipal state became a major player. The municipal electricity 'undertakings' were particularly successful and ended up being more effective than their private sector rivals, and the years 1870 to 1920 were a golden age for municipal energy. But in international terms, Britain's electricity industry was a laggard, even though its gas industry was the most advanced in the world. Its geographical fragmentation prevented the electricity industry from capturing economies of scale. The one exception was the advanced regional electricity system that emerged in the North East of England. Over the early twentieth century, there were repeated attempts to reform and reorganise the gas and electricity industries. All failed. There were too many vested interests, and measures to encourage voluntary amalgamation had no effect.

During the second phase, from 1920 to 1945, the national state intervened. The first major intervention was the creation of the Central Electricity Board from 1926. This state-owned public corporation rationalised electricity generation and constructed the first National Grid. This led to a remarkable turnaround, and Britain's electricity industry rapidly caught up with that in the US and Germany. However, electricity distribution and the entire gas industry were left in a fragmented state.

The third phase, between 1945 and 1979, was nationalised energy. The Labour government's nationalisation programme of 1947–48 forced through amalgamation and brought over 1,500 separate entities under two vertically integrated state-owned enterprises. Ownership transferred to the state and therefore indirectly the citizens of the country. One industry leader put it succinctly: the electricity industry 'is owned by the people of

England and Wales and they have to supply our capital requirements'.[13] During this phase the electricity and gas systems were dramatically expanded. Infrastructure was built on a massive scale – the supergrid, a new fleet of coal-fired power stations, nuclear and hydroelectric generation, liquified natural gas facilities, a natural gas transmission network and much more. It was the apotheosis of the 'load-hungry utility' that first emerged in the North East in the 1910s.

Gas and electricity competed vigorously, transforming the fabric of everyday life. Nationalisation provided the framework for a renaissance in the gas industry. The Gas Council oversaw three innovations within a decade: oil-to-gas, liquified natural gas, then North Sea natural gas. The programme to convert the gas system from using 'town gas' (derived from coal) to natural gas was one of the most impressive mega-projects in British history. In the space of ten years, the industry built a vast new gas transportation network and converted 35 million appliances for 13.4 million customers.

The nationalised energy industries were exemplars of an entrepreneurial and developmental state. However, over the 1970s inflation led to deteriorating financial performance. It is a myth that the nationalised energy industries were unproductive. However, they did struggle to reconcile the social and economic objectives they had been set once the asset-building phase was over.

Margaret Thatcher's election in 1979 led to another major state-directed reset, which set off the fourth phase: privatised energy. The real driver was financial stringency and a desire to evade the new Public Sector Borrowing Requirement. The Conservatives were determined to reduce state borrowing, and moving the energy industries into private ownership would accomplish this through a fiscal sleight of hand. Privatisation, as it came to be called, was something Chile pioneered but Britain quickly followed and pushed to the extreme. The primary objective was to improve efficiency. There were two levers. The first was moving the industries from public into private ownership based on the belief that the latter was superior. The second was splitting up the parts of the system that were monopolies (networks) from the parts that could be made competitive (generation and retail).

Parcelling up the industry in this way also made it easier to sell it off to investors. Politicians were moved to one side, and unelected independent regulators emerged in their place. These system architects became incredibly powerful and redesigned the industry around their own ideological commitment to private ownership and markets (in that order). Rather than paying for infrastructure from general taxation, with the rich paying a higher share than the poor, consumers split the cost equally. Very little infrastructure was built. Companies focused on sweating the assets inherited from the post-war generation (meaning focusing on driving productivity from the existing asset base rather than building new infrastructure) and generating profit.

The privatised model entered a new sub-stage around 2010 that I have called 'zombie privatisation'. The privatisation of energy had not gone to plan. The gas and electricity industries never experienced the spectacular efficiency gains that were promised. Consumers did not benefit from lower prices for long. After 2003 electricity prices began their inexorable rise, and by 2009 were 17 per cent higher than in 1990 when electricity was privatised. The hope that markets and competition might replace the state and regulation turned out to be just a dream.

From the early 2000s climate change introduced a problem that the privatised system was not designed to solve. The industry had to flip from sweating assets to building a gargantuan amount of infrastructure – from wind farms to electricity networks. In response to the new challenge the system architects started making tweaks. To convince companies to do things that were unprofitable, like maintain enough power stations to keep the lights on or build large wind farms, the state had to spend billions on subsidies. These handouts have created all sorts of distortions, much to the irritation of economists, but

Figure 0.1. Investment levels by the energy industry, Britain 1950–2023

Gross fixed capital formation by the networked energy industries as a percentage of GDP

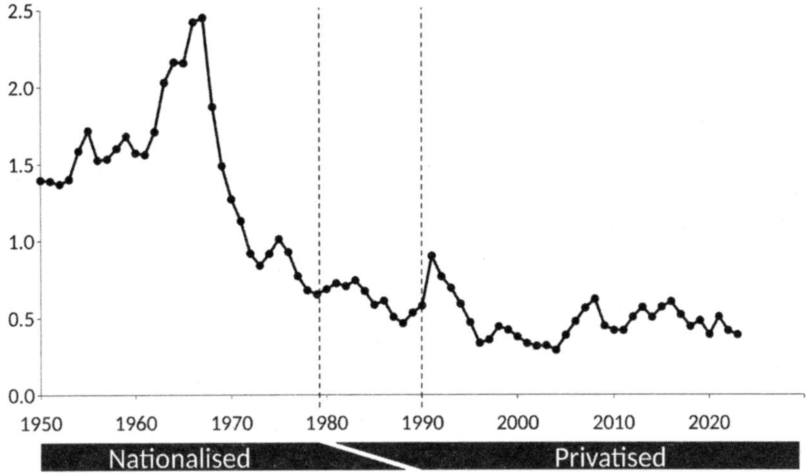

Note: Network energy includes gas and electricity production and generation, transmission, distribution and retail. Excludes oil and gas exploration and offshore extraction..

Source: ONS, Volume Index Capital Services (VICS), annual, UK, 7 November 2024; ONS, GDP at market prices.

ones that are incredibly difficult to remove. Despite protestations to the contrary, the industry intensely dislikes free market competition and would much prefer to subsist on subsidies.

Far from privatisation leading to a golden age of 'popular capitalism' with ordinary Britons owning shares, the energy sector became dominated by foreign ownership. Initially, it was American utilities and European state-owned giants. Over the last decade, the industry has increasingly moved under the control of asset managers like Macquarie and BlackRock. Regulation did not wither; it got much more complex. Each intervention had unintended consequences, leading to ever more adjustments. It was a process of 'institutional layering'; new organisations, regulations and programmes were layered on top of the existing set.[14] Today's energy system is so complex that few understand how it works. This makes coordinated action across companies almost impossible. To address this, one part of the company National Grid was effectively renationalised between 2022 and 2024 to act as a central planner. However, thanks to a series of half-measures, the central planner has been stripped of any power to deliver its plan. The privatised energy system has become like a zombie: the model is dead but the ideology lurches on. The system is beyond redemption, riddled with contradictions. A new system is required.

How might the British energy system evolve? In the final chapter I propose two scenarios for the future.[15] These scenarios are purely speculative, extrapolations from dynamics in the present. Scenario one is the emergence of a highly centralised version of energy capitalism I call the 'Central Return Generating Board'. The state takes a more interventionist approach than it has over the past forty years. The primary objective becomes ensuring investment and protecting private sector returns. The planning system is overhauled, and renewables are given lucrative subsidies. The frantic obsession with 'delivering at pace' blocks any fundamental reform. A wave of small-scale initiatives fails, foiled by complexity. Asset managers and executives do very well. Bills continue to rise. One of the political parties runs on a platform that 'net zero' is a con and green industries are being unfairly subsidised. The cancellation of net zero will not stop the rise of renewables and electric vehicles, but Britain may fail to meet its international climate commitments.

I have termed the second scenario 'mutualised energy'. This would require an ambitious reset by a brave political party. Public ownership was an extraordinary tool for building infrastructure at pace while delivering benefits for citizens. It can be so once again. In this scenario the parts of the system that are natural monopolies would be partly or fully nationalised to take advantage of the state's lower cost of capital. The state would also take ownership stakes in renewable generation projects rather than just providing subsidies. Markets would be reformed, with regional price signals to accelerate the development of demand-side response technologies (like domestic batteries and vehicle-to-grid electric vehicles). Decentralised energy would flourish with cooperatives, local authorities and citizens taking advantage of the falling cost of batteries and solar equipment. Bills would fall. Social and democratic consent for decarbonisation would be maintained.

My initial motivation for writing this book was to use history to demystify energy. Over the early 2020s, as energy prices rocketed, friends and family suddenly became interested in the industry I worked in. Most conversations began with people confessing they found energy incredibly confusing. Given the importance of electricity and gas to everyday life, one might think that the industry would at least try to be intelligible to interested citizens. The opposite is true. There is a widespread attitude that 'ordinary people' don't want to understand energy – they don't care; they just want their lights to work.

I used to think this, but now I believe that the complexity of the system is what deters citizens from engaging. In the decade since I began working in energy my own confusion has only grown. Over the years I found the phrases used by industry insiders to be revealing. Things were described as 'counter-intuitive', 'back to front', 'like water flowing uphill'. One senior executive once confessed to me that 'this place isn't the real world – it isn't like any normal business'.

Complexity is a self-preservation strategy developed by industry insiders to protect themselves from scrutiny. It favours established players who understand the complexities and have the resources to influence policy (in other words, lobby). Jargon-filled language is a form of exclusionary behaviour allowing only the initiated to participate in a debate. Some even revel in this, arguing that debates about energy policy should be kept hidden away from the public gaze.

As I began to write, the book grew in scope as I realised that debates about the future of energy desperately needed some historical perspective. Most people in the industry have only ever worked under the privatised model, and most online datasets go back only to the early 1990s. Despite being surrounded by infrastructure built by past generations, the energy industry has a very poor understanding of its own past. Most industry insiders and politicians think they know why privatisation occurred, but few have an appreciation of why energy was nationalised in the first place or how the nationalised industries worked. The modern-day obsession with quantitative forecasting out to 2050 or beyond has exaggerated the loss of memory. Historical anecdotes are only ever wheeled out for decoration. In 2024, the company National Grid launched a marketing campaign featuring slick videos about the construction of the first grid in the 1930s and the supergrid in the 1950s. Unsurprisingly they made no mention of the crucial role public ownership played in both programmes. In recent years an alliance of techno-futurists have become obsessed with nuclear power (mainly as a way of feeding artificial intelligence data centres with power). Various glossy online blogs celebrate the British nuclear programme of the 1950s and 1960s, but the fact that nuclear was state-owned is completely ignored.

The lack of engagement with energy history perpetuates the belief that 'there is no alternative' (TINA) to the current privatised model. This is capitalist realism at its finest; we have been convinced that it is natural and inevitable that everything in society must be run by profit-seeking firms.[16] The political scientist James C. Scott observed, 'History at its best . . . is the most subversive discipline, inasmuch as it can tell us how things that we are likely to take for granted came to be.'[17]

History is a living subject. Our views of the present are constructed upon a scaffold of ideas about the past. As Marx observed, it is often in moments of crisis that societies 'anxiously conjure up the spirits of the past'. The word 'conjuring' is particularly appropriate. Britain's privatised energy system was built upon a series of myths about how the nationalised industries worked: that they were bureaucratic and inefficient and that they underinvested. In fact, they were efficient, innovative, entrepreneurial and superb at building infrastructure. These are attributes we want today's system to have, especially the ability to build things at pace. Over the 1990s and 2000s, stories about the 'bad old days' were exaggerated and have ossified into what are taken to be historical truths. These representations have become so engrained that no one even bothers to fact-check them. For example, at an energy conference I was surprised to hear a very senior industry figure proclaim that the nationalised electricity industry was 'reassuringly expensive'. This would make today's industry 'disturbingly profligate'. Electricity prices for domestic consumers between 2021 and 2023 were higher than at any point between 1948 and 1990 (adjusting for inflation). At the same conference others argued that the one thing the nationalised industries were good at was long-term planning, as justification for developing a twenty- to thirty-year infrastructure 'roadmap' and all the subsidies to go with it. But the nationalised energy industry did not do anything of the sort. Infrastructure was planned in three- to seven-year waves. The idea of planning what should get built and where for the next twenty-five years was considered ridiculous.

Many in the British energy industry will be outraged by the term 'zombie privatisation'. I don't make the argument lightly. Many colleagues I respect will profoundly disagree, and this book won't help my career. The term has been deliberately chosen to describe a historical process: the way that the British energy system has become a muddled and dysfunctional hybrid. The privatised model has been adjusted so many times that it is no longer coherent. This has caused excessive complexity, which in turn makes the industry incapable of rapid action. The long list of reform programmes that are stuck in a death spiral is testimony to this. An analogy from computer programming is helpful. Software developers will often add patches to fix the bugs in a system. This works for a while, but at a certain point these patches start to make things worse, and the programmer must revisit the source code of the system. I will argue that we have arrived at this moment.

In March 2024, the United Kingdom became one of the first major economies to reach the halfway mark to net zero, having reduced territorial greenhouse gas emissions by 50 per cent compared to 1990 levels. The second half of the journey will be much harder than the first. All the low-hanging fruits have been picked, like deindustrialising and switching from coal to gas. As the Climate Change Committee made clear in 2024, Britain is not on track to hit its future targets. From queues to connect to the electricity grid to wind farms being cancelled, over the last decade the failures have mounted up. Powerful headwinds emerged in the early 2020s that the energy industry has not had to deal with simultaneously for a long time: interest rate rises, supply chain and labour market constraints, stagnating living standards.

To maintain social and democratic consent for net zero, bills must go down. People are repeatedly told that renewables are cheap. However, bills have repeatedly gone up. For the eighty years between 1920 and 2000, British citizens could reasonably expect electricity prices to fall, with some oscillations upward for a few years here and there. Since 2003, electricity prices have steadily, and then rapidly, increased. The war in Ukraine merely accelerated this trend. This war was not, however, some unanticipated 'Black Swan' event. As early as 2010 the energy regulator Ofgem conducted scenario-modelling factoring in a Russia–Ukraine conflict. Different factions in the energy industry endlessly debate the reason why prices have risen. There are many factors: gas-fired generation setting the price, increasing reliance on gas imports, rising network costs, ballooning subsidies. Yet for citizens and consumers the cause is irrelevant. To borrow a term from the great cybernetician Stafford Beer, the purpose of a system is what it does. From the perspective of British citizens, it would seem that the purpose of the energy system must be to steadily raise prices.

The institutions and ownership models that emerged in Britain in the 1980s and 1990s were not meant to solve a problem

Figure 0.2. Electricity prices in Britain, 1920–2024

Electricity price for domestic consumers – pence per kWh in 2000 prices

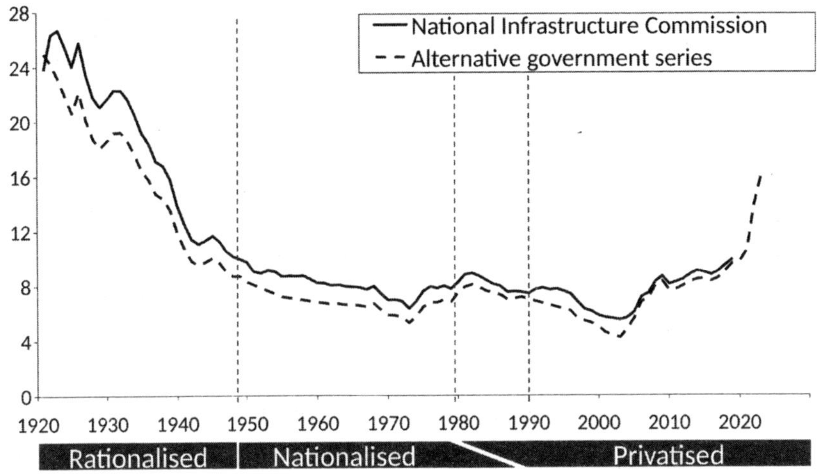

Source: Roger Fouquet for the National Infrastructure Commission, historical datasets. Price is the average faced by consumers, including network costs, tax and subsidies; alternative series is Digest of United Kingdom Energy Statistics, historical electricity data 1920 to 2024, accessed 30 July 2024.

like climate change. The privatised model was meant for sweating assets, not building them; for driving competition, not cross-industry cooperation; for taking politics out of energy, not facilitating democratic consensus. History suggests that we cannot revolutionise energy around new technologies without changing the founding principles of the system.

Countless books, articles and blogs have articulated the scale of Britain's economic woes. The last two decades have seen not just a relative decline in living standards compared to other countries, but for many people an absolute decline. There is a consensus across the political spectrum that one root cause is terrible productivity due to low levels of investment. Britain has some of the lowest investment levels among countries in the Organisation for Economic Co-operation and Development.

Energy is part of the problem. Low investment has led to an overreliance on gas-fired power stations constructed in the 1990s. Rising prices have contributed to deindustrialisation.

One school of thought blames this on 'red tape'; the planning system, regulatory bodies and the state just need to get out of the way, and the private sector will do the rest. In 2024, an essay restating this argument became a sensation, dominating the party conference scene. This is a comforting argument as it avoids the need for major structural reform of the state and the economy. Some have even suggested that structural reform would be 'nihilistic' and that 'radical incrementalism' is the more pragmatic path.[18]

The historical analysis presented in this book suggests that 'radical incrementalism' is not an option. In energy we have been trying this for two decades. Privatisation is the reason for Britain's low levels of investment in energy. The planning system and red tape play a smaller role. Between 1950 and 1979 the nationalised energy industries invested on average 1.5 per cent of the country's GDP in fixed capital. In the peak years of 1966 to 1967, investment reached 2.4 per cent. The nationalised industries faced numerous planning hurdles, which they constantly complained about. However, between 1979 and 1990 investment fell to 0.6 per cent and since 1990 it has averaged just 0.5 per cent.[19] Privatisation incentivised underinvestment due to a higher cost of capital and because deferring investment increased profits. Unbundling prevented coordination between the constituent parts of the system. Regulatory game-playing eroded trust between private companies and the regulators, further stalling necessary investments. Privatisation also led to excessive gearing (companies increasing their debt levels), so now companies are financially weak just as they are expected to increase investment.

The energy crisis of the 2020s is part of a wider crisis in state legitimacy. In *Failed State*, the journalist Sam Freedman portrays the British state as dysfunctional, with political elites frantically pulling levers to no avail. The political economist Abby Innes has gone even further and demonstrated with painstaking detail that the neoliberal state in Britain is suffering from the same pathologies as late Soviet Russia: bureaucratic rigidity, organisational fragmentation, farcical administrative complexity. Privatisation is one of the main reasons for the loss of state capacity. Worryingly, the dysfunction both Innes and Freedman describe is also prevalent in the privatised energy system.[20]

Feeding more money into this system and expecting better outcomes is naïve. We must move beyond seeing the state's role as simply to remove barriers, ensure investability, de-risk and subsidise. Increasing investment levels requires a significant degree of societal buy-in. This will not be sustained under the current system because more investment by the private sector will only lead to bill increases, and more subsidies will only exaggerate the sense of unfairness. The pathway to higher investment involves de-privatisation. We need not reinvent the wheel. The nationalised gas and electricity industries are perfect examples of what Mariana Mazzucato has termed the 'entrepreneurial state'; they incubated and scaled new technologies, delivered mega-projects on time and on cost and successfully owned and operated assets.[21]

The historical narrative presented in this book contributes to broader debates about how societies should decarbonise. One position could be termed 'techno-optimism' or 'green capitalism'. Proponents of this view argue that the technologies required to reach net zero already exist or are emerging. Capitalism is working its magic and would work even better if there were a global carbon price. Market structures and institutions may require some incremental reform, but nothing dramatic. The state's role should be restricted to addressing market failures and helping to jump-start immature technologies with a mix of targeted regulations and subsidies.[22] Britain is often cited as proof of the wisdom of this position.

This camp has a selective definition of capitalism, which is assumed to be synonymous with the neoliberal strain that has been prevalent in the West since the 1990s. This ignores the achievements of a very different type of energy capitalism in the West after the First World War. The techno-optimists are correct that most of the technologies required to prevent catastrophic climate change already exist. However, they underestimate the crucial role that the state has played, and will need to continue to play, in scaling technology. Were it not for the actions of an entrepreneurial state between 1945 and 1979, Britain would not have developed nuclear, liquified natural gas, hydroelectric power or natural gas. The state also took on the vested interests that would have blocked the development of new technologies. This lesson applies today. Oil and gas companies, gas networks and their asset manager backers will not walk away from their assets without a fight. Some self-described techno-optimists are in fact fatalistic, not optimistic, in that they see energy policy as unchangeable. It is noticeable that the term 'energy transition' has delinked from the aspiration of stopping catastrophic climate change. This is to be optimistic about technology only within a pessimistic world view about the capacity of society to be organised along different principles.

Another position is that of 'green Marxism'. Proponents argue that capitalism is the cause of climate change, not the solution. Capitalism is defined by the profit motive and private ownership of the means of production. Under capitalism, what is socially beneficial is not always profitable and what is profitable is not always socially beneficial.[23] In *The Price Is Wrong*, Brett Christophers has made the most precise critique of 'green capitalism'. His argument is that while wind and solar generation may be cheap, the issue is that they are insufficiently profitable when compared to oil and gas. Consequently, all over the world renewables have been heavily subsidised to ensure adequate levels of profitability for the owners of capital. Globally, 80 per cent of large-scale renewable generation capacity scheduled to be built between 2024 and 2030 is on some form of subsidy.[24] Other green Marxists go a step further and argue that capitalism rests upon a 'metabolic rift' whereby society expropriates value from nature. This leads to the concept of 'degrowth', which proposes that societies give up on striving for continuous economic growth.[25] At the other end of the spectrum are Marxists who argue that the problem is not economic growth, but the lack of social and democratic control over production and investment decisions. Some are even positively utopian, reasoning that technology (especially solar and batteries) is paving the way for a socialist future of distributed ownership of energy assets.[26]

This book broadly supports the green Marxist position (although I think my argument could be also described as Schumpeterian). However, the argument that we need to do away with capitalism lacks specificity. The political economy of today's energy system is *very* young, having only been developed in the 1980s. Moving on from a privatised model of energy capitalism that has had its time is a more pragmatic approach than ending capitalism in its entirety. Christophers is broadly right that the privatised (or liberalised) model will not scale renewables fast enough, but he conflates markets with capitalism. Price signals and markets are compatible with greater levels of state, mutual and municipal ownership. Without price signals it will be difficult to develop sufficient levels of storage and demand-side response to complement intermittent renewables. In other words, neoliberal capitalism won't save the planet, but prices and public ownership might. I am optimistic about the potential for technology to create a radically different kind of energy system. The 'mutualised energy' model discussed in the final chapter shares some features with the vision of *Fully Automated Luxury Communism* presented by Aaron Bastani.

Finally, a few words on the boundaries and limitations of this book. This is not a comprehensive history of the science and technology behind the energy system. Nor is it a roadmap for the future mix of technologies. There are countless other books that offer this perspective. In the later chapters I will offer a broad sketch of what is needed to decarbonise the system, which of course involves building a lot more renewables, but exactly how the generation mix should split among solar, wind or nuclear is not in scope here. As I hope will become clear, I find these kinds of forecasts to be of limited use if the energy system does not possess the capacity to make them a reality within a tolerable cost envelope.

The historical narrative in this book is focused on the political economy of energy. The story is therefore somewhat elitist in focusing on capitalists not workers, producers not consumers, politicians not citizens. This reflects that the energy system *is* elitist. Citizens have had little say in how the system is run.

The first five chapters are purely historical pieces. Chapter 6 shifts from historical analysis to the present, which means it is inevitably influenced by my own experiences and involvement in certain debates. The final chapter is a work of speculation about the future. To help the reader get a sense of the scale of investments made in the past compared to the present, I have, where appropriate, adjusted financial values into 2024 prices.[27]

There is nothing in this book that can claim to be academically original. I have relied heavily on existing histories of energy, particularly the works of Leslie Hannah, Robert Millward, Martin Chick and Dieter Helm. These authors wrote histories about the administration and industrial structure of energy. This tradition seems to have become less fashionable in recent years, and I hope this book can revive interest in an older literature that deals with some timeless questions of ownership and control. I have supplemented it with archival research. However, material is scattered across multiple sites, in part due to the decision at privatisation to leave it to companies to maintain the records. Some did, but many did not. In a vindictive move politicians decided against requiring files be deposited in the National Archives. With that decision the past became more distant.

This book is also not a study of the entire energy system. Ultimately this would entail studying the entirety of the economy. This is a book about networked energy: electricity and gas supplied through networks. Within that scope, it is mostly about electricity, which was the larger of the two industries from the early twentieth century. Non-networked energy is only partially covered. Coal features only as it relates to electricity and gas. Agriculture, forestry, waste and offshore oil and gas are not covered. One must draw the boundaries of a system somewhere. I have focused on networked energy because it is pivotal to the decarbonisation strategy of Britain and other countries.

Telling the story of gas and electricity together is important. These industries were and are intertwined, locked in competition and co-dependence. They shared the same feedstock, coal, for nearly a century. The actions of the state impacted both in similar ways. Since the 1990s their interdependency has strengthened, with gas flowing into power plants to produce electricity.

This is a study of networked energy in one country, Great Britain. Despite this geographical shortcoming, it is a study of relevance for other countries. Britain is the birthplace of the privatised energy system and has taken that model to the extreme. As such, it is something of a canary in the coal mine for other countries to watch. Unfortunately, the canary is already dead. It is time for Britain to regain its nerve and show other nations how to climb out of the pit.

1

Localised Energy, 1810–1920

On the night of the 31 December 1813, Westminster Bridge witnessed a pivotal moment in the history of energy. Along either side gas lamps were installed by the London Gas Light and Coke Company (GLCC), which had been incorporated by Royal Charter just one year earlier. The lamps were switched on, and for the first time the bridge was illuminated. The GLCC's founder, German impresario Friedrich Albrecht Winzer, had demonstrated the viability of gas lighting on Pall Mall in 1807. The Westminster scheme was a much more complex feat of engineering. The gas that fuelled the lamps flowed through underground pipes from a nearby gas production facility, the Great Peter Street Gasworks. It was only thanks to the skill of the GLCC's chief engineer, Samuel Clegg, that the facility was ready in time. Clegg had been badly burned after an explosion a few months before. Even on the day it was uncertain that the equipment would work. Clegg had to light the lamps himself because other employees were fearful of another explosion.[1]

Spectators on Westminster Bridge that night witnessed one of the first instances of networked energy: energy carried from sites of production to sites of consumption via an infrastructure network. In the eighteenth century, luminosity was provided by tallow candles made from animal fats. Gas was the first alternative, and it would change the urban landscape. Before gas lighting, Westminster Bridge was so dark at night that James Boswell copulated on it with a prostitute in 1763.

Britain was not the first country to manufacture gas from coking coal (the process of heating coal in the absence of oxygen to a temperature above 600 degrees Celsius). There is evidence of gas being piped through bamboo in China in the second century CE. Britain was, however, the first place in the world to scale the technology. This was partly due to the abundance of coal in Britain, which powered industrialisation and urbanisation. It was also the result of the application of formal scientific research to industrial processes.

The Gas Light and Coke Company expanded following the success of its network strategy at Westminster Bridge. By 1820, 300 miles of gas pipes had been laid under the feet of Londoners bearing the company's motto *Fumo dare lucem* ('Light from smoke'). The company achieved economies of scale through bulk purchasing of coal inputs and by increasing the size of its gas manufacturing plant. By 1851 gas was half the price of tallow candles per unit of light.[2] That year gas illuminated the Great Exhibition and the next year the House of Commons.

Gas was a new industry of the Industrial Revolution. Gas lighting spread from London to other urban areas, and by 1830 there were 200 companies across Britain. Almost all towns with a population greater than 10,000 had the technology. From Britain, gas lighting spread across Europe and the US. Britain became an exporter of engineering services with companies like the Imperial Continental Gas Association heavily involved in the construction of gas works in Hanover, Berlin, Antwerp and Vienna. Between 1830 and 1870 gas lighting then spread to smaller towns and gas lamps entered shops, factories, railway stations and some middle-class households.[3]

Gas was arguably the first integrated large-scale network industry – something usually associated with the railways. The next networked energy industry to emerge was electricity. There were many events in the late 1870s and early 1880s that might be considered the beginning of electrical utility service in Britain. Each moment was claimed by the town or city in question as 'the first . . .' The equivalent to the Westminster Bridge lighting occurred in the small town of Godalming, Surrey, in 1881. That year Godalming became the first place in the world to use electric street lighting, following the expiration of its gas lighting contract. The electricity was generated by a water wheel on the river Wey. But Godalming's innovation was a false start. The scheme was unprofitable and was shut down a few years later. Gas lighting was restored.[4]

The next breakthrough involved a technology transfer from the US. Thomas Edison's incandescent lamps and electricity generation plant were on show at the Paris Exhibition in 1881 and the Crystal Palace Exhibition of 1882. Edison's representatives in London worked with various banks and entrepreneurs seeking exclusive rights to manufacture and market the 'Edison system'. The first pilot project was at the Holborn Viaduct power station, comprising two jumbo generators shipped from New York. It was the world's first coal-fired power station. The scheme began in January 1882 with incandescent lighting installed in hotels, stores, restaurants and other private buildings in the high-end neighbourhood. Despite the excitement the project was loss-making and ended up being costlier than gas lighting. It was shut down in 1886 and the properties reverted to gas.[5]

Electricity and gas networks were infrastructure-heavy industries, meaning that many things needed to be constructed before end consumers could turn on a gas mantle or light bulb. Building a system was expensive. In the 1890s in London it took roughly £840 of capital investment (in 2024 prices) per domestic light bulb installed. The cost was roughly split fifty-fifty between generation equipment and the distribution cable network.[6]

In the first phase of development, gas and electricity companies were 'vertically integrated', meaning that they covered every step in the process: manufacturing (gas), generation (electricity), distribution and retail (marketing, sales, metering, billing). Vertical integration made sense for such early-maturity industries because engineers and entrepreneurs needed to synchronise all the parts of the system – addressing bottlenecks as technology developed to reduce overall system costs. It is often claimed that Edison's genius was developing an entire system that knitted together the various components in the chain. However, Edison was merely following the example set by gas.

After some difficult false starts, electricity gained momentum in the 1890s. Supply companies sprang up across the country, focused on lighting offices, factories, stations, warehouses, some homes and even football games. Generally local industrialists supplied the equity capital and only later turned to capital markets for debt financing.

The transfer of electricity technology from the US was more successful in Germany and France. In a pattern that was repeated for decades, British firms were often behind the technology frontier. In Britain, the famous battle between Edison's direct current (DC) and Westinghouse's alternating current (AC) systems was less than decisive. The DC system had an economic operating radius of about 1.5 miles from the generating station and was therefore suitable for small-scale urban schemes. However, DC persisted for a long time, which slowed the emergence of the 'universal system' (three-phase with combined AC and DC). An alternating current frequency refers to how quickly a current changes its polarity; fifty hertz means it changes from positive to negative at a frequency of fifty cycles per second. To function, electrical equipment must be synchronised to the same frequency. In the US and Germany the 'universal system' emerged earlier as smaller firms merged, and their voltages and frequencies were standardised from the 1890s. Meanwhile, in Britain the situation remained disorderly for decades.[7]

Late-nineteenth-century Britain was an open economy nested in a global economic system. Networked energy only developed thanks to the circulation of ideas, engineers, entrepreneurs, technology and capital between countries. For example, the Godalming scheme was built by the German Siemens brothers. British engineer John D. Gibbs and Frenchman Lucien Gaulard developed the first transformer in 1882. Three inventors in three countries simultaneously invented the three-wire system in the early 1880s – Thomas Edison (US), John Hopkinson (Britain) and Wilhelm von Siemens (Germany). Edison's secretary and pioneer of the first large regional system in the world in Chicago, Samuel Insull, was a British emigrant who travelled back and forth across the Atlantic throughout his life. Insull's Chicago system relied on imported steam turbines from England, which were invented by the Englishman Charles Parsons in 1884. Through Parsons, Insull became friends with Charles Merz and the two exchanged letters for decades with profound consequences for the development of the British electricity grid in the 1930s.[8]

There was an inventiveness to the way the British muddled along. Direct current systems not only survived but were optimised in clever ways. To address the high distribution costs of the DC system, British engineers used storage batteries connected in series. The batteries were charged when demand was low and discharged when it was high. This approach had the benefit of being highly reliable. Power stations could be shut down for hours for maintenance without impacting the supply of lighting. The electricity companies, referred to as 'undertakings' at the time, in Chelsea and Colchester pioneered the method in the 1890s and in the case of Chelsea it was still in use until the 1920s.[9]

The closest thing that Britain had to an Edison, Tesla or Westinghouse was Sebastian Ziani de Ferranti. He was even nicknamed the British Edison, with an 1889 cartoon portraying him as a modern-day colossus straddling the Thames. In 1888 Ferranti developed the first British instance of the 'modern' electricity system to supply lighting to the Grosvenor Gallery. Ferranti bypassed regulatory restrictions on laying underground cabling by building an overhead distribution network. Then at the age of just twenty-two, Ferranti became chief engineer for the London Electricity Supply Company and began working on a bold plan to develop a vast generating station at Deptford, chosen because the land was cheap and had good access to coal and water. Ferranti was the first British engineer to see beyond the small-scale DC schemes: the Grosvenor project used a

700-horsepower generator, large for the time. But Deptford was gigantic, with a maximum capacity of 150,000 horsepower. Ferranti's most important contribution was the development of the first high-voltage AC transmission lines, using a paper-based insulator he had designed. Yet as with Godalming, Holborn and Grosvenor, the Deptford scheme was a failure and was abandoned in 1891.[10]

Competition and the state

Building an electricity or gas undertaking was a speculative venture that involved significant risk. The technology was immature, upfront costs were enormous and there was uncertainty over long-term demand. Early ventures need to raise capital equivalent to fourteen times their annual revenue in the first few years of operation.[11]

Competition was intense. From the outset, electricity was in a battle with gas. Edison had devoured gas engineering manuals, looking for ways to compete. With the advent of electric lighting the gas industry had to diversify into heating and cooking. The DC system was then on the receiving end when the AC system emerged as superior. After a fire at the Grosvenor Gallery power station in 1890, the rival St James' Company swept in to poach customers. While the technology was nascent it made sense to let different systems and firms compete for territory and see which technology won.[12]

Duplication was tolerated. In the middle of the nineteenth century, London, York, Birmingham and Edinburgh had multiple gas companies with the streets strewn with competing pipelines. If a company could not outcompete its rivals, another option was to buy them up. From the late 1860s, the Gas Light and Coke Company acquired and merged with multiple operators in London, supplying them from a new large gas works in East Ham.[13]

In the Victorian and Edwardian periods, gas and electricity undertakings were what economists term natural monopolies.

In simple terms, it was cheaper for one firm to supply gas or electricity than having several rival firms do so. Building a network incurred significant upfront cost. If another firm wanted to build a second network, it would have to incur the same costs, but it wouldn't have any guarantee of being able to poach the customers of the first network. These high barriers to entry thus favoured a single monopoly provider. Networks also exhibited positive returns to scale, meaning that as the network grew in density the cost of adding each new user tended to fall.

Network dynamics created another problem; once built, a gas or electricity firm had a captive user base, so it could jack up prices. Network monopolies created the opportunity for companies to extract 'economic rents'. The concept of 'economic rent' refers to situations where the owner of an asset has the power to charge prices in excess of the cost of production.

Why not just allow competition between companies for the same patch? Surely, this competition would lead to lower prices. Counter-intuitively, the answer is no. In 1847 a parliamentary commission concluded:

> The existence in the same town of two rival gas companies does not appear to us at all calculated to benefit the consumer . . . Competition between companies is never long lived. Either one of the competitors is ruined, and the survivor makes the consumer pay for the cost of the contest, or the two coalesce, and levy rates to pay a dividend upon the capital.[14]

By 1859, the political economist Edwin Chadwick argued that competition was to blame for the high costs and poor quality of service in gas and water.[15] This dilemma is sometimes called 'the two-tap problem': having two systems compete for the same households leads to duplication and ultimately customers pay for both networks.

Yet it took decades before the state intervened to protect citizens from destructive competition. The state's first foray into gas and electricity regulation was to establish rights of way for private companies. In practice, this meant permitting digging up the ground to lay pipe and cable. This was vital, as early projects had been held back by the high cost of distribution. Some early schemes relied on laying cables in the gutters as they had no legal power to underground the cables.

The characteristics of energy networks – monopoly, the potential for stimulating economic growth and negative externalities (noise, fumes, explosions, digging up roads) – made more comprehensive regulation necessary. However, in the first half of the nineteenth century regulation was either absent or ineffective. There were parliamentary statutes, but these were nonbinding or unenforced.[16] Regulation first emerged in the 1840s after a series of parliamentary enquiries which led to controls on prices and profits. An act of 1847 limited dividends (profits) to 10 per cent and defined maximum prices, which could vary locally. Legislation also set rules around the laying of mains, the condition of metering and pipes, and the prevention of public nuisances (leaks and explosions – in the 1850s, 25 per cent of London's gas supply was lost to leaks).[17] In practice, the new legislation was useless as monitoring was almost nonexistent. From the 1850s, gas prices stopped falling at a rapid rate, increasing pressure on the state to intervene further.[18]

The situation improved in the 1870s with the development of the sliding-scale method. This mechanism meant that companies could increase dividends only if they reduced prices below a benchmark price level. Over time the dividend level was reduced in parliamentary acts from 10 per cent in the 1870s to 4 per cent by 1896. The sliding scale was not universal, and in 1900 half of all private gas companies were on a simpler maximum price model. In London, companies could choose when or even whether to adopt the scale, and there was no discernible impact on the performance of those that did.[19] There were other weaknesses in the regulation, in particular no standards on the quality of gas supplied and no obligations to supply households in an area, leading to cherry-picking. Profit restrictions were easy to evade. Companies could establish subsidiaries to supply labour and equipment and then buy from these entities at inflated prices to accumulate profits outside the regulated framework. Companies could also 'water the capital base', which meant spending more money on replacing equipment to inflate the overall value of the assets so that the overall returns were higher.[20]

By the time electricity began to scale in the 1890s the state had learned many lessons from gas networks and made regulations tougher. The foundational legislation was the 1882 Electricity Lighting Act, which controlled licences to operate, tariffs and rights of way. It also contained a crucial innovation: local authorities had the right to acquire private undertakings after twenty-one years. The logic was simple. While technology was uncertain the state wanted private companies to take the risks. But giving local authorities the right to acquire acted like a 'sword of Damocles', which reduced the risk that companies would extract excessive profits.

The legislation was strongly influenced by the Liberal politician Joseph Chamberlain, who headed the Board of Trade in William Gladstone's government from 1880 to 1885. As mayor of Birmingham (1873–76), Chamberlain had brought the water and gas utilities under the city's ownership and control. Edison's representatives in Britain strongly opposed the 1882 act, calling it 'vexatious and harassing', and private companies argued that their tenure should be extended to seventy years. The industry also criticised the provision that allowed local authorities to buy the assets at 'scrap iron prices', meaning based on the book value of the assets and not the value of the lost revenue. Following years of intense debate, the law was amended in 1888 to increase the tenure from twenty-one to forty-two years.[21]

Municipal energy

From the 1870s, the state entered as a major force in networked energy. There was a massive expansion of energy infrastructure between 1870 and 1914, with an increasing share provided by the local state along the Chamberlain model. This was something of a golden age for municipal energy. At a time when the central state's role in the economy was limited, local authorities had more freedom to act. The 1870 Gas and Water Act made provision for local authorities to set up their own utility companies. All they required was Board of Trade approval rather than an act of Parliament. Between 1895 and 1900 the number of municipal electricity undertakings increased from 39 to 164. By 1900 Britain had the most municipalised electricity system in the world, with 71 per cent of firms in local authority ownership. Only Norway had a similar level. In Germany, the figure was just 18 per cent, in the US 13 per cent and France just 2 per cent. In gas, the private sector was more dominant, and only 28 per cent of undertakings were municipal, compared to 94 per cent in Sweden, 84 per cent in Denmark, 50 per cent in Norway, 30 per cent in Germany and 2 per cent in the US and France.[22]

Local authorities entered the market only after the electricity and gas industries had matured and organisational forms were stable. Municipal energy was also a response to the failures of private sector provision. There was an emerging consensus that municipal ownership was necessary to address the problems of natural monopoly and the failures of regulation. The *Birmingham Daily Post* summarised it well in 1882, saying there was

> a general feeling that for the purpose of preventing the creation of a new monopoly in private hands, to ensure the control of the streets, and then to promote public convenience, and also to limit as far as possible injurious competition with Corporation gas lighting, the supply of electric lighting ought to be in the hands of the local government authority.[23]

The municipal energy movement predated the rise of socialism as an ideological and electoral force. Intellectuals like the Webbs and the Fabians had very little influence on it. In the 1850s the liberal political economist John Stuart Mill advocated municipal ownership of the water industry.[24] The same arguments influenced staunch Liberals like Chamberlain, who in 1874 justified municipal ownership in terms that would be considered radical today:

> In the first place I distinctly hold that all monopolies which are sustained in any way by the state ought to be in the hands of the representatives of the people – by the representative authority should they be administered, and to them should their profits go, and not to private speculators. In the second place . . . I am inclined to increase the duties and responsibilities of the local authority, in whom I have myself so great a confidence, and I will do everything in my power to constitute these local authorities real local Parliaments, supreme in their special jurisdiction.[25]

Chamberlain's support for municipal ownership was not universal. He restricted it to towns that possessed no extensive estates or other sources of revenue, and was insistent that a council should not be allowed to restrain a private electricity company from emerging just to protect its municipal gas interests. There were other benefits. The widening of the franchise from the 1860s meant that politicians were under pressure to address issues stemming from urbanisation. Local authorities could fund public health projects like sanitation using the income from energy undertakings. Shopkeepers, businessmen and wealthy elites encouraged the trend to relieve pressure on rates, hence municipal gas and electric utilities first emerged in newly incorporated towns.[26]

Municipal energy was ultimately pragmatic. Towns with other sources of income from facilities like ports were less likely to adopt the model. Municipal gas undertakings were more popular in the North and Midlands than the South. These were areas that had experienced the fastest population growth and had the greater need for new urban amenities. Towns with Conservative MPs had a lower tendency to municipalise, but the effect was weak and there were Conservative councils like Bournemouth and Blackpool that had large municipal energy providers.[27]

How did the performance of municipal energy undertakings compare to that of private ones? This was a vibrant debate in the early 1900s. An anti-municipal campaign was spearheaded by the Liberal politician Lord Avebury, with the electric traction entrepreneur Emile Garcke as an influential string-puller behind the scenes. The campaign reached a climax in the summer of 1902, when a series of sixteen articles criticising 'municipal socialism' was published in *The Times*.[28] Defenders of the municipals argued that they were more cost-effective as they could borrow money at a lower interest rate. Political entities are, in theory, constantly replenished with new citizens and so are more likely to pay back a loan than a business. Municipals could also forgo profit. The other side of the debate claimed that the growth of the municipals was temporary and driven by uneconomic pricing – essentially setting prices too low and wages too high in order to buy votes. Private companies were more efficient and better asset stewards thanks to the profit motive. The municipals were 'living off their capital, and in a few years their plant and equipment will be worn out', claimed one critic.[29]

This mirrors the argument made in an influential article by the economist Armen Alchian in 1965: private firms are more efficient because managers are continuously monitored by shareholders who can sell their rights and because they face the threat of takeover or collapse. State-owned enterprises are not subject to the same disciplining pressure because the owners (the population) cannot sell their property rights.[30] Alchian's argument was contested within orthodox economics by Eugene Fama, who argued that the labour market incentivised managers to perform well regardless of who owned the firm.[31]

As is often the case, the economic debate rested on ahistorical notions about how state-owned enterprises actually functioned in the past. Municipals were not charities, but commercial entities much like the companies they competed with. Chamberlain even likened the activities of a municipal authority to that of a joint-stock company. Municipals did not reduce profit levels to zero, they just distributed the profits in a different way: to the local state and not exclusively to the owners of capital. In the case of municipal gas, at the end of the nineteenth century about 25 per cent of gross trading profits were transferred to local authorities. Like the companies, the municipal public corporations needed to raise capital to fund infrastructure expansion. By 1919 municipal electricity enterprises had raised just as much capital as private companies had. However, whereas companies raised both debt and equity, the municipals raised only debt to ensure that local authorities remained the sole owners.[32]

In 1913 the economist Ashmore Baker published a remarkably modern quantitative study comparing private and municipal electricity undertakings. Baker's study confirmed the long-observed fact that municipals sold more electricity, at a lower price, with lower capital costs (borrowing) and lower operating costs. Between 1909 and 1919 the municipals had 37 per cent lower costs per unit of energy sold, and translated this into 30 per cent lower prices.[33] Baker was one of the first to recognise that scale had a significant impact on the efficiency of an electricity undertaking. Even after controlling for scale, municipal undertakings had lower unit costs and passed this on to customers in the form of lower prices. Municipals were also able to borrow money at a lower rate of interest, which translated into less capital expenditure on physical equipment (CapEx) per kilowatt (kW) of maximum load (the maximum amount of electricity demand that could be delivered at one time).

Baker also found that municipals and companies had almost identical labour costs. The municipals actually paid lower wages, debunking the idea that they were spending lavishly on workers to buy votes. Municipals also had lower coal input costs, meaning that they were either better located or better buyers. The starkest difference in cost structure was in management salaries. Companies had to pay significantly more for 'leadership' with no discernible impact on performance. The overall effect was remarkable; Baker estimated that the municipals 'earned more than 2–3 times the gross profit per pound of capital than the companies'.[34]

Baker also showed that municipals were better agents of electrification than the private companies. Between 1900 and 1910 municipals reduced prices to stimulate demand for electricity. In contrast, the private companies had kept prices constant and volumes had remained relatively flat. Municipal electricity suppliers were the disrupters of the era. It was an innovative business model that created a powerful 'flywheel' effect; lower costs were translated into reduced prices, which in turn drove up demand, which generated economies of scale, which led to even lower costs.

In gas, it was a similar story. Municipal gas enterprises had lower prices, lower costs and similar profit levels. However, unlike in electricity, municipal gas undertakings were larger than privately held ones. Municipals also had lower consumption per customer, which reflected the fact that they were often serving poorer areas where private companies did not want to venture.[35]

The critical role of the municipal state is poorly understood in various popular conceptions of the history of energy. For example, Carlota Perez's influential work on 'technological revolutions' argues that financial institutions were the most important actors in the 'frenzy' phase of electricity. Yet in Britain it was not so much banks as municipal governments that drove the frenzy.[36] Municipal capital was well entrenched and refused to become subservient to private capital. Advocates of privatisation in the 1980s and 1990s liked to present their policies as 'returning' energy assets to the private sector. However, this ignored that state ownership built much of the electricity system in the Victorian and Edwardian periods.

Citizens and consumers

Networked energy had a dramatic impact on everyday life. In the first half of the nineteenth century, gas lighting was the preserve of rich households. From 1887 the Welsbach gas mantle dramatically improved domestic lighting and, accompanied by the development of prepayment meters, gas was brought within the reach of poorer households. The incandescent light bulb continued the trend, producing light far more efficiently than the gas mantle. In its early decades of development, electricity was a luxury product – it is telling that some of the earliest demonstration projects involved illuminating art galleries and high-end hotels. Over time the cost of bulbs and electricity fell and consumption of lighting – in terms of total lumen-hours – increased 129 per cent from 1900 to 1920.[37]

Better lighting was an enabler of other things – socialising, work, education. Improved street lighting even reduced crime rates. The smog of Victorian cities was so bad that sometimes the days were dim. The Pre-Raphaelite painter Ford Maddox Brown, trying to finish his magnificent murals in Manchester Town Hall, wrote that 'without the gas on many days I could do nothing'.[38]

There was nothing universal about electricity and gas service. Undertakings, whether municipal or private, did not have an obligation to supply all households. Many homes, especially rural ones, did not have access. Even in the region with the most advanced electricity system, the North East, several towns did not have access to power in 1910.[39] Some of the earliest examples of wind being used to generate electricity were by rural households and farmsteads. In 1909, one company advertised equipment that combined home-mounted wind turbines with storage batteries and even electric vehicles for rural communities.[40]

Electricity also impacted industry and transportation, although less so than in Germany and the US. By 1921, 65 per cent of electricity consumption was by industrial and commercial users, 24 per cent domestic and 12 per cent traction.[41] Electric tramways greatly improved urban mobility and sprang up in cities and small towns from Manchester to the Isle of Thanet. Between 1900 and 1915 the number of electric tramway firms grew from around 40 to 170. Their influence was particularly significant in the North East, Yorkshire and the

North West, regions that had the most miles of track. The success of the municipal electricity movement proved to be a platform for municipally owned electric rail. By 1915 municipal firms had built more than double the length of track than privately owned electric traction companies.[42]

Over the first decades of the twentieth century, electricity started to outcompete gas in the home, but gas consumption was very sticky. The British gas industry was the largest in Europe, second only in the world to the US. In per capita terms it was the biggest; one in four citizens had access to gas versus one in seven in the US. The gas industry was in a prosperous period of growth just as electricity was emerging. Gas firms didn't seem to fear the competition, perhaps myopically, and continued to invest in new technology. The gas industry then went through a technological transformation at the turn of the century with mechanical stoking, vertical retorts and 'water gas' technology improving productivity.[43] Between 1882 and 1914, coal prices rose 30 per cent but gas prices fell by 12 per cent, promoting the switch from coal to gas in cooking.[44] From the 1890s, there was a rapid uptake of gas cookers. In 1892 only 2 per cent of London Gas Light and Coke Company customers had gas cookers, but by 1911 it was 69 per cent.[45] Gas cookers were far cleaner than coal fires and opened new culinary options. Gas was still used for half of all public lighting by 1937.[46] Domestic consumers seemed to prefer electric lighting, not least because it was safer, but gas persisted in lighting for a long time. In 1900 electricity was twenty-five times more expensive per unit of energy than gas but only seven times more efficient. What changed the dynamic was that electricity prices fell by much more than coal and gas prices.[47]

International comparisons

Between 1813 and 1920, networked energy went from a handful of small-scale lighting projects to large regional systems across Britain. This was capitalism at its most dizzying creativity. In 1900 Britain was an energy-intensive economy with the highest energy consumption per person in the world except for the US. This was largely thanks to its abundant coal. A knock-on effect was that Britain had the highest gas consumption per capita in the world, 3.7 times higher than the US. Yet Britain's electricity industry was a laggard. By 1920 Britain had much lower electricity consumption per person than the US, Norway, Germany and Sweden, and it was barely ahead of France, Italy and Spain.[48]

The weakness of electricity was not just due to the strength of gas. In some parts of the country there were deep-seated problems due to fragmentation. Figure 1.1 gives a sense of the patchwork quilt of municipal, private company and holding company undertakings in Yorkshire. London was the most extreme example. By 1914 it had ten different frequencies, multiple voltages, thirteen private and fifteen local authority supply undertakings in the London County Council area, with a further sixty-five in the Greater London area. By 1914 a German engineer called Georg Klingenberg published a scathing study of London's electricity system. Klingenberg was the head of the power plant division of a German engineering firm. His study compared London to the two cities that exemplified the second industrial revolution – Chicago and Berlin – and showed that on almost every metric London's system was worse. This may have understated the issue; of the ten largest cities in the Western world, London had the lowest electricity consumption per capita, the highest prices and the lowest load factor. Load factor is a measure of the efficiency of an electricity system, calculated by dividing the total consumption of electrical energy (kilowatt-hours or kWh) for a given period by the maximum amount of energy that could be produced in that period.[49] Consumption per capita of course reflected differing economies. Chicago and Berlin were much more energy-intensive city economies.

Were Britain's electrical woes due to the capabilities of its engineers? The high degree of variation in voltages and frequencies was a more acute problem than in other countries. One of the electricity industry's most eminent historians, Leslie Hannah, attributed this to the 'individualism of British engineers'.[50] Yet British electrical engineers contributed to many of the major technological innovations of the time – the transformer, steam turbine, AC transmission cables. Where Britain seemed to fall behind was in scaling up these inventions. The

Figure 1.1. Electricity undertakings in Yorkshire in 1934–35

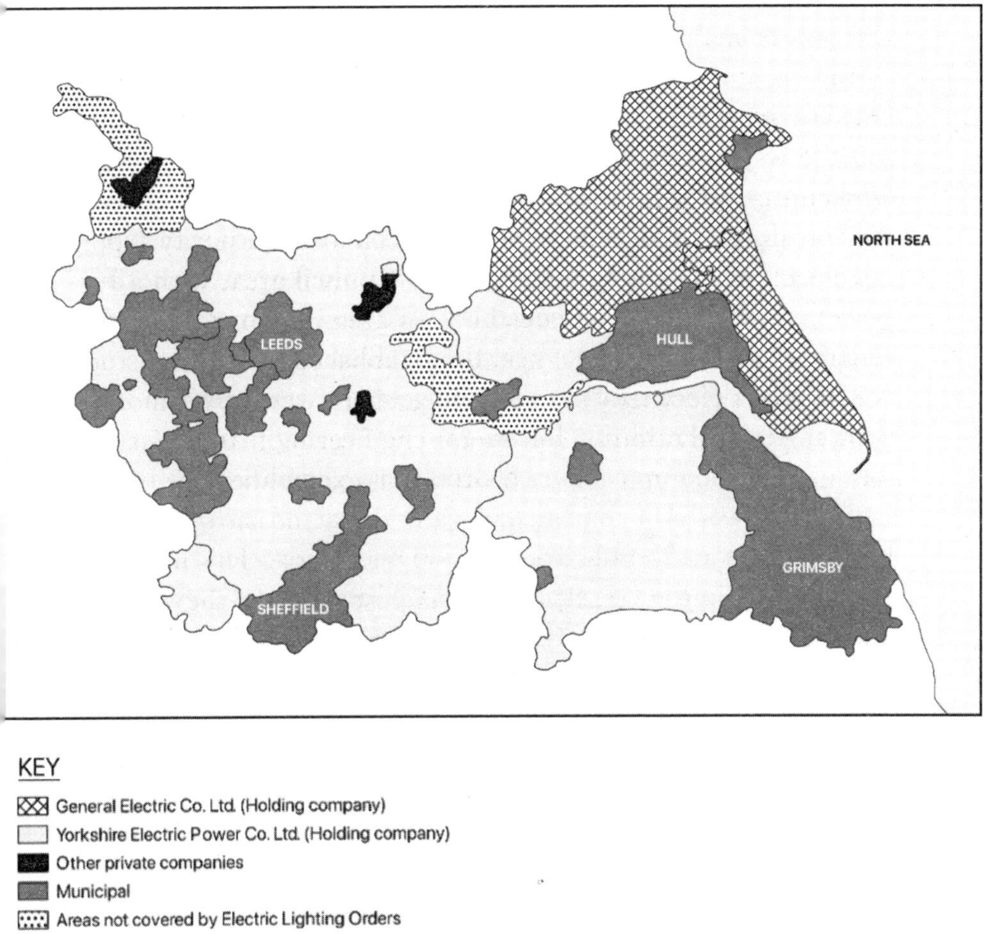

Source: G. T. Bloomfield, 'Yorkshire Electricity Board Area', British Electricity History, britelechist.uoguelph.ca.

transformer is a useful example. A British engineer was one half of the duo who developed and tested it in 1882, but it took European and American engineers to commercialise it. An electrical journal in 1887 complained:

> It is a not very complimentary reflection for European electricians and capitalists that although all ideas and experimental work needed to have come from Europe . . . it should be reserved for an American firm to take up the system and make it the commercial and practical success which the Westinghouse company is now doing.[51]

One contemporary theory was that Britain's geography did not suit the way electrical technologies evolved in the early twentieth century. In the 1890s, high-voltage transmission lines and the transformer reduced the cost and complexity of transporting electricity over long distances. This unlocked hydroelectric power or 'white gold' (renewable-based power generation and electricity grids have always been intertwined).

The first demonstration of point-to-point transmission was the Lauffen-to-Frankfurt line in 1891 in Germany. In a marvellous case of showmanship, a hydroelectric generation station in Lauffen powered a man-made waterfall at an exhibition in Frankfurt via a 109-mile transmission line. Hydroelectric power grew rapidly in the US, especially in California and New York, and in the Nordics, Central Europe and Spain. This drove down the cost and price of electricity, which increased consumption. This dynamic was especially important in the electrification of manufacturing in these regions.

Britain lagged a long way behind other countries in hydroelectricity as it simply did not have as many suitable sites, which were clustered in Scotland and North Wales. In 1938 only 5 per cent of Britain's electricity supply came from hydro, the lowest of any European country. Yet the hydrological explanation for British backwardness is inadequate. Germany had much higher electricity consumption levels, but only 10 per cent of its supply came from hydro. And countries like Italy and Spain generated more than 90 per cent of their electricity from hydro plants but had lower electricity consumption than Britain.[52]

Why did Germany and the US develop more advanced electricity systems? In his classic book *Networks of Power: Electrification in Western Society, 1880–1930*, the historian Thomas Hughes developed a compelling thesis for how electricity evolved as a complex system in the early twentieth century. Hughes argued that by the 1890s electricity had acquired an internal momentum with mass, velocity and direction. This set off a period of self-reinforcing expansionism that culminated with the dominance of regional systems by the 1920s. Regional systems involved a single organisation operating as a monopoly provider in an area. The system was built around large generating stations (both coal and hydro), high-voltage transmission lines and substations with transformers to step voltage up and down.

The systems that developed in Berlin and Chicago exemplified the archetype, and the latter had a direct impact on British thinking. In 1892 the British emigrant Samuel Insull became the leader of the Chicago Edison Company. Insull's crucial contribution was to realise the criticality of having diverse types of electricity demand that peaked at different times of day, called 'diversity of load'. Increasing the size of the generating units, whether coal or hydro, led to efficiencies and reductions in unit costs. With these efficiencies Insull could reduce prices to drive up consumption in an area. However, if consumer groups had 'peaky' demand the generating stations needed to be sized to the peak and would be underutilised for other periods of the day. Insull focused on attracting groups of customers with different types of peak demand over the day to better utilise generation station capacity. Electric traction had peaks at the start and end of the day. Industrial processes that ran through the night were therefore complementary. Insull even had a measure for this, the 'diversity factor'. By 1910 Insull had articulated a vision for the electricity system that dominated until the late 1970s: the 'load-hungry utility' seeking out diverse forms of load to improve efficiency, drive down prices and push up consumption.[53]

London was the antithesis of the Chicago and Berlin systems. Undertakings were too small and fragmented to generate scale benefits, so prices were high. Industrial companies, urban railways and even some commercial premises chose to generate their own electricity, which reduced the diversity of demand. In an ingenious scheme, Selfridges on Oxford Street used a generator to light the store and charge battery-powered delivery vans. This was a critical difference to Berlin and Chicago. One reason was that German and American electrical equipment manufacturers dominated the market in Britain and sold generation equipment directly to urban rail companies and industrials, discouraging them from connecting to the public system.[54]

The situation in London was the most extreme example of a pattern evident in other towns and cities. The exception was in the North East of England, where the North Eastern Electric Supply Company (NESCo) operated. Newcastle had ten times the electricity consumption per capita of London thanks to a system that replicated the Chicago and Berlin model. Power was generated from a combination of coal and waste heat from industrial processes. The region was an industrial powerhouse with 20 per cent of the nation's coal mining output, 37 per cent of iron ore mining and 51 per cent of merchant ship building.[55]

In 1901 NESCo opened the Neptune Station, the first large three-phase generator in the country. Further huge stations were added to the system at Carville and Dunston, the first power stations with a control room. A sixty-six-kilovolt (kV) transmission line, the highest voltage line in Britain, connected generation to demand. NESCo was by far the largest utility in the country. Unlike other regions, the whole area was under a standard system, a three-phase current and forty-hertz frequency. In 1924 NESCo achieved a load factor of 56 per cent when the next best in the country, Manchester, was at just 32 per cent.[56]

NESCo's success was the result of several factors. The municipal authorities had sufficient revenue from the port and coal to fund urban sanitation, so were happy for NESCo to operate the electricity system. The company was also commercially smart and achieved scale quickly through mergers, helped by strong social ties among the region's industrial elite. Almost all the capital came from local sources until 1906, when the company raised debt through the investment bank Lazard Frères. Another factor was of course very cheap coal, which fuelled NESCo's large generators. With low prices, NESCo won contracts to supply industrial, ship-building, mining and traction facilities – unlike in London. In 1901 NESCo had just 1 gigawatt hour (GWh) of demand from industry, mining and chemicals, but by 1913 it had 188 GWh.[57]

NESCo's success was also thanks to the skill of two engineers who would have a large impact on British electricity, Charles Merz and William McLellan. Their firm, Merz and McLellan, was an electrical engineering consultancy that essentially designed the NESCo system. Charles Merz's father had founded NESCo, but rather than stay focused on the North East, Merz would go on to be the most vocal campaigner for the rationalisation of the entire British electricity system.

Gas did not have the same scale effects as in electricity. Gas was manufactured from coal and stored in the massive gasholders that dominated urban skylines for a century. It therefore made sense to manufacture the gas close to sites of demand and move it through localised networks. Cast iron mains were common from the middle of the nineteenth century, but these pipelines were leaky and hence operators wanted to keep the pressure as low as possible. Until the arrival of natural gas in the 1960s, high-pressure transmission did not make sense. Gas distribution was therefore more naturally atomistic, suited to a regional structure. There was nothing like the self-reinforcing momentum that emerged in the electricity industry.[58]

The pressure to reform

Municipal electricity and gas enterprises may have performed better than private companies, but there were wider structural problems they could not address due to their local scope. Britain had a highly fragmented electricity system of small undertakings, and the complexity of ownership froze the structure of the industry. There were simply too many firms operating at a suboptimal scale. Unlike in the US and Germany, the British system lacked strong financial institutions that might have forced through rationalisation. The problem of fragmentation was most acute in electricity but also existed in gas. This suggests that it was the political economy of energy – specifically, the patterns of ownership – that was the root cause of Britain's issues.

The repeated attempts over the early twentieth century to reform London's electricity industry illustrate the way fragmentation led to paralysis. Charles Merz was the leading proponent of the large regional-power-system model. Merz first turned his attention to London in the early 1900s, offended by the disorder of its power system. In 1904 he set up the Electric Power Development Company as a vehicle to give London a system like NESCo's. Merz's plan was simple: he would build large generating stations outside London and along the Thames, plus a new set of transmission lines into the city. The existing enterprises would buy 'bulk power' at a price substantially lower than the cost of them generating on their own. These firms could then shut down their small generating stations. It was a miniature version of the scheme that central government would apply to the whole country in the late 1920s.

Merz even persuaded Samuel Insull to testify as to London's backwardness and the need for change. The proposal gained the support of hundreds of manufacturers, who signed a petition in favour of it. However, on the London County Council the Progressive Party opposed the project on the grounds that it would erode municipal control, and the Conservative Party opposed the interference with private enterprise. Unsurprisingly, the gas companies also opposed it. The Merz scheme meandered through Parliament and select committees, but it never progressed to a third reading before Arthur Balfour's government collapsed. As one politician told Merz, the issue 'was politics not engineering'. There was an attempt to revive the scheme on the eve of the First World War, but it also failed.[59] In other parts of the country similar attempts to build larger generating stations and supply bulk power to areas failed, blocked by inter-system rivalries.[60]

The First World War added momentum to the shift towards large regional systems. In the US and Germany giant power plants were built to meet wartime demand, along with more interconnections to improve economies of scale and resiliency. Merz and McLellan became advisors to the Ministry of Munitions, and in 1916 the government agreed to fund interconnection between undertakings to create larger units. In 1916 McLellan was made director of the Department of Electrical Power Supply, but he was transferred to the Admiralty to work on submarine warfare before he could make any significant progress.

An engineer called Arnold Gridley had to take up the mantle and started to force through interconnections in 1917. Under Gridley's oversight, the Electrical Sub-Committee tightly controlled the approvals for new generation stations to focus investment on maximising output for the war effort.[61] The results were impressive; for example, the committee oversaw a quadrupling of the electricity generation capacity in Sheffield between 1914 and 1918.[62] Sheffield was at the centre of armaments production, with electricity demand booming due to widespread adoption of electric arc furnaces for steel making. Gridley oversaw a similar transformation in Coventry and the South West. Britain's achievements over the course of the war were admired in the US. The chief engineer of the US Electric Bond and Share Company observed that 'in Great Britain plans far more comprehensive than anything even talked of here are being laid years ahead for increasing, interconnecting and centralizing the supply of electrical energy'.[63]

By the end of the war, a pattern of techno-economic development had emerged in the US, Germany and Britain that would shape the energy system for the next half century: the load-hungry utility driving towards ever larger scale. The reformers ramped up the pressure. In 1917 the Board of Trade established the Williamson Committee, which argued that the main issue was that the 'linking up and interchange of power is now extraordinarily difficult and costly' because of the huge number of 'parochial and discordant' undertakings. The committee recommended setting up 'one central authority to regulate' the industry with five Electricity Commissioners. These Electricity Commissioners would have the power to set up new district electricity boards, effectively forcing through interconnection. The boards would be publicly owned and have the power to consolidate generation, provide regional transmission and purchase in bulk from the most efficient generating stations.[64]

This was essentially Merz's NESCo system and London plan at a larger scale. In 1918 Charles Merz joined forces with Viscount Richard Haldane, the secretary of state for war between 1905 and 1912. Haldane chaired a parliamentary committee on the best use for British coal, and the resulting report once again recommended that the country adopt the NESCo model. The Haldane-Merz report fired a broadside at the electricity industry's parochialism and the state's feebleness:

> Parliament was apparently convinced that the generation and supply of electricity must be dealt with in a big way . . . They were, however, apparently afraid to insist on the amalgamation of the existing lighting enterprises which . . . were and are still each limited to a few miles in area.[65]

The report recommended consolidation into sixteen electrical power districts, which would construct super-sized generation plants. Merz and Haldane also advocated tight central government control over generation and transmission and the control of power prices at the high-voltage level.[66]

There was a backlash from Conservative MPs and sections of the industry to such heavy-handed state intervention. The report was watered down and became the 1919 Electricity Supply Act. It was a fudge. The Electricity Commissioners became a mere coordinating body, who could recommend but not compel interconnection. Their main instrument would be to establish joint electricity authorities responsible for coordinating electricity supply in an area, but only if the existing utilities decided they wanted it. Essentially, reform was voluntary.[67]

The 1919 act was a failure. The Electricity Commissioners were toothless. The industry doggedly opposed and frustrated reform at every turn. No one was more belligerent than George Balfour, an industrialist and Conservative MP for Hampstead. In 1909 Balfour had merged his company with another to create Balfour Beatty. The firm would go on to be a major supplier of engineering and construction services to the electricity, rail and gas industries. George Balfour was also a fierce opponent of the Haldane-Merz plan. He argued that interconnection would emerge spontaneously if it was in the interests of private firms.[68] This ignored the fundamental cooperation problem: even if a group of undertakings could agree that they needed to rationalise, agreements would break down over who would take the lead. This fed off municipals fearing domination by larger and worse-run private firms, a justifiable fear given the municipals were more efficient and effective. Interconnection also required a degree of standardisation of frequency and voltages, which was extremely expensive.

By 1920, many politicians and industry leaders were of the view that Britain was an electricity laggard based on its low electricity consumption per capita. This was a somewhat arbitrary metric, but it was the one that mattered to many contemporaries. Local affiliation was the most powerful force at work. Heterogeneity and fragmentation had a path-dependent impact. They made coordination difficult because of the number of actors that had to be corralled to make any significant change. The situation was not because Britain had an underdeveloped scientific or technical culture. The North East had built a truly world-class regional electricity system, and municipal electricity enterprises successfully drove prices down and electricity consumption up over two decades. The issue was political inertia. The state tried to solve the problem of fragmentation through persuasion. It failed. By 1920 the British energy system had entered a stalemate with all but a few visionaries in a state of procrastination.

2

Rationalised Energy, 1920–1945

In 1920, John Maynard Keynes observed:

> The most serious problems for England have been brought to a head by the war but are in their origins more fundamental. The forces of the nineteenth century have run their course and are exhausted. The economic motives and ideals of that generation no longer satisfy us: We must find a new way.[1]

The story of networked energy in the interwar period exemplified these words.

The history of energy between the two world wars is poorly understood in political circles today. For the right, the decades before nationalisation in the 1940s were a utopia of free enterprise. On the left, it is seen as a nightmarish time of destructive competition. Both accounts rely on the myth that the state did not intervene until after the Second World War. Yet it was a Conservative government led by Stanley Baldwin that set up the Central Electricity Board (CEB) in the late 1920s. This pioneering public enterprise reset the political economy of energy and oversaw a remarkable transformation of the electricity industry. The CEB built the first National Grid and brought swathes of the industry under direct state control. Conservative and industry voices who argued that the 'dead hand of the state' would stifle innovation were proven comprehensively wrong. In many ways, the CEB started something in the 1920s that the Labour Party simply finished in the 1940s.[2]

The failures of voluntarism

Repeated attempts to reform the electricity system during the early twentieth century culminated in the 1919 Electricity Act, which ended up being ineffective. The Electricity Commissioners had no power, and voluntary interconnection was rare. In 1925 there were nearly 600 electricity undertakings, and a laissez-faire mindset still lingered. For example, in 1924 the Electricity Commissioners agreed that all undertakings should be placed on a standard frequency, but they had little power to make this a reality and by the mid-1920s there were seventeen different frequencies being used across the country.[3]

There were also calls for amalgamation and rationalisation in gas. At the end of the First World War, the gas industry was also fragmented, with small-scale firms and little cross-industry collaboration. Competition with electricity intensified in the interwar period, which depressed returns. The gas industry accepted its inevitable retreat from lighting and focused on cooking and heating and marketing to domestic housewives. Organisations like the British Commercial Gas Association provided some coordination on marketing campaigns and standardisation of tariffs and appliances, but successes were limited.[4]

Some examples of scale emerged. In the 1920s, various gas companies in the North East merged to be better able to compete with the North Eastern Electric Supply Company (NESCo). Between 1922 and 1935 the London Gas Light and Coke Company (GLCC) absorbed six of the large London gas companies. There was, however, little evidence that these acquisitions improved outcomes for citizens, and a parliamentary committee noted that 'the affairs of that company have not been well managed'.[5] The number of gas undertakings fell only slightly, from 797 in 1921 to 706 in 1937. Joint holding companies were formed that rolled up firms, but in an opportunistic manner with little geographical coherence.[6]

Holding companies in electricity had a varied impact during the 1920s and 1930s. The organisational form was really a means to evade profit regulation. In some parts of the country, they grouped together small undertakings and rationalised systems – for example, in the East Riding of Yorkshire, Lincolnshire, Cornwall and the Midlands. In London, the London Power Company was formed in 1925 to amalgamate the generation capacity of smaller firms. However, many holding companies were geographically dispersed.[7]

Some of the holding companies were huge. London's eleven largest holding companies collectively owned 155 subsidiaries with 1.2 million customers.[8] Britain's holding companies were less influential than in the US, however, where the collapse of Samuel Insull's empire in the early 1930s following the Wall Street Crash of 1929 was a national scandal. Nevertheless, as early as 1920 the Electricity Commissioners highlighted that the dubious practice was driving up prices for consumers and increasing profits for capitalists.[9]

In 1922, George Balfour, the Conservative MP who owned Balfour Beatty, created the country's largest holding company, Power Securities Corporation. This giant company contained electricity undertakings spread across Scotland, the Midlands, Wales and London. It also included three major engineering suppliers (Balfour Beatty, Babcock & Wilcox and British Thomson-Houston). In the mid-1920s Balfour used the power of his holding company to block attempts at reform, refusing to cooperate with the commissioners unless legally compelled. Balfour was not alone, and parliamentary investigations highlighted how the holding companies had frustrated rationalisation.[10] By 1935 the holding companies had made little positive impact. Most counties still resembled a patchwork quilt, with multiple electricity firms.

Britain was not alone in struggling to rationalise its electricity system. Across Europe and the US, interconnection agreements between companies were rare. However, the situation in Britain was at the extreme. Fragmentation persisted for so long because of 'path dependency', a term used to describe how past events or decisions significantly influence the options available later on. In conventional economic thinking the best firms and products win. When path dependency is factored in, competition between firms does *not* always lead to the 'survival of the fittest'. Increasing returns to scale (particularly strong in network industries), early-mover advantages and policies that favour incumbents can lead to a dynamic where some firms survive despite offering inferior products. In Britain, the fragmentation of networked energy created a path-dependent lock-in. It took a long time for the penny to drop among political elites that amalgamation would require state intervention. It is notable that in both Britain and the US progress was made on interconnection only during the First World War, when the military establishments essentially forced it upon firms.

It was Stanley Baldwin, Conservative prime minister from 1924, who was the first front-bench politician to grasp the scale of the problem. Baldwin's Board of Trade president noted that 'electricity is so inefficient today in this country that it has always been amazing to me that the Labour government did not attempt to nationalise it'.[11] Baldwin appointed Lord William Douglas Weir, chair of a Scottish engineering firm, to chair a commission to investigate the matter. The resulting publication, the Weir Report, was one of the most important documents in the history of British energy.

The report dismissed Britain's lack of hydroelectric power as an adequate explanation for why the country lagged others in electricity consumption. Britain's abundant coal, high levels of urbanisation and industry located close to urban areas meant that it was well suited for a highly efficient interconnected system. The Weir committee assembled an impressive list of witnesses, including Samuel Insull from Chicago, whose testimony was given great weight in the final report as the world's pre-eminent electricity expert. The report pulled no punches in laying the blame at the feet of politicians: 'The policy of persuasion can only be written down as a failure . . . delay and procrastination are widespread . . . the resultant loss to the country has been heavy and becomes daily heavier.'[12]

The Weir Report recommended rationalising generation into a smaller number of larger stations and building a nationally interconnected network. The recommendations were accepted in full. This was not the first time such suggestions had been made, of course: so what had changed? A crucial catalyst was the perception that the situation in electricity supply was sapping Britain's industrial strength and contributing to economic decline.

Between 1870 and 1914, Britain fell behind the US as the leading global economy. The US was at the forefront of various technological developments in these years (mass production, chemicals, the internal combustion engine). It was in electricity that the gap between Britain and the US was most pronounced. Over 1870–1914, the average growth rate in labour productivity for British utilities was 1.4 per cent as compared to 4.0 per cent in the US. There was also an emerging consensus across the political spectrum that economic growth required the agglomeration of British industry into larger-scale units, as had happened in the US. Across numerous industries British firms grew larger in size in the 1920s. The fragmentation in the electricity industry stuck out like a sore thumb.[13]

The Weir Report included a crude but simple table showing electricity consumption per person in various cities and countries, with Britain at the bottom. In a parliamentary debate Lord Weir drew a direct relationship between electrification and national regeneration:

> To those who believe that this country has passed the zenith of its supremacy, and that we can only look forward to gradual degeneracy in those spheres where we formerly led the world, this Bill can make small appeal and I can understand their attitude of leaving things as they are.[14]

The Central Electricity Board

Battersea power station is one of London's most striking buildings. Built between 1929 and 1955 it is still one of the largest brick buildings in the world. Today it is prime real estate. Following a regeneration programme in the 2010s it is now home to shops, fine dining and luxury apartments. But this temple of commerce was once a 'temple of power', and its vast scale meant that it came very close to being cancelled before a single brick was laid.

In the late 1920s London's electricity system was a mess. In response to criticism a group of private companies formed the London Power Company (LPC) in 1925. The goal was to pool their resources and build larger, more efficient, stations. Battersea power station was the centrepiece of the plan. In 1927 the company proposed the idea to various authorities but faced significant opposition. In April 1929 a letter in *The Times* brought the issue to a head. The signatories included mayors, doctors, presidents of royal institutes and other elites. The letter complained that the power station would be unsightly, and that pollution would cause damage to vegetation, buildings, paintings and public health. Battersea became a cause célèbre. The King's private secretary wrote to Neville Chamberlain, then minister of health, to endorse the letter in *The Times*.

London's increasingly voracious demand for electricity and the limited number of suitable sites meant that Chamberlain had to reluctantly inform the King of the cabinet's decision to go ahead with the station. The King was far from satisfied and expressed surprise that the site should have been approved without greater scrutiny. Battersea 'A' power station was built between 1929 and 1935. To address public concerns, the company hired Sir Giles Gilbert Scott to design the grand art deco exterior and installed experimental 'gas washing' technology to reduce the pollution levels. The fiasco reinforced the argument that electrical infrastructure needed more coordinated planning. One obvious solution was to move large power stations outside of towns and cities. But this could only be accomplished with transmission lines to carry power around the country. It was in this context that the Central Electricity Board began its work.[15]

The Weir Report recommended creating a new organisation, the Central Electricity Board, outside the control of the Electricity Commissioners. Its mission was to construct a new national electricity network, rationalise generation and standardise frequencies.[16] Baldwin acted swiftly, and for a time setting up the CEB became his chief preoccupation. He could act decisively safe in the knowledge that the Labour Party also backed the Weir Report's recommendations. It helped that influential Labour politicians like Herbert Morrison and Clement Attlee had served on joint electricity authorities and therefore knew first-hand the issues in the industry. Both the private sector and municipal undertakings opposed the passage of the bill, but most begrudgingly accepted that the writing was on the wall.

The CEB was created by the Electricity Act of 1926. The board was a not-for-profit entity responsible to government, not Parliament. Although board members were appointed by a minister, they could not be easily removed. Baldwin was particularly insistent that it was not a government department but rather a business-like board 'managed by practical men'. And keeping the CEB outside the civil service meant that it could pay higher salaries. Its grand headquarters overlooked Trafalgar Square in Central London (in the same building as National Grid's offices today). Baldwin asked Samuel Insull to be chairman, but he turned the offer down. This was a lucky escape, as the CEB's reputation would surely have been tarnished when Insull's American empire collapsed. Charles Merz was the natural candidate. The Weir Report essentially argued for a national system that reflected the model Merz had developed in Newcastle in the early 1900s.

Yet Merz was passed over for fear that his commercial activities would bring the impartiality of the board into question. Baldwin went with Sir Andrew Duncan, aged just forty-two at the time, a lawyer and industrialist. Duncan's lack of electricity expertise was seen as a strength, as he was not tarnished by the dire situation in the industry. Duncan's merits were his charm, patience and skills as a negotiator. He had even been knighted for the way he had resolved an industrial dispute in coal mining in 1921. Duncan shared Baldwin's determination that the CEB should not resemble the civil service, that it should be seen to work with the industry. Duncan chose Archibald Page as his chief engineer and general manager, a former Electricity Commissioner. Supporting Page were, predictably, engineers from Merz & McLellan and NESCo.[17]

The CEB needed to raise capital to fund the new network infrastructure. This was accomplished by issuing non-voting fixed-interest stock (bonds). The rate offered was between 4 per cent and 5 per cent (averaging 4.3 per cent). Stockholders had no voting rights and did not own any equity. The government was the sole owner. By 1933 the board had raised £53.1 million. Lenders would have to be extremely patient, as the securities would not be paid back in full until the 1990s. By 1947 the board had paid back only 2.6 per cent of the loans. The CEB had the option of using a Treasury guarantee, but Duncan refused to use it. This helped the organisation evade government scrutiny of its finances. The CEB was in many ways more autonomous than any private corporation at the time because, other than government, it did not have voting shareholders to deal with.[18]

The CEB's plan was relatively simple. It would select the best generating stations and buy power from them. By constructing a National Grid, it could transmit the power and sell it to the existing local undertakings. Those local undertakings would then shut down their smaller stations. The overall efficiency of the system would improve and the cost per unit of electricity would fall. The top tier of selected generating stations was the most efficient ones in the country, designated to supply base load. Base load is a crucial concept in electricity and refers to the minimum level of electricity demand required over a twenty-four-hour period. Base load generators are stations that can run round the clock, and when added together meet the total base load requirement. In the second tier were stations that were used only to meet peak demand.

Through selection the CEB controlled the location, design and operating plans of all new major power stations. In return, the CEB guaranteed all operating costs, installation and construction costs, and the capital charges on stations within certain limits that related to an approved rate of return. Non-selected stations could stay open only with the permission of the CEB. It could also compel selection into the national scheme at any time. The CEB essentially took over responsibility for planning generation infrastructure. Unselected stations were free to remain operational and could make short-run decisions over how much to generate from one day to the next, but they had to gain CEB approval to build anything new.[19]

Station selection was, in theory, based on techno-economic criteria like the cost of coal, availability of water and potential for expanding the plant. However, Duncan realised that success required more than engineering prowess. He needed to keep the industry onside to ensure that the settlement was durable beyond the lifetime of the incumbent government. Selecting a station would confer significant prestige on the engineers who ran it, winning their support for the overall strategy. The Electricity Commissioners had recommended selecting only 118 stations, but in the end Duncan went with 140.[20]

The CEB's selection approach provides a neat natural experiment for the effectiveness of public and private ownership. There were four categories of station: selected and unselected, municipal and private. Economic historians have analysed the performance of the stations in all four categories and found that selected stations had 20 per cent lower cost per unit of output than unselected ones. Contrary to one of the dogmas of neoliberal politics today, in this instance the state was very good at picking winners. Moreover, contrary to the popular conception that public ownership is less efficient than private ownership, selected municipal and private stations had the same level of productivity.[21]

The National Grid

The centrepiece of the strategy proposed by the Weir committee was the construction of a network to connect the selected power stations and existing local undertakings. Increasing the voltage reduced line losses (the energy lost in transmission). A voltage of 132 kV was chosen, which was double the highest-voltage line in Britain at the time. This was still far lower than the voltages used for transmission lines in North America and elsewhere in Europe, which were generally above 200 kV.

Engineers observed that the map of the proposed network looked like a 'grid iron', and the term 'grid' stuck. The National Grid was built in nine regional schemes, a modular approach that infrastructure experts cite as crucial to the success of mega-projects. Once the board approved a scheme, a local office was set up with devolved power. The 'undertakers' then conducted a conference over several weeks to maintain local support. Devolution also meant that each scheme didn't have to wait on approval by the central committee.[22]

The project moved at lightning pace. The CEB was established between 1926 and 1927. On average it took four months for the CEB to review and approve the plan for each region. Most of the construction took place between 1929 and 1934, with just over 3,000 miles of high-tension transmission line and 297 substations erected by 1938. The CEB built at a rate of around 500 miles per year. By comparison, today's privatised electricity transmission networks are targeting a rate of just 62 miles a year for the next decade.[23]

The speed of building was influenced by how quickly the board could do three things: secure wayleave agreements (access to land), order goods and services and construct the infrastructure. The board's annual reports contained neat data tables tracking all three. By 1930, 70 per cent of the route had

Figure 2.1. The first National Grid as of 1933

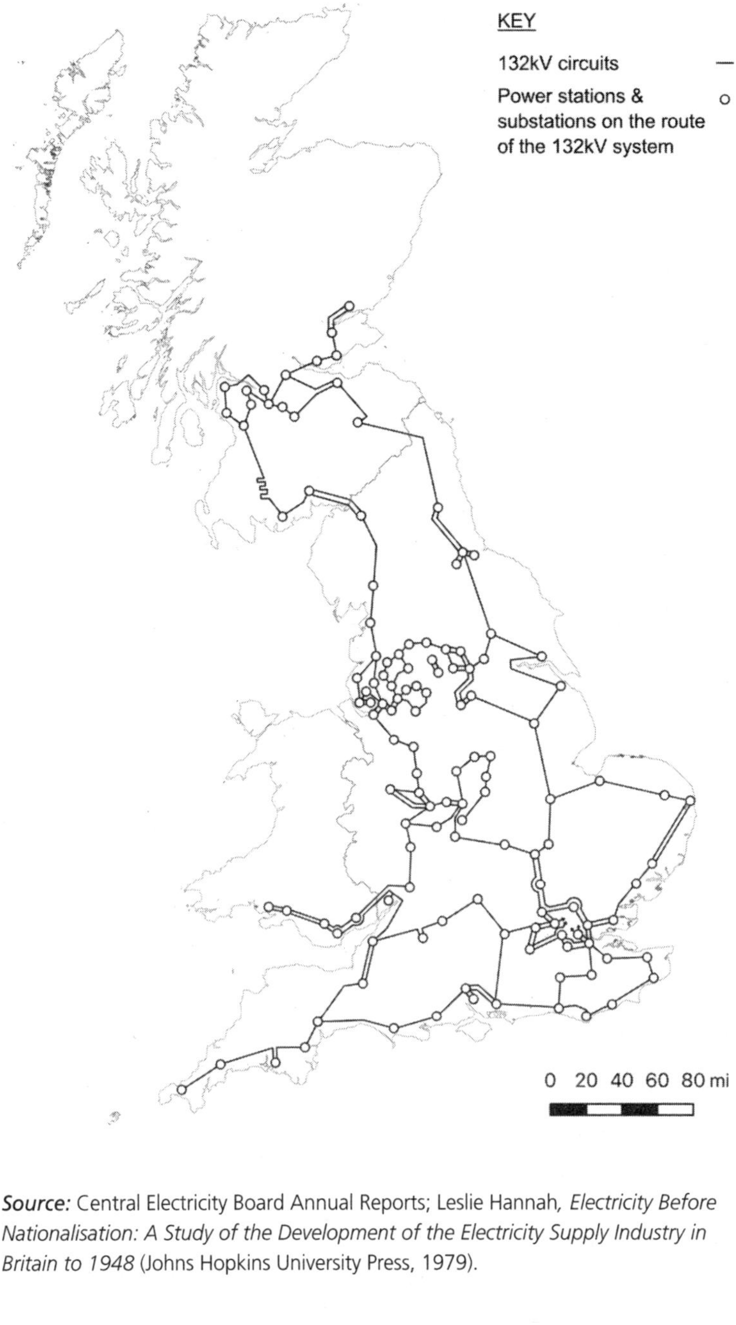

Source: Central Electricity Board Annual Reports; Leslie Hannah, *Electricity Before Nationalisation: A Study of the Development of the Electricity Supply Industry in Britain to 1948* (Johns Hopkins University Press, 1979).

wayleave agreements secured. By 1931, 80 per cent of the contracting was complete. All contracts for equipment and services were with British firms. The board worked closely with suppliers on the development of new types of switchgear, transformers and control apparatus. By 1931, half of all the transmission towers had been erected.[24]

In parallel the CEB rationalised generation and standardised frequencies, meaning that multiple counties could move on to the new trading arrangements soon after a section was finished. This meant that citizens started to experience the benefits without waiting for the whole national project to complete. More than 95 per cent of the grid was fully operational by early 1935, just nine years after the CEB was founded.

The board had to be extremely agile. It needed to expand the capacity of power stations in some areas in anticipation of the grid arriving, with the timing perfectly synchronised. Technology was constantly improved and optimised. The board coordinated dozens of small-scale 'micro inventions'. Physical infrastructure was adapted as the grid was being built to improve reliability or reduce costs. There was a series of 'world's first' inventions developed and deployed within a few years.[25] The frequency standardisation programme was particularly complex. New equipment needed to be installed in factories and power stations before the grid was energised. The 1935 annual report estimated that this work covered around 340,000 premises.[26] The 1937 annual report recorded that 'this vast work was carried out with hardly any interruption of consumers' processes'.[27]

It was a project on a massive scale using 150,000 tons of steel, 28,000 transmission towers, 12,000 tons of aluminium and 200,000 porcelain insulators. All that infrastructure had a profound impact on the British landscape. The CEB faced strong opposition in some areas over the visual impact of the towers, most notably in Keswick, Ashdown Forest, the South Downs and the New Forest. The Council for the Preservation of Rural England, founded in 1926, proved a highly effective opponent. In the Midlands, a part of the route passing through

Frampton-on-Severn was particularly contentious. The Bishop of Gloucester wrote a letter in *The Times* complaining that 'the whole proposal seems to be as indefensible as it is unnecessary'. The cleric was joined by the rural district council and the local archaeological society. The CEB conceded and relocated the line inland to avoid the village. There were other examples of local inquiries leading to route modification.[28]

Overall, however, the CEB seemed very successful at using persuasion to quell opposition. There were only a handful of cases in which the board had to ask the government minister to override objections raised by local authorities.[29] In total the board had to deal with 22,000 landowners to secure access rights and wayleaves. The programme went to great lengths to persuade landowners to accept standard remuneration (for example, five shillings per tower) and resisted escalating to the secretary of state for a compulsory purchase order. The board needed to use this option for only 600 cases (2.7 per cent).

The CEB had estimated the project would cost £26.7 million (£1.9 billion in 2024 prices). Unlike most mega-projects today, the first National Grid was completed on time and at cost.[30] It was extraordinary value for money when compared with the cost of grid infrastructure today. It is estimated that between 2025 and 2035 the various transmission grid companies will need to spend nearly £20 billion for just 620 miles of transmission lines.[31] Today's companies' costs are around fifty times more expensive per mile than those of the CEB's National Grid. The board's 1934 annual report also calculated that the value case for consumers in lower prices had been delivered almost exactly in line with projections.[32] The board was also an extremely lean organisation by modern standards: in 1934 it employed just over 1,200 people.[33]

Initially the grid was not so much a 'National Grid' but rather a series of interlinked regional grids. For most of the 1930s, it was operated from seven separate regional control centres that kept supply and demand in harmony. Control room engineers found that running a grid required understanding culture as much as electrical engineering. Demand for electricity reflected the BBC's radio schedule, with spikes at the end of popular shows. In an extraordinary act of inquisitiveness, the control centres experimented with synchronising the seven grids as one in 1936. It worked and created the single largest integrated power system in the world.[34] The staff may have been scolded, but their seniors realised that full harmonisation would improve the reliability of the system. Between 1937 and 1938 the first National Grid control centre was established in Bankside, South London, next door to where Charles Merz had first trained as a power station engineer. From 1938 the system was run as a single integrated system. Except for one serious blackout, in 1934, the grid proved highly reliable.[35]

The CEB was an ingenious policy innovation. The debates about public versus private ownership were temporarily solved by a typical British compromise. Creative language allowed the Conservatives to deny it was nationalisation. The founding statements were deliberately ambiguous:

> We propose not a change of ownership but a partial subordination of vested interests in generation to that of a new authority for the benefit of all, and this only under proper safeguards and in a manner which will preserve the value of the incentives of private enterprise.

Some in the industry were less diplomatic. The Council of the Institution of Electrical Engineers complained that the plan was an 'intolerable interference with the responsible management of selected stations . . . [and] the salvation of the industry is not to be brought about either by the waving of weird grid-irons or by the multiplication of authorities'. George Balfour called the CEB 'licensed burglars'. The generating stations he owned ended up selling more power, but Balfour was frustrated that the price was effectively capped so he could not extract higher profits.[36]

Despite the ambiguous language the CEB *was* nationalisation. A Conservative government had run roughshod over private property rights. The state might not have owned the power stations, but it had almost total control over what they did. Effectively, the state took responsibility for planning all major electricity infrastructure. It also became the sole owner and operator of the most critical component, the National Grid. It was an exercise in central planning and state-directed coordination unlike anything seen before, and one of the most radical exercises in industrial policy in British history.

The CEB's institutional legacy was significant. It set the organisational model for the period of nationalisation – the public corporation. Financing infrastructure through non-voting stock also became the norm in the 1950s. It may seem odd today that the party of Margaret Thatcher initiated the journey to nationalisation, but in the interwar period the Conservative Party embraced corporatist ideas. Many Conservatives advocated state involvement to promote agglomeration of firms. One faction, the 'Tory etatists', led by Harold Macmillan, went a step further and embraced nationalisation.[37] By the late 1930s, there was very little difference between this wing of the Tories and the Labour Party on matters of energy policy. While many Tories remained sceptical of nationalisation, it was hard to argue with the successes of the CEB. The CEB demonstrated that competition and state ownership were perfectly compatible, which further calmed Tory nerves. Public ownership was used for the natural monopoly parts of the system, the network, while competition was encouraged in the other parts, in generation and supply.

The CEB was part of a pan-European trend of greater state involvement in the economy and specifically in energy. Across Europe in the late nineteenth century, the role of the central state was restricted to establishing rights of way with light regulation of prices and profits. This changed in the period from 1914 to 1945, with the central state ratcheting up regulation and taking direct ownership of networked industries like energy, telecoms and rail. Even in the US, the federal government took a more proactive role in the 1930s with projects like the Tennessee Valley Authority and the Rural Electrification Agency.[38]

State involvement was a response to technological and economic forces within the electricity system. By the end of the First World War, it was clear that there were significant benefits to system integration. Interconnection allowed engineers to reduce the 'reserve margin' of plants and increase the size of generators. Bigger generators were more efficient and ran at lower cost. Combining transmission lines with larger generation stations was particularly effective. Transformers allowed engineers to stitch together different subnetworks with relative ease. Technological factors were the main reason for state intervention in electricity. This is supported by the fact that nothing like the same technological factors existed in gas and there was not the same pressure on the state to intervene.[39]

The Labour Party and left-wing ideology had very little influence on the formation of the CEB. In 1918 Labour passed Clause Four of its constitution, which set the objective 'to secure for the workers by hand or by brain the full fruits of their industry . . . upon the basis of common ownership of the means of production, distribution and exchange'. However, only the 1918, 1923, 1931 and 1935 Labour manifestos included a commitment to nationalise electricity. The 1922, 1924 and 1929 manifestos did not. In the 1920s, guild socialism emerged as a force in Labour politics, arguing for worker representation on public corporation boards. However, there would be no workers on the CEB. Indeed, the 1920s were a disappointment for Labour.[40]

Electric boom

The CEB's plan to concentrate generation in only the largest and most efficient stations was a success. By 1935 just twenty-eight power stations provided the majority of the electricity to the country.[41] The board also reduced the 'reserve margin' from

40 per cent in the 1920s to 10 per cent in the late 1930s. The best measure of efficiency was the system load factor. It had stagnated between 1922 and 1927 at 28 per cent to 30 per cent, but after 1927 steadily improved to reach 38.8 per cent by 1940.[42]

The CEB also succeeded in translating more capacity and better system efficiency into reduced prices. The price of electricity fell dramatically between 1920 and 1940. On a like-for-like basis (meaning adjusted for inflation and converted into the price per ton of oil equivalent) the price of domestic electricity fell 39 per cent, whereas the price of gas rose 58 per cent and the price of coal rose 16 per cent.[43] In 1920, electricity was almost twenty times more expensive to heat and cook with than coal, but by 1939 the gap had narrowed to four times.[44]

Falling prices understate the improvement to living standards. It is important to consider not just the price of energy, but the price of the service that it provides. This means taking account of the efficiency of the equipment used to provide light, heat, transport and motive power. In 1930, the price of electricity was five times the price of gas, but the electric light bulb was ten times more efficient than gas lighting. People switched to a costlier fuel for a lower price per unit of light (lumen-hours). Between 1920 and 1940 the price of lighting as an energy service fell 73 per cent.[45]

The overarching mission of the CEB was to drive up electricity consumption. The board accepted very low returns or even losses in the early years to increase sales and spread the cost of the infrastructure over a greater number of units. The Weir committee had set a goal of 500 kWh of electricity consumption per person by 1940. Remarkably, the CEB delivered on this target almost exactly.[46] The interwar years witnessed a massive increase in demand for electricity across industrial, domestic, commercial and traction. Overall sales per head of population grew 6.4 times between 1921 and 1938. Electricity demand for domestic purposes grew a staggering 18.8 times, commercial 7.7 times, industry 5.6 times, public lighting 4.8 times and traction 3.2 times.[47] Consumption of lighting and heating as energy services grew

176 per cent and 69 per cent, respectively, between 1920 and 1940. The growth in the consumption of lighting was particularly remarkable when considered in a longer-term perspective. Lighting consumption went from 10 trillion lumen-hours in 1900 (80 per cent gas-fuelled) to 150 trillion lumen-hours in 1950 (95 per cent electricity-powered). The world was literally 15 times brighter by 1950.[48] From the 1920s, both private and local-authority-constructed houses had electricity installed as standard. In 1919, only 5 per cent of houses had electrical wiring, but by 1937 this figure was 66 per cent, over years where the housing supply grew at 2 per cent per annum.[49] The number of electrical sockets per house also increased following the Electricity Development Agency's hugely popular 'Wizard in the Wall' campaign in the 1930s.

The 'consumer revolution' in energy appliances is often associated with the 1950s and 1960s, but it started in the 1930s with home appliances like irons, hoovers and electric cookers. Electricity undertakings focused marketing and sales on domestic housewives. The Electrical Association for Women was founded in 1924 by Caroline Haslett, who would go on to serve in high office during the nationalised period.[50] Evidence that the electricity industry was targeting the domestic market is visible in the price record. Between 1921 and 1939 domestic prices fell more steeply than industrial prices.[51]

The interwar period was one of intense competition between gas and electricity. The gas industry was resilient and by the end of the 1930s was still the largest in the world. Between 1921 and 1937 gas sales continued to grow, although at a declining rate. Whereas electricity prices fell, gas prices rose 58 per cent in real terms between 1920 and 1940. Gas undertakings therefore had to focus on areas where price was less significant. Gas lost the market for domestic lighting but held its own in public lighting with sales doubling from 1920 to 1937. Gas undertakings also doubled down on cooking and heating. In the 1930s, gas cookers were the height of modernity, increasing from 210,000 to 1.5 million between 1932 and 1938.[52]

The gas industry could claim, with justification, that the CEB had effectively put the force of the state behind electricity and that this had disadvantaged gas. One of the reasons gas demand remained sticky was that gas pipes were built into the fabric of homes. In the 1920s gas undertakings lobbied hard to ensure that all council housing had gas as standard. A 1933 act of Parliament respected the council's right to choose and did not mandate dual connections to all homes, but the emphasis on 'freedom of choice' for citizens meant that most councils installed both gas and electricity as amenities. Working-class citizens were not passive in this. They became skilled negotiators with councils for access to both types of energy supply.[53]

Electricity is often seen as the archetypal 'general purpose technology' (GPT). GPTs are infrequent technological shocks that generate long-run positive effects on economic growth across multiple sectors.[54] Electricity comprehensively changed industrial production. Steam-powered factories tended to have a large engine in the centre of the factory with belts and pulleys linked to machinery. Electricity could be routed to small motors in individual machines, which created more flexibility in the layout of the factory. Electricity was therefore crucial to the development of the modern production line.[55]

In 1920 Britain lagged far behind the US and Germany in the electrification of industry. Without access to a reliable and cheap electricity network many manufacturers chose to build their own generation plant. In the East Midlands, a region with the potential for the lowest-cost electricity thanks to abundant low-grade coal, businesses as diverse as the Kelham Sugar works, Ketton Cement works, British United Shoe Machinery Company and Boots Pure Drug Company opted to generate their own power.[56]

The CEB succeeded in driving up industrial electricity consumption, which grew from 2,000 GWh in 1921 to 11,600 GWh in 1939. The fall in prices persuaded industry to use electricity from the National Grid and not rely on off-grid self-generation. This was pivotal to increasing diversity of demand. Self-generation accounted for 75 per cent of industrial electricity consumption in 1907, but this had fallen to 50 per cent by 1935 and 33 per cent by 1948.[57] The grid also allowed manufacturers to move to the outskirts of urban areas where land was cheaper. Electrification did have a positive impact on British manufacturing. Yet by 1938 there was still a huge gap compared to the US, which used three times more electricity per worker than Britain.[58]

How did Britain compare to other countries? In 1927, the output of the electricity system in the US was five times greater than in Britain. The CEB closed the gap, and by 1937 it was only three times.[59] However, Britain was still significantly behind. Economists use a measure called total factor productivity to evaluate how efficiently a country or sector converts all its inputs (or factors of production) into outputs. In the utilities sector, total factor productivity grew by an average of 3.9 per cent per annum in the US between 1920 and 1940, compared to just 1.8 per cent in Britain.[60]

Britain may have lagged the US, but it compared better to the rest of Europe. Electricity consumption per person increased more between 1920 and 1938 in Britain than in any other European country. For several years in a row the annual reports of the CEB celebrated that the growth in electricity consumption was higher in Britain than in the rest of the world, especially during the Great Depression.

Britain was not the first country to construct high-tension transmission lines, which were widespread around Europe and the US before the First World War. In one sense, the CEB was merely playing catch-up. Yet there was an originality to what the CEB accomplished. Britain's grid was not designed around hydroelectric facilities located far away from urban centres. It was instead designed to connect coal-fired generation and urban centres in a 'meshed network'. The use of a lower voltage was more suitable for this goal. Only Britain developed a truly unified network before the Second World War. It was not until 1967–75 that the US system developed a cross-continental grid system.[61] Credit must go to the generation of engineers who learned their craft in the North East and applied the same principles to the national system under public ownership. In 1932 there were so many Tyneside engineers in London working for the CEB that William McLellan hosted the first annual dinner of the NESCo Association at the Waldorf for thirty homesick former NESCo employees.[62]

The National Grid and war

Sir Andrew Duncan left his role as chairman of the Central Electricity Board in 1934 to become executive chairman of the British Iron and Steel Federation. By then Duncan was widely recognised as one of Britain's great living industrialists. Following his extraordinary achievements in electricity the government tasked him with the even harder job of reorganising Britain's struggling steel industry. However, with the advent of the war Duncan's talents were needed elsewhere. When Winston Churchill became prime minister in 1940, he selected Duncan as minister of supply, a critical position in the war cabinet and a post he held until the end of the war.

One of Duncan's most pressing responsibilities was increasing the output of industrial and munitions factories. By 1942 over 300,000 people were employed in more than forty Royal Ordinance Factories (known as ROFs). The ROFs were dedicated to critical wartime production of explosives, arms and ammunitions. By the start of the war, almost all industrial processes used electricity, and electricity permeated every sphere of modern warfare – not just munitions factories but barracks, encampments, searchlight stations and aerodromes. Supplying all these facilities with power was a significant logistical challenge. But it was a challenge made slightly easier thanks to the National Grid whose construction Duncan had overseen.

The National Grid was thus a critical asset in the war effort. It enabled a rapid increase in electricity production at low cost. Rather than having to build new power stations next to every new factory, the CEB could simply build a spur off the grid and add to the capacity of existing stations connected *anywhere* to the grid. The strategy also conserved materials and labour, which were in short supply. Thanks to the wisdom of the CEB's engineers, the grid had been built with optionality in mind. For example, substations had been designed to make it easy to add new connections. Electricity consumption increased dramatically – by 70 per cent between 1937 and 1944. Yet over the same years capital expenditure on the grid increased by only 25 per cent.[63]

The National Grid unlocked something even more important, geographical flexibility. Placing the economy on a war footing involved a dramatic and sudden shift in the geography of electricity demand. Siting munitions factories was a challenge. For safety reasons they needed to be far from urban centres and in areas less vulnerable to German bombing. With the grid, Duncan could locate factories where it was most strategically suitable, in the West of England, South Wales and the North West. Before the war, the counties of the South West and South Wales were net exporters of power and the South East of England a net importer. Over the war the flows flipped. The grid handled the change with ease.[64] As an aside, this is the best example from energy history of a rapid shift in the geography of electricity demand analogous to today's potential boom in electricity-hungry artificial intelligence data centres.

The grid also made the war economy more resilient. An interconnected system blunted the impact of enemy attacks. Even if power stations or sections of the grid were damaged, power could be rerouted and supply restored relatively quickly. The decision by control room operators in 1936 to test synchronising all regions proved fateful. The grid was run as a single integrated system throughout the war, although not without challenges, as one regional control room was destroyed by bombs, and the central control room was moved from Bankside into the lift shafts of a disused Underground station in 1941. Inter-regional tie lines were reinforced, paid for with a novel funding mechanism. The

Treasury covered half with grants, and the CEB picked up the other half. This set a precedent for the post-war period of the state directly funding energy infrastructure.[65]

Remarkably, the grid enjoyed relative immunity from serious dislocation by war damage. The rate of reliability improved over the course of the war. By 1944, 94 per cent of electrical faults were quickly cleared with no impact on supply, up from 85 per cent in 1937. Of all the incidents that led to a loss of supply during the war, only half were due to the war and only 15 per cent of these were due to enemy action. A bigger issue was defensive barrage balloons that came free from their moorings and drifted into the path of the grid.[66]

If the grid was a kind of physical platform that created flexibility, the CEB was a kind of organisational platform. From 1939 the CEB set up a national pool of strategic spares holding critical components like transformers, generators and switchgear. This common pool resource, to be shared by the entire industry, was critical to the war effort. If a substation or station was hit by a bomb, engineers could call on the reserve and have the assets back in operation within a few weeks.[67] The grid was thus like a many-headed hydra, or, in the words of the board, a 'continually improving asset'.[68]

Unfinished business

The CEB's mandate did not reach down into distribution and retail, which was left in the hands of the many private and municipal undertakings. This made it difficult to transfer the full benefits of the National Grid to citizens, as the CEB had little influence over the price of electricity charged to end consumers. Moreover, the large number of different voltages across the country also loaded considerable cost and inconvenience onto citizens because appliances did not always work in different areas.

Since the 1919 act, the Electricity Commissioners had succeeded in setting up only eight joint electricity authorities or joint boards.[69] There were a few successes, notably in Birmingham and the South East of Scotland, but these efforts took years of tortured negotiation.[70] There were many other failures. In 1939 the public intellectual W. A. Robson called the London Joint Electricity Authority 'unscientific and undesirable . . . a weak federal body, cumbersome in structure and feeble in function'.[71]

There was some consolidation of distribution undertakings in the 1930s, triggered by the work of the CEB. Before the construction of the grid there were very few mergers of electricity undertakings, no more than five a year from 1895 to 1930. In the 1930s there was a merger boom, with dozens a year. The reason was simple: the grid incentivised consolidation as firms could increase their scale and sell power to the whole country and not just their locality. Despite these mergers and the work of the commissioners, by the end of the 1930s there were still over 600 electricity undertakings, and the smallest 400 of them accounted for less than 10 per cent of national sales.[72]

It was a similar story in gas. In 1945, a parliamentary committee headed by Geoffrey Heyworth, the chairman of Unilever, noted that only 65 of the nearly 1,000 undertakings were above the 'threshold' that the committee considered of optimal scale. The Heyworth committee advocated compulsory purchase of all undertakings and division of the country into ten regions. This was the first time a parliamentary committee had come out in favour of outright national ownership.[73]

In 1929, the Labour politician Herbert Morrison put forward a proposal to reorganise electricity distribution around a small number of regional boards. The McGowan committee of 1936 recommended reducing the number of undertakings, accompanied by legislation to give adequate compulsory powers for reorganisation. The committee did not advocate nationalisation but suggested that provision should be made for using public ownership as a lever if necessary. This was rejected by the government due to fears that it would be disruptive. The industry could point to the improvements that had occurred during the

1930s and argue that there was no need for such drastic action. It was not until 1942 that a parliamentary report recommended nationalisation of electricity to force through agglomeration.[74]

By the mid-1940s, the Labour Party was firmly committed to nationalising electricity and gas. This led to a battle within Labour over *how* to run the industries. On the one side were followers of Herbert Morrison. In 1933, Morrison wrote *Socialisation and Transport*, which summarised his views on how to apply socialist principles to publicly owned services following his experience running the London Passenger Transport Board. Morrison was scathing about the role of workmen, noting that 'the majority of workmen are . . . more interested in the organisation, conditions, and life of their own immediate workshop than in those finer balances of financial, industrial, and commercial policy which are discussed in the Board room'.[75] This was managerial elitism at its worst. Morrison's model for the public corporation was one with the 'good chaps' as high custodians of public interest.[76] On the other side of the debate was Ernest Bevan of the Transport and General Workers Union, who argued for some form of worker participation on boards.[77] Morrison would go on to win the argument.

There were some within the electricity industry who favoured further rationalisation and public ownership. Once again, it was engineers from the North East who relentlessly kept pushing for reform. The general manager and lead engineer for NESCo, E. H. Woodward, argued that scale mattered above all else, and he was ambivalent as to whether this was accomplished under public or private ownership.[78]

The most passionate industry advocate for nationalisation was Thomas Graeme Nelson Haldane, the nephew of Lord Richard Haldane, Lord Chancellor under the Asquith and MacDonald governments and co-author of the Haldane-Merz report in 1918. After reading engineering at Cambridge, T. G. N. Haldane moved to Newcastle to work for Merz and McLellan, where he was apprenticed to Charles Parsons (inventor of the steam turbine). Haldane was a brilliant engineer who picked up Merz's relentless focus on order and coherence. In 1927, Haldane co-authored a paper on the design of city distribution systems and the problem of standardisation, which became a classic design manual for engineers. The paper articulated an approach that combined standardisation with adaptability, so it was easy to add components to a network as demand grew. Following this, Haldane worked with Merz on the design of the National Grid. Then at the age of just thirty he became the first engineer in Britain, and possibly the world, to construct and test a ground-source heat pump at his family estate in Scotland.[79]

Haldane could have had a comfortable life working as a partner at Merz and McLellan, but that was not the engineering culture in which he was raised. In 1934, he wrote a pamphlet called *The Socialization of the Electrical Supply Industry* under the pseudonym 'G. H.'.[80] It was published by the Fabian Society and Herbert Morrison commented on a draft. Haldane reasoned that repeated attempts to reform the electricity system before 1926 failed because government had been weak. He saw the CEB as a fudge, which had only been approved by Parliament because 'it interfered as little as possible with vested interests'. The Weir commission had mistakenly confined its attention to generation and transmission, which meant that there was 'no adequate provision to secure to the general public the benefit of economies [of scale] effected'.

Haldane argued that the whole electricity industry needed to be taken into public ownership and reorganised 'on the basis of large regional areas'. Regional boards would be given the power to standardise, drive economies of scale and extend electricity service to rural areas. Each board should have two representatives from government, one from the local authority and two from the labour movement. Consultative committees would ensure proper engagement with trade unions and citizens. The existing electricity undertakings would be purchased using government bonds. Haldane's support for nationalisation was based on engineering logic more than ideology. In 1932, he had visited the USSR but was thoroughly unimpressed. Haldane simply saw public ownership as a means to developing the most efficient electricity system.[81]

Haldane's intervention nearly cost him his job. A director of one of London's electricity companies hired a private detective to uncover the identity of the anonymous author and threatened Haldane's employer, Charles Merz. Merz had to pay for the publication of a counter-tract to smooth over the matter. Undeterred, over the following years Haldane worked in the background to persuade politicians of his vision. The fact that his uncle was Richard Haldane certainly helped.[82]

In 1936, Herbert Morrison made a speech in the House of Commons that closely followed Haldane's argument. In a 1941 letter to G. D. H. Cole, the influential guild socialist and Fabian, Haldane wrote:

> The present need for Government action seems imperative. I believe the whole industry now recognizes the need for reorganisation, but the various interests seem quite incapable of agreeing amongst themselves on a voluntary basis. It would seem that reform must be initiated from outside by Government action.[83]

Haldane's wisdom and bravery were rewarded. A few years later, Clement Attlee's Labour government would nationalise the whole industry. In 1948 Haldane became president of the Institution of Electrical Engineers. The stage was set for the engineers of the North East to transform the energy system once again.

3

Nationalised Energy, 1945–1979

This organisation, when it decided to do something, my God they do it right, no mucking about.

– Phil Johnson, Central Electricity Generating Board engineer, 'An Oral History of the Electricity Supply Industry'

A new type of British nation emerged after the Second World War, and energy was pivotal to the nation building. The Marxist intellectual Tom Nairn wrote of the times that 'the old idols of gentlemanly sloth and corpse-like "stability" had to give way to the over-riding demands of one new, hard god: production'.[1] Coal, gas and electricity were seen as pivotal to expanding the productive capacity of the country. 'To electricity belongs the Present and the Future', ran one post-war advertisement, an example of a kind of electrical millenarianism that seized the times.[2]

As in other European countries, there was a dramatic shift towards the state as an owner of industry. Energy was arguably the most important component of the nationalised political economy. The electricity industry was the country's biggest capital spender in the 1950s and 1960s, accounting for 7 per cent to 10 per cent of total capital formation. Lord Citrine, chair of the electricity industry, was Britain's most powerful business figure. No individual before or since was responsible for such a large share of national investment.[3]

Despite their importance to the post-war economy, the mechanics of the nationalised energy industries are poorly understood – and economists have shown a distinct lack of interest. Even seminal books on the history of energy skip from why nationalisation happened to its unwinding, missing out the bit in the middle.[4] The popular interpretation is that nationalisation failed because it was inherently inferior to private firms operating in markets. Nationalisation is seen as one of the reasons why Britain fell behind other European economies like France and Germany in the late 1970s (even though these economies also had extensive state ownership). In this model, privatisation from the 1980s simply unwound something destined to fail.[5]

The lack of interest in nationalised energy is peculiar. It is common for people to praise the Victorians for building the railways, but rare for the Central Electricity Generating Board or the British Gas Corporation to be acknowledged for building much of the modern energy system. The only reason so many British homes have central heating today is because of the natural gas conversion programme of the 1970s. Some energy historians have been complicit, overlooking the role that public ownership played in incubating technologies like nuclear and liquified natural gas.

Nationalisation was a means, not an end. For R. H. Tawney, the historian and socialist, success depended not on the 'mere change of ownership but on the degree to which advantage is taken of the opportunity . . . to carry through measures of re-organisation which private enterprise was unable . . . to undertake, and . . . increasing production'.[6] This chapter will uncover a hidden history obscured by the privatisers in the 1990s. Nationalised energy delivered on Tawney's vision, building infrastructure on a gargantuan scale, developing new energy technologies and extending heat and light to all citizens.[7]

Establishing nationalised energy, 1947–1951

In 1940 there were only a handful of nationalised industries. By 1949 there were twenty-five. Electricity, gas, the Bank of England, coal, rail and aviation were all brought under state ownership.

The newly nationalised industries accounted for 10 per cent of the workforce, 17 per cent of GDP and 19 per cent of investments.[8] Electricity was nationalised in 1947 and gas followed in 1948. The existing private owners were issued with fixed-interest stock as compensation. In one swoop just over 1,500 gas and electricity undertakings were merged into two state-owned enterprises.

What explains such a dramatic shift in political economy? One interpretation focuses on ideology. In the 1930s, the credibility of capitalism had been damaged by high unemployment, financial crisis and exchange rate instability. This lent weight to the argument by British socialists that capitalism was both immoral and economically inefficient. They further argued that as the economy grew more capital-intensive, producers would group together and form protective cartels. For socialist thinkers, nationalisation was essential to prevent the emergence of an insidious form of monopoly capitalism.

Public ownership had supporters in both political parties. In 1918, the Labour Party's commitment to nationalisation was enshrined in Clause Four, which was really a pragmatic measure to unite a broad coalition of trade unionists, socialists and middle-class activists.[9] By the 1930s nationalisation also appealed to Conservatives. In 1938, Harold Macmillan even described the Labour Party's nationalisation programme as 'mild' compared to his own.[10] Tellingly, the Conservatives never unwound the nationalisation of energy during their long period in government between 1951 and 1964.

Nationalisation was popular for practical reasons. It was seen as a necessary lever to address the persistent issues in gas and electricity.[11] Advocates could point to the success of the Central Electricity Board and argue that full nationalisation was the logical next step. A view emerged that the state had waited too long to properly deal with electricity transmission and generation and should not make the same mistake again with distribution. 'No half-measures' became the mantra. In 1942, Paymaster General William Jowett captured it well in a report on electricity: 'We should not hesitate to embark on bold measures of reconstruction . . . [as] there comes a time in the history of a nation when he who tinkers is lost.' By 1945, there was a broad consensus across political parties and in industry that government-led reorganisation was necessary. Viewed from this perspective, nationalisation was the logical conclusion to a process.[12]

Not everyone on the left was convinced that nationalisation was necessary. Some in the Labour Party, inspired by Keynesian ideas, were convinced that the success of economic planning during the war demonstrated that public ownership was not required for the successful regulation of the economy. A crucial ingredient to convincing the dissenters was the argument that nationalisation could unlock a better future. The state could ensure that gas and electricity became universal services, with the extension of supply to all rural areas. Here the British left took inspiration from the Tennessee Valley Authority and Rural Electrification Agency, pillars of the New Deal in the US. Public ownership was also presented as a way to set uniform prices. 'Postalisation', as it was termed, was the idea that a service should have a universal price like a postage stamp.[13]

Champions of private enterprise did not put up much of a fight. Having repeatedly failed to reorganise voluntarily, most companies accepted that the time had come for a more radical approach. Some even saw it as an opportunity. Both gas and electricity were facing a massive bow wave of capital expenditure. German bombs had destroyed plant and equipment, especially in the case of gas. Once electricity came out in favour of nationalisation, the gas industry did not want to be left out in the cold, unable to access the funding that would be made available to its competitor. One industry insider claimed that 'the gas industry was even anxious to be nationalised'.[14]

Under the Labour government from 1945 to 1951, a new type of state emerged: a 'developmental state' focused on reconstruction and increasing Britain's domestic economic output through construction. Consequently, the gas and electricity industries developed something of a frenzied obsession with building infrastructure.[15]

One feature of the developmental state was a firm belief in the power of planning: the conscious direction of the national economy by the state. In practice, this meant setting target growth rates, channelling state investment into sectors that had the biggest impact on the productive potential of the economy and carefully managing supply chains. In theory, this would avoid the economy-wide underinvestment and unemployment that had characterised the 1920s and 1930s. Moreover, it would reduce uncertainty for the private sector, with the state signalling the long-term direction of the economy.

Planning had to be highly flexible in the immediate years after the war. The focus of the Investment Programming Committee (IPC) was on managing the acute shortages of raw materials and labour. The electricity and gas industries were not the only ones with surging investment needs. There was little 'picking winners' in the sense of favouring particular technologies. Resources were allocated on a 'production-minded output-maximising' basis. In modern management parlance, it was an 'agile' process. The planning authorities were constantly calibrating where to direct resources based on real-time information flows. It was a huge operation. Between 1946 and 1949 the gas and electricity industries were building at a much greater rate than ever before in their histories but only received 2.9 per cent of the nationwide allocation of steel.[16]

Defining features

After the nationalisation acts in 1947 and 1948, the gas and electricity industries took shape as institutions with six defining features: public corporation status; commercial objectives; vertical integration; polycentric power structures; a 'cult of the engineer'; and pay-as-you-go funding.

Both industries were owned and controlled by public corporations headed by boards that were independent of government, based on the model of the Central Electricity Board. Corporation accounts were separated from national budgets, which was supposed to reduce Treasury interference and encourage innovation. Electricity was always kept on tighter reins than gas, mainly because the latter was much smaller. The autonomy given to the gas industry debunks the notion that public ownership necessarily entailed governmental intervention. It was given considerable funding, allowed to switch feedstock to oil and then natural gas despite the impact on the domestic coal industry, and was largely left alone.[17]

The corporations had two main objectives: to act in the public interest and to break even *over a period* (meaning they could 'take one year with the next').[18] Boards comprised experienced individuals from within the energy industry, trade union representatives and local politicians. Emanuel Shinwell, minister of fuel and power, argued in 1946 that there was no one better able 'to judge the public interest than the people who are running the industry'.[19] This comment highlights that the elitism of Morrison's approach to the London Passenger Transport Board had made its way into nationalisation.

The nationalised industries were not in the public sector as we mean it today; they were commercial state-owned enterprises. The output was not offered for free, as is the case with the National Health Service or schooling. For example, commercial ambition led both the Central Electricity Generating Board and the British Gas Corporation to set up international engineering consultancy businesses, which sold services worldwide. Leaders were aware of their broad duties to 'the public' in a general sense, but their primary focus was to serve citizens as consumers. One senior electricity leader later reflected that 'the whole concept . . . was that you were serving the community, and the whole ethos of the place and the management of it was the customer came first'.[20]

Nationalisation of gas and electricity created vertically integrated organisations spanning the full value chain. The theory was that this would improve coordination between production, transmission, distribution and retail. One of the reasons socialists were so focused on public ownership was that they saw fragmentation as inefficient, but they also believed privately owned monopolies would simply abuse their market power. Vertical integration went hand in hand with public ownership.

In the 1980s and 1990s the architects of privatisation were incredibly successful in portraying the nationalised industries as bureaucratic monoliths. This was an unfair and inaccurate characterisation that did not reflect how the organisations were structured. The gas and electricity corporations were 'polycentric' organisations with multiple centres of power, regional autonomy and decentralised decision-making.

In the first decade of nationalisation there were two organisational tiers: a central authority and regional area boards (fourteen in electricity, twelve in gas). At the centre were the Gas Council (which became the British Gas Corporation) and the British Electricity Authority (the BEA, which became the Central Electricity Authority and then the Central Electricity Generating Board). These central authorities would remain relatively free from political intervention in day-to-day activities until the early 1970s. The BEA was responsible for all generation and transmission and sold 'bulk' electricity to the area boards. In the first decade of nationalisation, it exercised some control over the area boards: approving expenditure, controlling reserves and comparing the performance of boards. However, once funding was approved, usually annually, the area boards had considerable freedom on how they spent the money.[21]

The area boards were to be 'autonomous bodies', in the words of Shinwell. They were responsible for all customer-facing activities (sales, marketing, servicing) and the distribution networks. As one area board manager later recollected, the central authorities 'had very little influence on the way I ran the London Electricity Board. It was an autonomous board, I had my own statutory powers and so on and so forth and it was very, very difficult for [them] to really intervene too much.'[22]

The architects of nationalisation debated the right balance between centralisation and decentralisation. Shinwell favoured giving the area boards a high level of freedom, whereas Herbert Morrison wanted a stronger centre that could encourage 'socialist competition' between the regions, using statistical reporting.[23] Morrison's ideas were more influential in the early years, but from the late 1940s the trend was towards decentralisation. Lord Citrine, chair of the Central Authority from 1947 to 1957, made the change in direction clear:

> Our policy is a policy of decentralisation . . . there will be errors, there will be occasions when we shall find that one particular Board is dealing with its problems in quite different ways from another . . . You cannot have autonomy devolving . . . without differences showing themselves.[24]

He warned the audience to not nag him to 'standardise' the moment differences emerged.

The North of Scotland Hydro-Electric Board (founded 1943) was given almost total autonomy and reported to the secretary of state for Scotland as opposed to the minister for fuel and power. After their election in 1951, the Conservatives introduced an even more decentralised structure, creating two Scottish boards that operated totally independently and had full control over generation, transmission and retail. In 1957, the Conservatives broke up the Central Electricity Authority into an Electricity Council and the Central Electricity Generating Board (CEGB). The CEGB retained responsibility for generation and transmission, but it was taken down a peg and placed on equal footing with the area boards. By 1960 the chair of the CEGB went as far as to state that the area boards were 'legally and financially completely independent'.[25] The CEGB also adopted a regional organisational structure from 1958, with five regions having considerable freedom to build infrastructure.[26]

One of the reasons why decentralisation gained traction was that it played off the belief that public ownership was a way to wrest control of industry away from financiers and bureaucrats and give it to engineers and workers. In 1947 Morrison wrote:

> We must again turn to our technical men and to our scientists and rely on them to take the lead as they did when this country's industrial wealth was first built up . . . In the battle before us our mechanical engineers are our armoured divisions.[27]

A popular view across both left and right was that British decline was the result of its elites lacking engineering and business experience. Technological futurism seized political imagination, epitomised by Harold Wilson's famous words in 1963 that 'the Britain that is going to be forged in the white heat of this revolution will be no place for restrictive practices or for outdated methods on either side of industry'.[28] Techno-futurism became techno-chauvinism, with stories about the future based on protestations that Britain was an inherently inventive country with a raft of inventions it could claim as its own (steam, electricity, nuclear).[29]

In this context, both gas and electricity developed a kind of 'cult of the engineer', which had a significant impact on decision-making.[30] Lord Citrine ran the electricity industry through a board of equals consisting of a chief engineer and area board chairs who were mostly engineers. There was no chief executive officer. Within the British Electrical Authority, the chief engineer was the most important position in a management trio which included the chief commercial officer and chief accountant.[31] The primacy of engineering manifested itself in high expenditure on research and development. The gas industry had four research facilities that became global centres of innovation. The CEGB had three and ran one of the best-paying graduate schemes in the country to attract top scientific talent.[32] From the mid-1950s, both gas and electricity spent significant sums on training engineers in the new 'science of management'.

How would the engineers pay for all the infrastructure they intended to build? There were three options: borrowing, bills and funding from the state. In the first decade after the war, both gas and electricity directly raised fixed-interest stock, but stockholders had no voting rights and did not own equity.[33] Between 1948 and 1955, the British Electrical Authority did six offerings, each between £100 million and £200 million (between £3.4 billion and £6.9 billion in 2024 prices) with returns of 3 per cent to 4.5 per cent. After 1955, all capital was raised by the Treasury.[34] The Gas Council was given more freedom and was permitted to borrow up to £1.2 billion from 1965 on its own balance sheet (£26 billion in 2024 prices) with a Treasury guarantee.[35]

A second way to pay for capital investments was from consumer bills in the present, termed 'self-financing' (which included bills and depreciation). However, higher bills meant lower consumption. Holding bills down was crucial to incentivising consumers to buy new appliances. Higher consumption also meant spreading the fixed costs of infrastructure over more units.

The third route was funds from the Treasury, which could fund through transfers, loans or fixed-interest stock issues (guaranteed by the state). A key feature of the financing arrangement was the low cost of capital. The state could borrow money at a lower rate than private sector firms. This meant that the nationalised energy industry could undertake projects with very long or uncertain payback periods – like building networks or nuclear plants.

The economist Dieter Helm has characterised the approach used as 'pay-as-you-go'. The post-war generation paid for investment out of current income rather than through borrowing and future bills. The only question was whether to ask citizens to pay as consumers or as taxpayers. Paying from consumer bills was regressive because all citizens paid the same price regardless of income level. Paying from tax was more progressive, as the rich bore a higher share of the cost.[36] It was a simple, transparent and flexible approach. In the 1950s and early 1960s, the electricity industry was in a building phase, so only 20 per cent to 40 per cent of investment was self-financed from bills.[37] When the build phase was over, self-financing levels were raised. Pay-as-you-go was not a blank cheque, however. Over the 1960s and 1970s the Treasury steadily ratcheted up financial controls to slow spending.

Pay-as-you-go was the most suitable funding mechanism for a generation of politicians and engineers who saw it as their obligation to build an endowment for future British citizens. This may seem counterintuitive. On the surface a 'save then spend' approach may seem more prudent. But as the economic historian Avner Offer so lucidly explains:

> Governments succeed where markets fail because they do not commit to long-term contracts . . . A financial balance is a hoard. Once spent, it is gone . . . Pay-as-you-go is a claim on the community's indestructible real tax base. In effect, it is a claim on a share of GDP – how much to be revealed when it becomes due for payment.[38]

Mega-projects in electricity

In his 1955 autobiography, Emanuel Shinwell, minister of fuel and power, complained that the Labour Party did not have a clear plan for what to do once public ownership was in place. 'I had believed, as other members had, that in the Party archives a blueprint was ready . . . [but] I found that nothing practical and tangible existed . . . I had to start on a clean desk.'[39] This may have been the view from Whitehall, but many in the electricity industry were extremely clear. The industry's leadership was the same as it had been before the war, with the tragic exception of Charles Merz, who died with his two children in an air raid in 1940. The overarching objective was still the same as it had been in the Central Electricity Board: scale.

A generation of power system engineers had spent years trying to make the case for system rationalisation and had learned the hard way that incremental change did not work. Now they were in the ascendancy and controlled an industry worth £831 million (£34 billion in 2024 prices).[40] Over the next two decades these engineers built a system that was the apotheosis of the 'load-hungry utility'.

The first test was to end the rolling blackouts that afflicted the nation over 1946 and 1947. The initial causes were coal shortages plus extreme cold. However, with demand for electricity growing as the economy recovered, the British Electrical Authority projected that there would be insufficient generation capacity within a few years. Group Captain Charles Verity was put in charge of speeding up power station completion rates. He inherited a situation of immense complexity, with ten government committees responsible for commissioning each site. Verity cut swathes through the bureaucracy and developed a kind of 'factory model' to progress each power station in parallel. His team carefully logged the progress on all sites and diverted resources to where it would increase the *overall* rate of completion rather than partial completion.[41]

Between 1948 and 1958, the total capacity of power stations grew 8 per cent per year. Years later there were complaints that stations were over budget, but in the context of the extreme pressure to increase build rates the achievement was impressive – especially so given that throughout the 1940s the power station programme faced challenges from planning authorities, local councils and rural preservation societies. Stations were cancelled, delayed or significantly modified at Lincoln, Durham and Bankside (London).[42]

Verity's approach worked only because in parallel the distribution networks were being reinforced, so a power station completed in one place benefited many locations. Before nationalisation, adding to the 132 kV National Grid involved complex legal and financial negotiations with the local electricity undertakings. After nationalisation it was much simpler. Engineers improved the layout of the network, which led to a significant improvement in reliability. London went from having one of the worst distribution systems to one of the best by the end of the 1960s. Standardisation was another priority. The variation in voltages and frequencies was finally cleaned up. Finally, consumers could be confident that their appliances would work all over the country.[43]

The objective of providing electricity as a universal service fit neatly with the industry's voracious appetite to increase diversity of demand. In 1947, 25 per cent of households lacked electricity, but by 1957 this was down to just 10 per cent. Following a rural electrification programme, 72 per cent of all farms had access to electricity. Rural electrification was uneconomical for private sector firms. But under public ownership the profit imperative was relaxed, and the industry could cross-subsidise from urban to rural areas. A calculation at the time indicated that these cross-subsidies had increased urban bills by just 2 per cent.[44]

With the blackouts ended and distribution networks set on a more rational path, the industry turned its attention to the long-term plan for the National Grid. The early years of the British Electrical Authority were marked by caution. Some leading engineers favoured simply reinforcing the existing 132 kV grid. Once again, North Eastern engineers had bolder ideas.

In 1948, T. G. N. Haldane became president of the Institution of Electrical Engineers. Ever the radical, Haldane challenged conservatism and developed an idea his mentor, Charles Merz, had articulated in the 1920s. Haldane argued that building a new grid with a higher voltage was the optimal way to meet rising demand. It would extend the benefits of pooling generation capacity to the whole country, which would drive up the system load factor, reduce the spare plant margin and improve reliability. Haldane introduced a novel argument: a new 275 kV grid would reduce the cost of moving coal by train. Power stations could go to where the cheapest coal was, with electricity carried to centres of demand via the grid.[45]

Haldane's intervention was critical. At the BEA, John Hacking (deputy chairman) and V. A. Pask (chief engineer) were irritated at being upstaged by an outside consultant engineer.

They changed tack and started to lobby for a new network. D. P. Sawyers, head of transmission, capitalised on the momentum and in 1950 took such a proposal to Lord Citrine. Citrine loved the idea but insisted on a catchier name than 'superimposed grid'. Thus the 'supergrid' was born.

The supergrid was a plan so outlandish that visiting American engineers called it 'unnecessarily ambitious'. It was double the voltage of the existing grid and would require 1,150 miles of overhead cabling with forty-six switching and transforming substations. Compared to the 132 kV grid, each line would carry six times the power, with towers double the height.[46] The new grid's centre of gravity was the East Midlands and Yorkshire, the regions with the lowest-cost coal-fired electricity generation in the country. In 1958, the East Midlands could generate electricity at a cost 21 per cent lower than the national average and 40 per cent lower than in London.[47]

The supergrid took less than a decade to approve, design and construct (1952–60). In 1950, it was estimated that it would cost £52 million (£2.0 billion in 2024 prices). The project was delivered on schedule and on budget.[48] This was a remarkable achievement given the ubiquity of manufacturing shortages. The engineers who designed the supergrid had the wisdom to build it with optionality. The land adjacent to substations was acquired to make it easier to extend them in the future. Certain sections of overhead lines were constructed with wide clearances to enable upgrading to higher voltages. This turned out to be wise, as electricity demand grew faster than expected. From 1965, 400 kV lines were added without needing to add entirely new towers to carry them.[49] In 1961, the electricity grid was even extended subsea, with the completion to France of the longest interconnector in the world. The grid builders also developed several innovative technologies. The transformers were so huge that they had to be kept just under the limit of what British roads could bear during transportation – 150 tons. Developing circuit breakers that could cope with the higher voltages was a particular challenge. Extensive use was made of standard equipment, which meant a handful of suppliers could compete to build interchangeable kit.[50]

The publicly owned electricity industry built an extraordinary amount of grid in the 1950s and 1960s. Nothing like it has occurred since. Across all voltages, network length grew 3.1 per cent a year. By comparison, in 2022 a government department estimated that between 2021 and 2050 Britain should target a growth rate between 0.8 per cent and 1.9 per cent.[51] The International Energy Agency has calculated that China is aiming to grow its transmission systems by 4.5 per cent annually between 2021 and 2050. Between 1955 and 1970 the comparable figure for Britain was 8 per cent.[52]

Of equal importance to the supergrid was increasing the scale and efficiency of power stations. In the early years of the BEA, the chief engineer, V. A. Pask, was reluctant to change designs due to concerns over the reliability of larger and higher-pressure sets. A turning point was the appointment of Stanley Brown as head of generation design and then as chief engineer in 1956. Brown was more radical and oversaw what became known as the 'Brownian Revolution': an increase in the size and pressure levels of sets, and the development of re-heat technologies, which when combined reduced the cost of generation. In 1959, the CEGB set itself the target of building the equivalent to half the entire existing generation capacity of the country in just five years.[53]

It was a revolution of stunning technical and economic success. The largest sets in the mid-1960s were nine times the size of the largest ones in 1929.[54] Bigger power stations plus the supergrid allowed the CEGB to build on the work of the CEB and further rationalise generation. In 1935, there were 395 large coal-fired power stations across the country with a total capacity of 7.8 GW. By 1960 the number of stations had increased a little to 409, but their total capacity was now 28 GW, a three-and-a-half-fold increase.[55] The geographical pattern of power also changed. Generation was concentrated in areas like the

Figure 3.1. The supergrid as of 1972

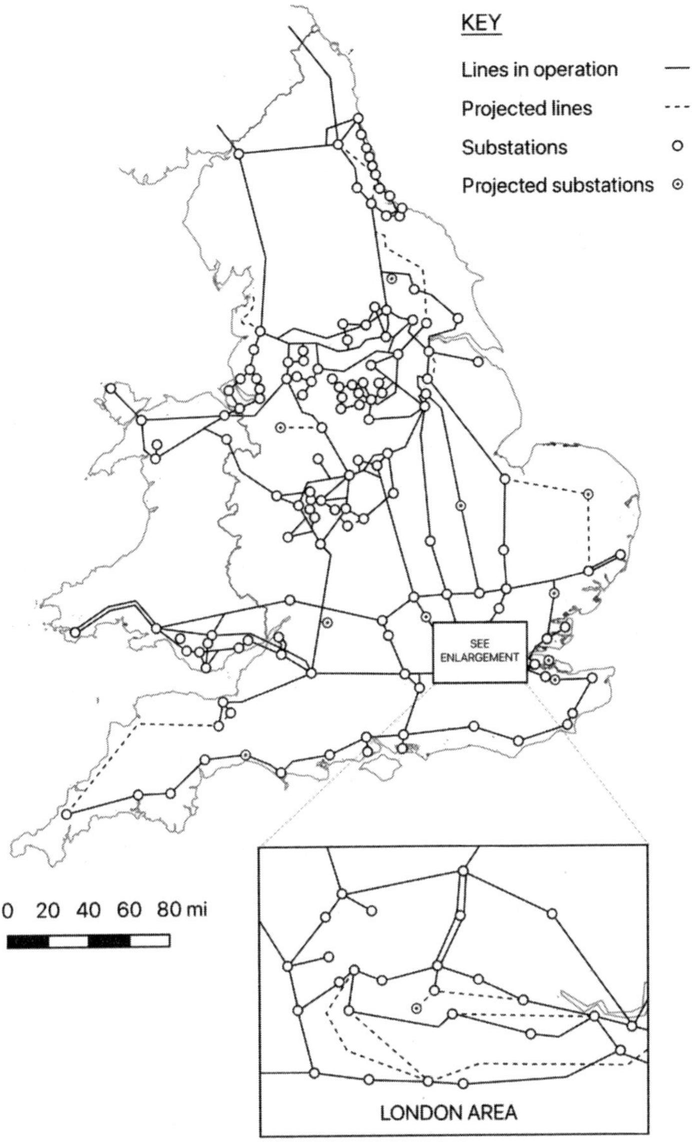

Source: Central Electricity Generating Board annual report, 1972–73.

East Midlands and Yorkshire with abundant and low-grade coal. Huge power stations lined the river Trent, which became known as 'Megawatt Valley'.

The CEGB pursued the concept of the load-hungry utility to its ultimate conclusion. Increasing the scale of generation stations and expanding the electricity network led to significant improvement in load factor and thermal efficiency. Load factor increased from 33 per cent in 1938 to 52 per cent in 1970. Efficiency was translated into lower prices and improved reliability, and this pulled more demand onto the grid. The share of industrial demand met by self-generation fell from 45 per cent in 1938 to 22 per cent by 1957.[56]

The generation programme faced constrained supply chains across equipment, materials, services and labour. The CEGB went to great lengths to keep the manufacturers of equipment, almost all British, up to date about the size and composition of its construction programme. This did not mean giving firms an easy ride. In the early 1950s, the BEA became increasingly concerned about the operation of 'rings' among firms supplying turbo-alternators, boilers and high-pressure pipework. These rings had considerable market power. The BEA initially agreed to pay the higher prices but put pressure on suppliers to expand their capacity. This carrot was accompanied by selective use of the stick. The BEA would periodically relax bottlenecks by turning to imports, which required government approval. This had the benefit of disciplining domestic suppliers.[57]

In the North West of Wales in the county of Gwynedd is the picturesque village of Dinorwig. In the nineteenth century, Dinorwig was home to one of the largest slate mines in the country, but over the twentieth century it fell into decline. Dinorwig's unique geology was of little interest to anyone except for a small community of feral goats that inhabited the old quarry. That changed in the 1970s. Thanks to two conveniently placed lakes either side of Elidir Fawr mountain, 'Dino' was the perfect place for a pumped storage hydroelectric facility. Pumped storage involved pumping water from a low reservoir to a higher one when electricity demand was low and releasing the water to generate power when demand was high. Constructed between 1974 and 1984, what became known as the 'Electric Mountain' was one of the most impressive feats of engineering in British history.

What made the site special was the potential to build a facility under the mountain without additional damming of the lakes. A short access road was the only surface feature. It was the largest pumped storage scheme in Europe, costing £425 million (£1.4 billion in 2024 prices). It had the capacity to provide 1,300 megawatts (MW) of power within six seconds of being switched on, and 1,680 MW for five hours straight. That equated to being able to deliver power to around 1.7 million households for five hours. The underground complex was the largest civil engineering project in European history. It had sixteen kilometres of tunnels, some of which were large enough to fit two double-decker buses side by side. The main machine hall under the mountain was the size of a hundred Olympic-size swimming pools.

Priority was given to the protection of the environment and the visual beauty of the Snowdonia National Park. The cabling to the site was undergrounded. The waterways had a diversion pass for fish. Local heather seeds were deposited at a university. The rare Arctic char that lived in one of the lakes were carefully transferred to other suitable lakes. A visitor centre was constructed that hosted a steady flow of 35,000 visitors a year, with exhibitions showcasing the local environment. After privatisation the centre became the responsibility of the company that owned the power station: it was closed in 2018 and then demolished.[58]

Dinorwig was the culmination of a forty-year programme to develop hydroelectricity in the British Isles. Britain had always lagged behind Europe and the US because it did not have as many suitable 'run-of-the-river' sites. In 1943, the North of Scotland Hydro-Electric Board (NSHEB) was established to develop hydroelectric power and electrify the remote parts of the Highlands. The NSHEB was one of the earliest expressions of the link between public ownership of natural resources and distributing the benefits of electricity to all citizens. Profits from the sale of surplus electricity to England were ploughed back into distributing power to the more remote, low-populated areas of the Highlands.[59]

The hydroelectricity construction programme was of a similar scale and pace to that of the supergrid. An official historian of the NSHEB described the years 1953 to 1958 as 'frenzied'.[60] At one point there were fourteen hydroelectric schemes under construction simultaneously. By 1960 there were 875 MW of hydro power in Scotland, a tenfold increase on 1947. In addition, four major pumped storage hydroelectric schemes were constructed in the 1960s. The hydroelectric projects were gruelling work, with engineers facing torrential rain, snow and wind. There was an extremely high casualty rate, with injuries and deaths on almost all projects.[61]

The development of pumped storage facilities such as Dinorwig was particularly consequential. Pumped storage was incredibly valuable for the electricity system as it could be used to meet peak demand without building lots of additional coal-fired stations. T. G. N. Haldane was one of the first British engineers to articulate this point in 1955, and he would go on to write a textbook on the subject.[62]

Pumped storage was incredibly complex, cutting across multiple engineering and scientific disciplines (hydrology, electrical engineering, geology). The Cruachan scheme in Argyll and Bute was opened by the Queen in 1965. Like Dinorwig, it was a labyrinth of tunnels and chambers that moved water around *inside* the mountain. The 'hollowed-out mountain', as it came to be called, took six years to build and was first properly put to the test on the night of the 1966 World Cup final. Over an hour period after the expected end of the game Cruachan kept the grid in balance.[63] Over the 1960s television ownership boomed; by 1968, 90 per cent of homes had one. Pumped storage power stations like Cruachan and Ffestiniog helped deal with rapid increase in demand that occurred at the end of popular television programmes when domestic devices, like kettles, were switched on simultaneously.[64] There were other, more dramatic incidents, as in 1972 during the Miners' Strike, when Ffestiniog helped reduce severity of the enforced blackouts.

The Scottish hydro programme and Highland electrification were funded almost entirely from general taxation. In 1960, it was estimated that a quarter of the NSHEB's service area was being supplied on an uneconomic basis. The state deemed the cross-subsidisation of Scotland's electricity industry a matter of social justice: the arrival of light and power was momentous for many rural communities. In 1951, at a ceremony to celebrate the occasion in Fort Augustus, a reverend even thanked God that 'after many years of hope deferred, our faith has been rewarded and power and light have come to us'.[65]

A common caricature of the nationalised electricity industry is that it was ruled by engineers obsessed with building things for the sake of it. Over the 1960s the Treasury took this view of the hydroelectric programme. Yet there was something very humane about British hydro. Vast power plants were built into the mountains of Britain, bringing power to some of the island's most iconic landscapes. Hydroelectric infrastructure was designed to service the everyday rhythms of British life: television, tea, football and strikes.

Just as the hydro programme was winding down, Britain's electricity industry embarked on a mission to develop an entirely novel technology – nuclear. Britain's love affair with nuclear energy began in the 1940s. It was seen as having strategic importance and a source of industrial power. One of the benefits of Britain having its own nuclear energy programme was the production of weapons-grade plutonium. The world's first full-scale nuclear power station was the Magnox reactor at Calder Hall, built between 1952 and 1956. It was intended as a demonstration project, so cost overruns and unfavourable economics were tolerated. In the wake of the Suez Crisis in 1956 the state became more concerned about energy security and decisively swung behind nuclear. In 1957, Prime Minister Harold Macmillan tripled the size of the nuclear programme.[66] For the CEGB this posed a challenge. Nuclear was expensive and had a shorter projected lifetime than coal-fired plants. To prevent bills from going up, the board had to drive even more efficiencies from the existing coal-fired fleet.[67]

The objectives of the first programme, in order of priority, were to create a market for British-designed reactors, support the export of those reactors, and develop cost-efficient energy supply. The problem was that nuclear was not cost-competitive with coal. The 1955 white paper made it clear that the first reactors would need considerable subsidies. Officials assumed that the economics would improve, but this assumption was undermined by cost overruns and falling coal prices.[68] The white paper of 1955 had been astonishingly light on detail and ignored nuclear decommissioning costs.[69] By 1960, the CEGB was pushing back the expected date by which nuclear would be cost-competitive with coal. The first nuclear programme ended up building 3.8 GW of capacity, which was more than the initial 1955 target. However, only two Magnox reactors were exported, and the cost was exorbitant. An economist later estimated that the Magnox programme cost nearly £10 billion more than a coal alternative.[70]

The second nuclear programme started in 1964, targeting 5 GW by 1975. It committed to another British technology, the Advanced Gas-Cooled Reactor (AGR), which was only in prototype stages. The CEGB was open to competition from other countries and by the late 1960s was in favour of switching to the American-designed Pressurised Water Reactor (PWR). The cabinet office overruled the CEGB on the basis that importing reactors would kill the prospects of the domestic nuclear industry. Like the Magnox reactors the AGRs also experienced significant cost overruns. The construction consortia needed to be reorganised twice to stave off financial collapse.

Christopher Hinton (CEGB chair, 1957–64) advised scaling back the nuclear programme, and Stanley Brown (chair, 1965–72) wanted it stopped.[71] The programme finished with ten AGRs with 6.5 GW of capacity, which was ahead of the target. The third nuclear programme started in 1974. Once again, there was a debate over whether to go with the US-designed PWRs or favour a new British technology (this time, the Steam Generating Heavy Water Reactor). On instruction from government in 1976, the CEGB was told to order four more AGRs to protect the National Nuclear Corporation. By 1979 the Conservative manifesto argued for just one PWR.[72]

These nuclear programmes were part of the fastest energy-technology deployment in the history of energy; nuclear went from basic scientific concept to first commercial station in only a quarter of a century.[73] Britain was a pioneer, but early advances had a downside. Britain locked in inferior reactors like the Magnox and AGRs and missed out on the superior PWRs that would be used in the French and Swedish nuclear programmes in the 1970s and 1980s. It is a myth that the CEGB was an uncritical supporter of nuclear, blinded by admiration for the complex engineering. Christopher Hinton was one of the most persistent critics of the UK Atomic Energy Agency.[74] National defence, strategic interests and protection of an indigenous British industry were more important factors. State ownership undoubtedly played a role. It gave politicians the ability to ignore engineers like Hinton. Moreover, the state could provide 'patient capital' and bear a low rate of return, meaning that nuclear was tolerated in a way it would not have been in the private sector. As the historian David Edgerton has neatly summarised, 'Privatisation exposed the real economics of nuclear power, long deceitfully concealed by the state.'[75]

It is fashionable today to imagine that the only reason Britain struggles to build infrastructure is because of planning restrictions. This rests on a belief that past generations never faced these challenges, and that organisations like the CEGB were given *carte blanche*. This is a myth. Under the Town and Country Planning Act of 1947 the board had to apply to the Ministry for Fuel and Power for permission to build anything. Local authorities and planning bodies were consulted in parallel. If there were objections, the application was submitted to the Ministry of Town and Country Planning. This usually led to a public inquiry with ministers making the final decision on whether to approve the project.[76]

In 1952, a parliamentary committee complained that these 'tedious procedures' were delaying station completion rates. Opponents included local authorities and residents. More vocal were a raft of quasi-governmental organisations like the Council for the Preservation of Rural England (plus its Scottish and Welsh branches), the Ramblers Association, the Nature Conservancy and the National Parks Commission. These organisations were emboldened following the Access to the Countryside Act (1949). Supergrid planners commented that compared to the first grid 'we've been in a completely different ball game, with planning officers that want to study our proposed routes in absolute detail and then make their own suggestions'. Another engineer complained about a route near Hadrian's Wall, saying, 'It's a good job Hadrian wasn't around now . . . He'd never get planning permission for all that.'[77]

The British Electrical Authority asked to be given more powers, but this proposal was squashed given the public perception that the industry was already being too autocratic. The 1957 Electricity Act made things even more difficult.[78] Lord Lucas led a campaign to include an 'amenity' clause. The government opposed the amendment but was defeated. The final clause meant that the board had to 'have regard' for 'preserving natural beauty, of conserving flora, fauna and . . . features of special interest and of protecting buildings and other objects of architectural or historical interest'. The board complained that this requirement was so broad it would be unworkable. From 1957 'amenity' had to be considered from the earliest stages of planning. The board believed that it had been lumped with 'an expanded national service'. Now it had to balance supplying power as economically as possible with the preservation of amenity.[79] The former could be quantified but the latter could not.

The CEGB felt stuck between two imperatives. Building power stations and transmission in rural areas would avoid the criticism that emissions would negatively impact urban air quality. However, rural projects would inevitably disturb areas of beauty and the environment. The supergrid made it harder to argue that a power station had to go in a particular place. A good example was Holme Pierrepont. It was a perfect site for a large coal-fired power station, with access to coal that was too low-grade for other uses. Consent was granted in March 1960, but after protests by planning authorities and the local council the Ministry for Fuel and Power pulled approval in 1961. The board had to change plans to building a giant plant at Ratcliffe-on-Soar, but only after a long public inquiry and many objections. The board had lost five years and felt it was 'prevented from using efficiently the low-quality Nottinghamshire coal for which power stations are the only market'.[80]

The CEGB's annual reports emphasised that 'unremitting attention was given to the task of minimising the impact of essential extensions' and 'no single problem gives the Board more concern than that of amenity'.[81] William Holford, the professor of town planning at University College London, was appointed as a part-time member of the CEGB from 1957 to 1973. A special project team called the 'Station Environment Group' was established. The board hired a small army of architects and landscape architects which were part of the design team from the outset of a project. The board employed so many landscape architects that there was a national shortage. Landscaping was used for most substations in the 1960s and 1970s, with some hidden behind newly planted forests. Expenditure on landscaping went from £4,860 in 1963 to £109,103 in 1966.[82] The board also used photographic and digital techniques to simulate 'zones of visual influence', a technique used to great effect in Dinorwig.[83]

The CEGB also invested in research and development to head off challenges. Following the loss of a legal case to a fishing club in Derbyshire, the board funded research to demonstrate that fish populations were not adversely impacted by hot water expelled from power stations and that they benefited from these 'fish Jacuzzis'.[84]

To avoid 'wirescapes' around substations the board used underground cabling rather than overhead lines. Undergrounding was anywhere between eight to twenty-three times more expensive, so the cost implications were significant. To preserve the view of Snowdon on Glaslyn Estuary, the CEGB was prepared to spend an additional £2.5 million on undergrounding the Trawsfynydd-to-Bangor route. The Ministry for Fuel and Power insisted that this was not enough and several more miles were undergrounded, doubling the cost. For comparison, the entire supergrid was budgeted to cost £52 million, and government expenditure on ancient buildings and historic monuments was only £1.25 million a year.[85] The annual reports were littered with similar examples. By the end of the 1970s, there was more high-voltage cable undergrounded in Britain than in the *entire* US.[86]

What price should be put on amenity? In a sense, the CEGB could never do enough. This was demonstrated one evening in 1960 when the chairman of the CEGB, Christopher Hinton, walked into the Royal Society of Arts to give a paper on the efforts the board was making to preserve amenities. Hinton was a brilliant mind. He had left school at sixteen to become a railway apprentice but went on to be one of the nation's leading nuclear engineers. He was also a pragmatist and realised that the work of the CEGB could not be left entirely to engineers. On this night, Hinton walked into a bear pit, with an audience filled with hostile rural preservationists. Hinton had asked to give the talk and was not combative. He acknowledged that 'it is no use to argue that properly sited pylons and transmission lines stride grandly across the country. To the average man they are (consciously or subconsciously) the tentacles of industry creeping out into a countryside which he would prefer to keep free.'[87] Elsewhere, Hinton warned against referring to towers as 'knights in shining armour', as 'knights in shining armour are a damned nuisance in the wrong place'.[88] Here he was mirroring one of the board's most significant landscape architects, Sylvia Crowe, who claimed that substations were 'like gallows' that would 'depress anyone', and that 'the landscape of the British Isles faced the greatest crisis in its history'.[89]

In his talk Hinton outlined the basic problem of NIMBYism. The power stations and transmission lines had to go somewhere. For people in the area the benefits were nil, but the immediate and visible impact of the infrastructure was considerable. Reducing the impact on amenity cost money. Underground cabling in one area would inevitably lead to the question why not do it in other areas. Hinton was not trying to win an argument. He concluded that this was a 'problem that cannot be removed'. No precise definition or set of rules could be called on to resolve the intractable dilemma.

It was only through skill, hard work and determination that the CEGB made progress. Over the 1950s and early 1960s there was a steady increase in the number of projects undergoing public inquiries. The board was at pains to stress respect for inquiries (in modern parlance, 'consultations') as part of the democratic process. For Sylvia Crowe, it was 'consulting to avoid delay', cooperating with all parties in design to prevent protests at a later stage. But success in these negotiations was often achieved at the cost of considerable delays and frustration over years, not months.[90] In language familiar today, the CEGB played the role of being on the side of economic growth facing down blockers. Its 1962–63 report complained that 'recent developments may trend in the direction of giving private and sectional interests too great an opportunity to impede' and 'become so burdensome as to restrict national progress and standards of living'. One of the reasons why the board accelerated building a smaller number of very large power stations after 1957 was that it would mean fewer consultations.[91]

Overall, the board dealt with these challenges very well. It ran a massive public relations campaign. One advert in *Country Life* showed a pylon being placed in the landscape by a giant hand with the question 'Where would you run the pylons?' The text underneath focused on the benefits that electrification would bring to rural communities: 'Pylons down here will mean a better life up there.' Another advert appealed to people's sense of obligation to the future, with a picture of two children looking at a miniature pylon on a table with the line 'Will they write to "The Times" about it?'[92] A 1963 short film dramatised the arrival of a CEGB wayleaves officer (played by Desmond Llewelyn, Q in the Bond films) in a village pub to explain how routes were selected, why undergrounding would cost ten times more and how the grid would bring down bills.[93] Persuasion worked. For example, the supergrid programme managed to secure wayleave agreements for 99 per cent of the route without using compulsory powers.[94]

Mega-projects in gas

In 1976, the chair of the British Gas Corporation looked back on the previous decades and reflected that in 1950 'few would have given the gas industry much of a chance of survival'.[95] But nationalisation gave the industry something it had been lacking since its inception: scale. In 1948, the Gas Council sat atop the largest integrated gas company in the world. It could now dedicate meaningful resources to take the fight to electricity. In the 1960s, the British gas industry would lead the world in making a series of technological breakthroughs – deriving gas from oil, importing liquified natural gas (LNG) and converting the whole system from coal gas over to natural gas.[96] Nationalisation provided the framework for a renaissance in the industry.[97] In the 1970s, following repeated oil price shocks, the state decisively backed gas as a crucial component of Britain's industrial strategy.

In the late 1940s, the existential challenge facing gas was that there was no obvious way to gain the same economies of scale as in electricity. In 1945, the Heyworth committee concluded that 'a national grid is not practicable'.[98] In the first decade of public ownership gas got off to a bad start. Gas prices rose whereas electricity prices fell. In response to coal shortages, area boards had to turn down gas pressures at certain times of day.[99]

One thing in the favour of gas was that the nationalisation act gave the Gas Council significant powers. Critically, it could borrow up to £250 million (£10.5 billion in 2024 prices), which it could use to fund research and development.[100] Coal shortages led to a search for new feedstocks. The Gas Council oversaw the establishment of regional research centres that developed two innovative technologies for making gas from oil. The Gas Recycle Hydrogenation (GRH) process was developed at the Midlands research station. The first operational plant was in Bristol in 1965. The Catalytic Rich Gas (CRG) process was developed by the London Electricity Board and first used at the massive Bromley gas works.[101] These oil-to-gas technologies were cheaper than coal-to-gas and allowed gas to disconnect from coal prices, unlike electricity. These technologies were highly innovative and were licensed to Germany, Italy and Japan. In parallel, the industry's main research facility, Watson House, was given greater powers to set standards across the industry.[102] By the early 1960s, the Gas Council was at the centre of a successful innovation ecosystem.

As in electricity, network infrastructure was a critical enabler. The regional area boards refurbished and expanded the distribution pipeline network between 1948 and 1960. In 1958, the construction programme peaked with around 20,000 miles of new gas mains laid at a cost of around £100 million (around £2.6 billion in 2024 prices).[103] For comparison, the entire gas distribution network in Britain today is around 180,000 miles long, so in a single year the area boards constructed over 10 per cent of it. All construction came in under budget. In parallel the boards rationalised their coal-to-gas manufacturing facilities. In 1949, there were around 1,000 gas production facilities, but by 1958 this was down to 536 and just 192 by 1968.[104]

As in electricity, the Gas Council's other priority was to stimulate demand. In the late 1950s and early 1960s, the gas industry developed a sophisticated marketing strategy. 'Mr Therm', an anthropomorphic dancing flame, was one of the best-known advertising campaigns of the post-war period. Originally developed by the London Gas Lighting and Coke Company, it was borrowed by the Gas Council. The 'High Speed Gas' campaign from 1963 was equally successful. In a Gas Council film, Fanny Cradock taught viewers about the benefits of cooking with gas, and the world of culinary delights that awaited, such as triple-cooked chips and soufflé. In addition, roving home service advisors travelled the country giving cooking demonstrations.[105]

Transporting natural gas over long distance by pipeline was first developed in the 1930s in the natural-gas-rich US, where after the Second World War pipeline construction expanded dramatically. However, Britain lacked access to natural gas, so the industry hatched an ambitious plan to bring it onshore. In 1958 the Gas Council, in collaboration with the oil and gas company Conoco, developed the world's first liquified natural gas (LNG) tanker, the *Methane Pioneer*, which was repurposed from an old cargo ship. In 1959, it made trips across the Atlantic with thousands of tons of LNG onboard. Around the same time, the Gas Council agreed to purchase gas from a vast reservoir in Algeria under the Sahara called Hassi R'Mel. Two more ships were developed in 1963, the *Methane Princess* and *Methane Progress*, and huge new LNG processing facilities were constructed in Algeria and Canvey Island, Essex. In 1962 work began on a 200-mile pipeline from Canvey Island to Leeds, with spurs off it to eight of the twelve area boards. This pipeline – Feeder One – became the 'backbone' for the rest of the gas transmission network that was constructed over the next decades.[106]

In 1965, British Petroleum (BP) struck oil in the West Sole field in the North Sea. In popular historical imagination North Sea oil is 'a vision of buccaneering capitalism at its most adventurous' (Jeremy Paxman).[107] This ignores the fact that the capitalists involved were given a leg up by the state. Developing North Sea oil and gas was an immense engineering challenge that involved a neat division of labour between the private sector and the state.

Oil and gas companies formed consortia to undertake exploration and bring the gas 'to the beach'. From there, the nationalised gas industry undertook processing (including adding the infamous odour), transportation and sale. The first licences were awarded in 1964 in line with the new Convention on the Continental Shelf, which gave countries with coastlines sovereignty over oil and gas resources under the North Sea. The first volumes of gas came onshore to Easington, County Durham, in 1967. The development of North Sea gas was possible only because of nationalisation of the gas industry. Not only did the nationalised industry provide the onshore transportation infrastructure, but the Gas Council was the monopsony buyer of North Sea gas, signing twenty-five-year take-or-pay contracts (an agreement where a buyer is obligated to either take a minimum quantity of something from a seller or pay a penalty fee).[108] These contracts reduced the risk for the exploration companies because they were guaranteed revenue regardless of how much demand materialised.[109]

The discovery of natural gas in the North Sea created a conundrum. It had a higher calorific value than town gas and had the potential to be much cheaper, but there would be a huge cost to making the switch. Natural gas had a different chemical composition to town gas. The industry's main research centre, Watson House, tried desperately to come up with a way of blending natural gas and town gas while maintaining the safety of the system but concluded that it was not possible.[110] The entire existing infrastructure base – from pipelines to appliances in homes – would need to be replaced. Some politicians opposed conversion, most notably Margaret Thatcher, who argued in 1968 that 'this policy involves the wholesale displacement of existing gas-making plant . . . What we shall be doing . . . is writing off not obsolete equipment, but brand-new technologically up-to-date equipment' (a perfect example of the sunk-cost fallacy).[III] The National Coal Board also opposed the switch because it would reduce the demand for coal.

In 1966, the Gas Council and government made the decision to convert the entire industry over to natural gas. It started with a pilot for 7,885 customers in Canvey Island in 1966–67 to learn how to do conversion at a small scale. Once the methodology was honed, it was rolled out nationally. The British conversion programme opted for a quick conversion cycle, two to three days, as the Gas Council took the view that speed was essential to winning public support. This was a much shorter time frame than in other countries and incurred significant risk. In Canvey, one-third of all consumers complained, and in the early years of the programme about 15 per cent of appliance conversions had some kind of fault. London was particularly challenging due to the density of the city, traffic, intricate pipeline networks and the threat of IRA bombings. The Central London conversion programme was suspended twice due to mounting complaints. However, the Gas Council embraced an ethos of failing fast in order to learn.

The conversion programme adopted a modular delivery approach, with regions responsible for planning when each post-code underwent conversion. This was crucial because changing appliances had to coincide with retrofitting the existing pipeline network. Working region by region and street by street also had the advantage of allowing learnings to be applied from one area to another.

Households were given a 'C-Day' when a fitter would arrive and replace or adapt all their appliances. Workforce manuals placed great emphasis on making the first interaction with the customer pleasant and reassuring. Within ten hours the network turned the gas back on. The process was even quicker for some types of consumers, with hospitals and hotels facing only a few hours of supply interruption. There followed an eight-week 'call back' period where operatives returned to resolve any issues. In some cases, where customers were being difficult or there were multiple faults, the home service advisors would attend to demonstrate the benefits of cooking with natural gas. The resulting cake was of course a neat bribe. All of this was done at no direct cost to the end consumer. If customers refused, as a last resort the conversion authorities had the right to shut off the gas supply and force entry.[112] However, overall the British public were remarkably cooperative. Only two premises in a hundred could not be entered immediately on their 'C-Day', and only one in a thousand ended up needing its supply cut off.[113]

Conversion was immensely complex. A census of appliances between 1967 and 1969 revealed that there were nearly 8,000 different types that would need replacing or adapting. For each appliance there was a standard conversion set and a procedure to help the gas fitter work at pace. Given the broad array of appliances, there were more than 4,000 different conversion sets with about 1,400 procedures. Information constantly flowed back and forth between the engineers on the front line and a central Technical Advisory Panel. Storerooms were set up around the country, like today's Amazon warehouses, all employing the latest inventory-management techniques.[114]

Natural gas meant that the economics of gas resembled electricity more closely. For the first time there were benefits to creating a national network that could bring gas from a handful of points along the coast down the country and inland. Pipeline technology had improved in the 1930s, but it was not until the 1950s that advances in metallurgy and pipe-laying techniques enabled building a whole transmission system.[115] In 1966, the transmission network had one pipeline of 320 miles, no compressors (large jet engines in bus-sized sheds that pushed and pulled gas around the network) and one terminal (very large industrial sites to process gas). By 1979 the network had been expanded to 3,047 miles of pipeline, eleven compressor stations and five major gas import terminals.

Finding natural gas in the North Sea may have been luck, geologically speaking, but the ability to bring it onshore was anything but that. The new National Transmission System cost around £110 million (£2.3 billion in 2024 prices). By comparison, in 2023 the National Infrastructure Commission estimated that a new transmission pipeline network for hydrogen of just 950 miles could cost as much as £22 billion and take ten years to construct.[116] Today's privatised operator is thus thirty-one times more expensive and much slower than the nationalised industry. In the peak years of 1967 and 1968, the gas industry built a staggering 600 miles of high-pressure pipeline per year.

Gas conversion would not have been possible without military-like central coordination. Initially the Gas Council fulfilled this role. In 1966, a Conversion Executive was established with powers over planning, technical standards, procurement and public relations.[117] The executive was the central brain. It set up a Technical Advisory Panel that developed standardised conversion procedures based on the census of appliances. The executive also gained agreement from all the equipment manufacturers to provide only natural gas appliances from 1968. New appliance standards were set by Watson House, demonstrating the wisdom of elevating its standing in the early 1950s. The executive also ran a successful public relations campaign on the benefits of conversion.

However, the Gas Council wanted more control and in 1967 commissioned McKinsey to investigate how this could be accomplished. This was one of the first instances of the energy industry's affinity for management consultants. Reflecting the enduring cross-party consensus on matters relating to gas, in 1971 the Conservative government acted on recommendations by the Labour Party from 1969. The 1972 Gas Act increased the power of the centre, dissolving the area boards and turning them into regional units of the new British Gas Corporation (although they still had considerable autonomy).[118]

Over ten years, 13.4 million customers and 35 million appliances were converted. The British programme was arguably the most successful in the world. The Dutch managed conversion for only 2 million customers in four and a half years, and the

Japanese only 5 million customers in twelve years. The speed is even more impressive considering that in just twenty years the gas industry had gone from the world's first LNG imports to complete conversion of the entire system. In 1966, the Gas Council estimated that conversion would cost £510 million (£10.5 billion in 2024 prices), with £400 million for changing appliances and £110 million for the new network. The whole programme came in on time and under budget.[119] The state had given the gas industry considerable freedom and financial backing. This trust was rewarded. The gas industry's 'self-financing' level was only 17 per cent in 1967 as conversion ramped up, but by 1977 it was up to 100 per cent.[120]

Public ownership was critical to natural gas conversion. The state's backing with 'patient capital' meant that the industry could place 'big bets' that would take a long time to pay off. Without state ownership, it is likely that vested interests would have blocked conversion, just as the fragmented gas undertakings had resisted amalgamation in the interwar years. Natural gas conversion essentially made the entire stock of coal-to-gas and oil-to-gas assets obsolete. Nationalisation also created a central organisation with significant control over the industry with considerable financial resources, which made it possible to coordinate the development of offshore fields with the build-out of the onshore transmission system. Other countries with more privatised systems, like the US, also made the switch from town gas, but not as swiftly and as comprehensively as did Britain.

Nationalisation also allowed the gas industry to take greater entrepreneurial risks in trying to compete with electricity. There were three successful technological innovations over the 1950s to 1970s (oil-to-gas, LNG, natural gas). The gas industry adopted a strategy like the one used by venture capitalists today: placing many technology bets simultaneously and rapidly pivoting as more information accrued about which technology would win. A culture of engineering innovation also played a role. It is telling that the man who announced conversion complete on 1

September 1977 in Edinburgh was Denis Rooke (chair of the British Gas Corporation), who had boarded the *Methane Pioneer* as a young engineer in 1958. At the ceremony Rooke called conversion 'perhaps the biggest peacetime operation in this nation's history' and reminded the audience that 'while we who worked on the job are congratulating each other on its successful accomplishment, we should not forget our customers. The biggest vote of thanks is surely due to them.'[121]

By the late 1970s Britain's gas industry was world-renowned. The British Gas Corporation set up an International Consulting Service that sold projects to Brazil, Canada, Norway, Russia, Spain, Thailand and Bangladesh. It was licensing technologies to the US and Japan. In Egypt and Algeria, the corporation supported the conversion of hundreds of thousands of households to natural gas. The corporation even developed a 'tech' business, selling control-system computer software to other countries.[122] In 1979 the corporation became the first nationalised industry to raise capital on the New York commercial paper market.[123]

The impact on citizens

Between 1950 and 1970, the British economy grew, wages rose and consumption increased. Energy was part of this socio-economic transformation. Electricity consumption per person increased four and a half times from 1948 to 1970. The slogan of the Electricity Development Agency summarised the profound changes occurring to everyday life: 'Electricity for all, and for every purpose.' It claimed there were 'Four Foundations of Modern Life: electric cookers, water heaters, refrigerators and washing machines'.[124] This was only a minor exaggeration. Every consumer durable index documented the rising use of these and other appliances. Between 1957 and 1962 the percentage of consumers with fridges rose from 11 per cent to 28 per cent, washing machines from 22 per cent to 45 per cent and TVs from 47 per cent to 84 per cent.[125] Marketeers portrayed appliances as labour-saving devices, but there is no evidence that they reduced the amount of time women spent performing domestic labour.[126]

Falling energy prices coupled with rising incomes drove up energy consumption. Between 1948 and 1968 electricity prices fell by 22 per cent in real terms and remained flat from 1968 to 1978. Gas prices fell by 11 per cent from 1948 to 1968, but following natural gas conversion fell by another 45 per cent by 1978.[127] Appliance quality and energy efficiency also improved. Between 1948 and 1979 consumption of energy services grew even more than raw energy consumption: consumption of domestic heat services grew by 133 per cent, lighting by 547 per cent and power for industry by 298 per cent. Citizens were willing to pay more for better energy-using products. The price of heating services increased over the 1960s and 1970s. However, the quality of heating services improved dramatically with electric heating, and from the 1970s natural gas–fuelled central heating. These quality improvements led to increased consumption of heating services.[128]

Citizens benefited from the intense competition between gas and electricity. This was particularly intense for local council authority housing, which went from under 10 per cent to over 30 per cent of housing between 1930 and 1970. In the 1930s, it was the gas industry that championed the 'right to choose', but in the 1950s it was the electricity industry making this argument. With gas resurgent there were now two load-hungry utilities in competition, driving up energy demand by building infrastructure into the fabric of buildings.[129]

Competition was most intense for domestic heating. In 1942, coal dominated, especially in working-class households, with electric or gas appliances used as a 'top-up'. In the 1940s to 1960s, electricity encroached on coal: domestic heat was just 17 per cent of domestic electricity demand in 1938, but by 1948 it was 40 per cent. Electricity area boards and appliance manufacturers pushed underfloor heating, water heaters and off-peak storage heaters.[130] The switch to electricity was in part driven by environmental regulations following the London Smog of 1952, which established smokeless areas. From 1956 to 1966, smoke emissions from domestic sources declined 38 per cent nationally, and as much as 76 per cent in London.[131]

The conversion to natural gas undoubtedly improved the everyday lived experience of citizens in towns and cities. A newspaper article in 1956 in the North East complained that the residents near the gas works 'have to contend with the most nauseating smell of gas permeating our homes and nostrils'.[132] Natural gas conversion eliminated the need for noxious gas works. Gas overtook electricity in heating following natural gas conversion. In 1970, only 40 per cent of central heating systems were gas-based, but by 1979 it was more than 80 per cent.[133] Central heating was revolutionary. As one consumer later recalled, people went from 'dreading the winter, to not dreading it at all'.[134] This shift in home heating reduced coal's share of final energy consumption from three-quarters in 1960 to only one-third by the mid-1970s.[135]

Evaluating performance

It is often said that history is written by the victors. The economists, politicians and bureaucrats who privatised the energy industries in the 1980s and 1990s succeeded in rewriting the history of the nationalised era. They characterised the state-owned enterprises as centralised, bureaucratic, inefficient and guilty of underinvestment. Many economists and political commentators have parroted this view.

The popular interpretation is incorrect. The nationalised gas and electricity industries were polycentric, innovative, highly productive and capable of building infrastructure at a pace and scale that outstrips today's private sector. In a sense, this is to be expected. As the economist Joan Robinson argued in 1978 it is a

> popular error that bureaucracy is less flexible than private enterprise . . . When large-scale adaptations have to be made, central control is far more flexible. It may take two months to

> get an answer to a letter from a government department, but it takes twenty years for an industry under private enterprise to readjust itself to a fall in demand.[136]

When compared with the Kafkaesque complexity of the present system, I imagine that many in the industry today would find the simplicity of nationalisation refreshing. In electricity the Central Authority met once a month, and Citrine was brutal in culling unnecessary meetings. Decisions were made with speed. After a debate in 1947 over the scope of authority of the North of Scotland Board, Emanuel Shinwell travelled to Scotland and took a short walk with Tom Johnston around the lake at Pitlochry. The pair arrived back to the assembled group of civil servants and Shinwell announced, 'I've decided the Board will retain its autonomy.'[137] That was the end of the matter. Planning was incredibly simple. The CEGB worked on a basic heuristic that 2 to 3 per cent growth in GDP implied a 7 per cent growth in electricity demand.[138] Both electricity and gas industries planned infrastructure in three- to seven-year waves. In 1981, the Monopolies and Mergers Commission conducted a detailed investigation into CEGB planning and revealed a process much simpler than the way the energy industry plans today.[139] Modern planning has far more in common with Soviet-style Gosplan, with a multiplicity of organisations involved in creating extremely complicated mathematical forecasts and twenty-plus-year plans.

Were the nationalised energy industries inefficient? Economists have three different ways of thinking about the efficiency of an economy or sector: productive, dynamic and allocative efficiency. Productive efficiency is simply a measure of the level of inputs used to produce outputs. A worker using machinery (capital) will typically be more productive than one without. In capital-intensive sectors like energy, the best measure of productive efficiency is total factor productivity (TFP), which measures output divided by the weighted average of labour and capital inputs. Data collected in the 1970s and 1980s indicated that between 1948 and 1968, TFP growth in electricity hovered around 3.4 per cent per annum, better than the manufacturing sector. The only nationalised sector with stronger performance was airlines. Between 1958 and 1985 TFP growth in gas was around 3.5 per cent per annum, also better than manufacturing.[140] In the 1960s and 1970s, the gas industry had one of the best productivity growth rates of any British industry.[141] For comparison, since the early 2000s TFP growth in gas and electricity has been negative.[142] Even publications by Thatcherites that were highly critical of nationalisation acknowledged that gas and electricity had strong productivity growth until at least the mid-1970s.[143]

How did Britain's gas and electricity industries compare to other countries'? In the post-war period, the US was the 'frontier' economy, the richest and most technologically advanced in the world. European countries could catch up simply by copying the US and importing technology. If a sector in Europe was catching up on the US, it was doing well. The economic historian Leslie Hannah has argued that the productivity of nationalised gas and electricity in Britain was weak when compared to the same sectors in the US, France and Germany. However, Hannah based his conclusion on output per worker, not TFP, and a statistical series that amalgamated gas, electricity and water. When water is excluded from the series, we see that output per worker in gas and electricity caught up to the US between 1950 and 1977.[144] The catch-up is even more impressive when measured by total factor productivity. In 2005, the economic historian Robert Millward revised upwards earlier estimates of TFP growth. His data series showed that between 1950 and 1973 Britain's electricity sector had an average annual growth rate in TFP of 5.5 per cent versus the US rate of 3.9 per cent. The equivalent metric for gas was 4.7 per cent in Britain against just 3.0 per cent in the US.[145]

Dynamic efficiency is the capacity of an economy or sector to generate new ways of doing things. On this measure, nationalised gas and electricity were highly efficient, innovative and entrepreneurial organisations. Contrary to the image of the state today as 'risk-averse', the Gas Council and the CEGB were risk-loving. They oversaw several technological innovations and were prepared to make 'big bets' on technologies like nuclear, the supergrid and LNG which were characterised by extreme uncertainty – the kind of uncertainty the private sector and financial institutions hate.

An article in the *Economist* in 2012 summed up the popular view that 'governments have always been lousy at picking winners'.[146] This does not fit the historical record. Nationalised energy picked some winners and some losers. LNG and then North Sea gas were bets that played out very well. Nuclear was more complex; Britain's early move created a technology lock-in. Once the PWRs were available, it was undoubtedly a mistake to stick with British AGRs just to protect the domestic nuclear industry. British nuclear was a strange case of a successful failure. Early successes made it hard to pull back or change path. The nuclear programme became 'sticky'; politicians were wedded to the policy because they were loss-averse and did not want to be the one to kill it. It was easier to let the nuclear programme muddle along.[147]

The primary objective of the nationalised gas and electricity industries was to build an endowment of assets for future generations. The CEGB motto was 'Power in Trust'. It saw itself as a mere steward of 'assets entrusted to them by the nation'.[148] The engineers who ran the nationalised industries were therefore focused on the long term. In 1959, at the opening of one of the huge hydroelectric schemes in Scotland, Sir Christopher Hinton reasoned, 'It seems to me that twenty, thirty and fifty years hence, people . . . will not think of the temporary financial difficulties . . . but will say how tremendously fortunate it was that this waterpower development took place when it did."[149] It is impossible to evaluate the performance of these organisations without understanding the centrality of this mindset. R. H. Tawney argued that patience was one of the virtues of public ownership, for it 'need not snatch an immediate profit at the cost of prejudicing the future of the industry'.[150]

Hinton was articulating an argument similar to one made by Keynesian economists, that discounting future consumption in favour of the present both was immoral and led to suboptimal economic outcomes. In 1952, Dennis Robertson, one of Keynes's good friends, argued that 'the State has claimed the right and assumed the duty of making and implementing on behalf of community one of the most fundamental economic choices, namely the distribution of productive resources between present and future uses'.[151] Governments often provide things like hydroelectric or nuclear power because businesses are impatient, and the state endures. State ownership lowered the cost of capital, which mechanically fed through to being able to accept a longer payback period on infrastructure projects.[152]

Allocative efficiency is the most counterintuitive way of thinking about efficiency. It is possible for an economy to be highly efficient at using labour and capital but produce the *wrong* outputs. Subsidising apple growing as a health measure may seem like an innocuous thing to do, but it might lead to a glut of cider and a shortage of beer. Mispricing often leads to allocative inefficiencies. In the 1980s, one argument that heavily influenced privatisation was that the nationalised energy industries had *overbuilt* because prices were set too low and therefore demand was too high. For this reason, it is important to investigate the complexities involved in setting energy prices.

The nationalisation legislation required that organisations should cover their costs taking 'one year with another'. In the late 1940s, this was taken to mean that prices should be based on average costs; the price should cover the construction and operating costs *pooled* across all parts of the industry over several years. This wasn't new: municipal and privately owned energy undertakings had long set prices using this rudimentary approach. Over the 1950s, economists came to see the practice as objectionable. Determining the 'right' price for electricity became a high-profile debate within academic economics, attracting giants of the discipline like James Meade and Ronald Coase.[153]

It was the nationalised electricity industry in France that pioneered the alternative approach, termed 'marginal cost pricing', in the 1950s. The basic idea was that the price of electricity should be set to equal the marginal cost of producing one additional unit. In the short run, this meant the operating cost of the plant (mainly fuel), and in the long run it also included the capital cost of replenishing the infrastructure. If prices did not equal marginal cost, consumers, businesses and economic planners would face the wrong signals. Underpriced electricity would mean that users would consume 'too much' but would not be paying for the full cost of the system. High demand could lead to overbuilding infrastructure, driving up costs for taxpayers and billpayers.[154]

In Britain over the 1940s and 1950s, there were repeated attempts to reform electricity pricing, but British economists were not as successful as their French counterparts. James Meade, director of the Economics Section in the late 1940s, tried to convince government of the merits of marginalism. Hugh Gaitskell, minister for fuel and power at the time, was sympathetic to Meade's argument that prices should be raised at peak times to reduce peak demand. However, Lord Citrine opposed this, arguing that it would not be in the public interest to raise prices. Herbert Morrison raised the same objection. He believed that universal service and a uniform price were intimately bound together. Proposals for a peak 'time of use' price were watered down into a seasonal peak price, which only lasted until 1949. The Economics Section kept pushing, but marginal pricing was a complex concept that officials found difficult to digest. The economists did not make it easy, with highly technical papers that paid little attention to practical considerations.[155]

In 1953, the economist Ian Little wrote an influential book that argued 'the electricity industry has completely failed to set up a pricing system which will enable it to produce amounts of electricity which are in the national interest . . . It was only interested in selling as much as possible.'[156] The effect of low electricity prices was to increase demand for electricity for certain uses that may have been better served by coal or gas. The battle with gas was particularly intense in heating. The popularity of electric space heaters was particularly problematic because the demand was so 'peaky'. Despite the massive expansion of capacity in 1963 the CEGB warned that space heating load was close to causing blackouts.[157] The area boards agreed that this was a problem but simply did not believe that consumers were price responsive, whereas economists thought they were (the same divide exists today). Industry managers argued that increasing prices would not only discourage the undesirable load, like space heating, but also desirable load like water and cooking. Instead, the boards promoted the use of off-peak heating appliances like underfloor heating and block storage heaters, with some success.[158]

Gradually the marginalist argument gained traction. The economist Ronald Edwards was appointed as chair of the Electricity Council in 1962 and he kept pressing for reform. A 'day and night' tariff was introduced for a portion of bills in 1962. The 'bulk tariff', the price at which the CEGB sold electricity to the area boards, was reset in 1965 using the marginal cost method.[159] Yet true marginal cost pricing was never fully implemented. This would have meant allowing coal prices to be determined on world level, which would have seen British mines suffer in the face of Polish competition. This was deemed incompatible with the public interest. British miners were not entirely protected, as in the 1960s coal mines were closing at a rate of three a fortnight and in 1968 alone 25,000 miners were made redundant.[160]

In summary, although productively and dynamically efficient, the nationalised energy industries were not as allocatively efficient as they could have been. Even after the reforms in the 1960s, the relationship between price and cost was tenuous. The economists had failed to convince politicians of the necessity of reform. In 1979, James Callaghan reportedly said of marginal pricing that 'as Chancellor I couldn't care less'.[161]

Even after the CEGB and Electricity Council decided that marginal pricing was necessary, there were twelve area boards that could resist. This was unlike France, where Électricité de France (EDF) had total control of every level of the industry. The problem was not so much public ownership as its decentralised form. It is also worth noting that while it may have taken the British more than a decade longer than the French to adopt marginal pricing, this was still a decade earlier than anything similar happened in the highly decentralised and privatised system in the US.[162]

Technocratic drift

Britain's nationalised industries had two objectives: to act in the public interest and to break even. These objectives were not incompatible, but there was a tension between them. Between 1947 and 1977 (the end of gas conversion) there was a tacit agreement between the state and the energy industries to focus on building infrastructure and universal service, with the break-even requirement relaxed. The state made up the shortfall. However, once the infrastructure was built and service extended to all citizens the focus shifted to breaking even.[163]

From the 1960s, the Treasury led the charge to reign in expenditure. Economists in the department were concerned that escalating expenditure was 'crowding out' private investment. Again, the Treasury imported various techniques from France. In the 1950s, EDF had developed the concept of using a 'test discount rate' to evaluate the merits of infrastructure projects. EDF first used the technique to decide between hydroelectric and thermal generation. Hydroelectric was expensive to build but generated savings over a long period of time because it had a lower operating cost than a coal-fired power station. The issue with hydroelectric was the risk of technological obsolescence – what if something better emerged in the future? Using a test discount rate flipped conventional wisdom on its head; longevity was a risk as well as a benefit. Using a high-test discount rate meant discounting the future more heavily, meaning a project needed to reach payback over a shorter period. The British Treasury used the approach in 1964 to evaluate two large hydroelectric schemes at Fada Fionn and Laidon. Hydroelectric projects had favourable economics in the late 1940s, when coal prices were high and interest rates low, but by the late 1950s coal was oversupplied and interest rates had risen. The two projects failed to pass the economic tests and were killed.[164]

The 1967 Treasury white paper took reform a step further and moved the gas and electricity industries towards long-run marginal cost pricing, required rates of return for existing assets and test discount rates for any new projects. In 1967, the test discount rate was set at 8 per cent. The 1961 Treasury white paper had recommended using a target rate of return but noted that 'social obligations might justify a lower target'. The 1967 report was the high-water mark for the influence of economists but proved too complex to implement.[165]

A further white paper in 1978 recognised the impracticality of the 1967 rules and moved back to simpler financial targets. From 1978 the required rate of return was set at 5 per cent across the whole portfolio of investments, so within that range there could be projects with a very low rate of return offset by projects with high rates.[166]

In parallel to these administrative changes, technological dynamics were also changing. There had always been some criticism of nationalised energy, but while a virtuous circle of rising demand, rising investment and falling real prices continued these criticisms never gained traction. From the early 1970s, the rate of improvements to steam turbine technology slowed down. Some argued that there were even diseconomies of scale. There was also an increase in cost overruns for generation projects. Over the 1970s the electricity industry had a lower total factor productivity than the French, US and German systems, although the British gas industry remained world-leading. Rather than producing power that was 'too cheap to meter', nuclear had proven to be extremely expensive. Essentially, the system reached a point of technological stagnation, which placed the nationalised energy industries under more economic pressure.[167]

In the late 1970s, performance declined across several nationalised industries. The oil price shocks of the 1970s set off inflation, which increased input costs. However, because governments wanted to restrain inflation, prices were held low. This just made the self-financing issue even worse. The energy industries were more successful than others in managing the issue. In 1978 and 1979, the electricity industry made a profit for the Treasury, and in 1977 the financial accounts of the British Gas Corporation showed that it was generating a healthy 8 per cent return on capital (after interest). However, by then it was too late to reverse the narrative of failure.[168]

The economist Massimo Florio has argued that from the 1970s the nationalised industries entered a phase of 'technocratic drift'. Until the mid-1970s, there was a voracious ambition to build infrastructure to meet ever-growing energy demand. However, by the late 1970s the context had changed. Slower economic growth meant slower energy-demand growth. The electricity industry reacted rationally, slowing down or halting various construction programmes, although perhaps not as quickly as it should have done. Without the same pressure to build infrastructure, these organisations lost something of their raison d'être. In addition, the Treasury imposed rules that required these state-owned entities to behave more like private firms. This was bound to lead to the next question: Why weren't they?[169]

4

Privatised Energy, 1979–2010

I used to say to the people . . . if you don't know what to do, think of what you would do in the Central Electricity Generating Board and then do the opposite.

– Ed Wallis, CEO of PowerGen,
'An Oral History of the Electricity Supply Industry'

When Margaret Thatcher came to power in 1979, Britain had some of the highest levels of public ownership in the world. The state was part of the material fabric of everyday life. A third of all homes were rented from the municipal state. Almost all infrastructure was publicly owned. Nationalised companies provided all homes with gas and electricity. There was a widespread consensus across the political spectrum that energy was so important that it had to be controlled by the state. Competition was something to be avoided because it would lead to negative outcomes, as it had in the early twentieth century.

In the 1980s energy policy dramatically veered in a new direction. By the mid-1990s, Britain was widely recognised as the global pioneer of industrial privatisation. The gas and electricity industries were broken up and moved into private ownership. Competition was now something to be embraced. Vertical integration was seen no longer as rational but instead as inefficient. The British state sold off £86 billion worth of critical national infrastructure across energy, water, telecoms and a host of other industries. This was the largest experiment in public divestiture ever undertaken among capitalist economies, with international ramifications. Governments all over the world imitated Britain or had the model forced on them by the International Monetary Fund and the World Bank. In 1993, with the tone and conviction of a zealot, the World Bank announced that it would 'aggressively pursue the commercialization and corporatization of, and private sector participation in, developing-country power sectors'.[1]

The popular interpretation of energy privatisation was neatly summarised by the *Economist* in 1995:

> Fat nationalised industries have been transformed into fit and profitable enterprises. Huge subsidies have been eliminated. The prices of . . . electricity and gas have dropped in real terms . . . Eager to learn from the success, scores of governments have studied the British example and much of Europe is now following in Britain's footsteps.

This remains the story the energy industry tells itself today.[2]

However, fifteen years later, in 2010, it was clear that privatisation had not gone to plan. Efficiency gains were modest. Consumers benefited from falling prices over the 1990s, but from the early 2000s prices started to rise to above pre-privatisation levels. Investment levels were persistently low. Bureaucracy had not been vanquished; it was worse than ever under the guise of regulation. Vertical integration had returned in the form of a small number of massive private sector organisations operating across the value chain. Competition had led to oligopolies. The industry had been 'de-nationalised' in the sense that it was now mostly owned by foreign giants like Eon, EDF and RWE, but this was not what the privatisers had in mind.

The causes and process of privatisation

Privatisation was born in the turmoil of the late 1970s, which broke the post-war consensus: stagflation, a belief that trade unions had become too powerful, a loss of faith in the state's ability to influence employment levels. Economic advisors to

Thatcher believed that inflation and slow growth were due, in part, to taxpayer money being poured into bloated state-owned industries. However, the evidence that the gas and electricity industries had an efficiency problem was weak. In a 1980 book, John Redwood, who headed Thatcher's policy unit, admitted that both had achieved impressive improvements in productivity over the preceding decades. More valid was the argument that these industries were vulnerable to political manipulation of prices, especially in the 1970s, which led to worsening financial performance. By the end of the 1970s, even Labour circles were open to reforming the nationalised industries and opening them up to competition.[3]

The real driver of privatisation was financial stringency and a desire to evade the new Public Sector Borrowing Requirement. Thatcher's government was determined to reduce state borrowing. Moving the energy industry into private ownership would support this goal through a fiscal sleight of hand. It would also raise revenue, albeit in a one-off manner and hence why Harold Macmillan termed it 'selling off the family silver'. Another important ingredient was a change in attitude towards employment. Once it had been accepted that there was a natural rate of unemployment determined by the market, the government could absolve itself of any responsibility for job losses. A related motivation was to erode union power.[4]

As with the long campaign for nationalisation, privatisation was an idea that acquired logic and meaning over time. The term itself traces back to the management guru Peter Drucker in the 1960s, who spoke of 'reprivatisation'. In the late 1970s 'de-nationalisation' was the more commonly used term, though it remained a vague notion about increasing the distance between government and industry. Years later, Nigel Lawson argued that the reforms were always driven by 'an ideological belief in free markets and wider distribution of private ownership of property'. However, the 1976 Conservative Party publication *The Right Approach* does not even mention energy privatisation, and the 1979 Conservative manifesto barely mentioned it. Thatcher had claimed that 'one could not have two rival enterprises seeking to sell electricity in competition with each other'. The Conservatives' 1983 manifesto was much more committed to privatisation of state-owned industries writ large but was vague on whether energy should be privatised. During Thatcher's first term, the ideological commitment to markets and competition wasn't really reflected in any significant changes to energy policy.[5]

Victory in the Falklands and the Miners' Strike of 1984–85 set the stage for more radical changes. The government was committed to breaking the power of the National Union of Mineworkers. Splitting up the Central Electricity Generating Board was one mechanism for doing this because it would remove the single contract between the electricity industry and the National Coal Board. The nationalised energy industries had sowed the seeds for Thatcher's defeat of Scargill, as the development of nuclear and natural gas had reduced the country's dependence on coal.

The advocates of privatisation shared the conviction that the nationalised energy industries were inefficient, had overbuilt infrastructure, and had built 'gold-plated' assets. A series of investigations by the Monopolies and Mergers Commission (MMC) in the 1980s seemed to confirm these views. The 1981 MMC investigation into the Central Electricity Generating Board highlighted that the corporation had overestimated demand and therefore overbuilt infrastructure – although it is worth noting that the overestimation was mostly driven by the optimistic economic growth assumptions the board were told to use. The investigation supported the view that the energy industry was moving from an asset-building to an asset-sweating phase, with technological development stagnating.[6]

An important theoretical intervention was made by the economist Stephen Littlechild in 1981. In an article called 'Ten Steps to Denationalisation', Littlechild argued for a three-pronged strategy: divide the larger nationalised industries into more manageable components, encourage competition where feasible and transfer assets into private ownership. Just a few years before, Littlechild had thought that any discussion of de-nationalisation would have been professional suicide. Yet by 1982, Littlechild's thinking was embraced by the various think-tanks that acted as vanguards of the Thatcherite revolution. By 1983 the financial secretary to the Treasury was passionately arguing for privatisation and the introduction of competition.[7]

Littlechild was just one of a group of influential economists who subscribed to the Austrian school of economics and the thinking of Friedrich Hayek. The group was clustered around the Institute of Economic Affairs (IEA), the Centre for Policy Studies, the University of Birmingham and the University of Surrey. These economists became extremely influential within the new 'regulatory state' that emerged over the 1990s to oversee privatisation. Littlechild became the director general of the Office of Electricity Regulation (Offer). Michael Beesley, the so-called 'grandfather of the regulators' from the University of Birmingham, was an advisor to various government departments. Colin Robinson of the University of Surrey and the IEA became a member of the Monopolies and Mergers Commission. Eileen Marshall became a managing director at the Office of Gas and Electricity Markets (Ofgem) and sat on the IEA advisory panel.[8]

A decisive moment was Nigel Lawson's move to the Department for Energy in 1981. Lawson had become heavily influenced by the thinking of the IEA and economists like Littlechild. His 'Market for Energy' speech in 1982 turned out to be revolutionary. Lawson argued:

> I do *not* see the government's task as being to try to plan the future shape of energy production and consumption. It is not even to try to balance UK demand and supply for energy. Our task is rather to set a framework which will ensure that the market operates in the energy sector with a minimum distortion and energy is produced and consumed efficiently.

Lawson argued that energy prices should be set by markets, and that 'the key lies in increasing the responsiveness of these industries to the forces of the marketplace'. He also argued it was time to 'question both the extent of the natural monopoly' and state ownership. These words would have been totally alien to politicians and engineers in the 1970s and gave an indication of the seismic changes that were about to take place.[9] Lawson was also one of the architects of the public sector borrowing targets and would go on to be chancellor from 1983 to 1989, where he would continue to champion privatisation.

Privatisation happened in three waves. It began with the state selling off its shares in Thomas Cook in 1972 and British Petroleum in 1979. Between 1983 and 1987, twenty-four industries were privatised, including British Gas in 1986. Between 1987 and 1991 a further forty industries were sold off, including electricity in 1988. There were four methods: public offerings, employee and management buyouts, trade sales and private placements.[10]

In energy, gas was first up. It began with the 1982 Oil and Gas Act, which clipped back the British Gas Corporation and split off some of its offshore activities. British Gas was then privatised in 1986 as an entire vertically integrated company with a twenty-five-year franchise. The 'Tell Sid' campaign of 1986 was one of the most famous advertising campaigns in British history and exemplified the concept of 'popular capitalism' that emerged in Conservative thinking. The government went to great lengths to ensure that consumers could buy shares in British Gas, even stuffing advertisements in bills. The 1986 act stripped the organisation of its monopoly on gas supply, but in practice it was extremely difficult for competitors to emerge because they would need to negotiate the terms of network access.[11]

There was some debate about whether to break up the corporation. In 'Ten Steps', Littlechild reasoned that privatising it as a single entity would be enough. Other economists argued that unbundling was essential to prevent the corporation from abusing its power. Within the government, Secretary of State for Energy Peter Walker argued for vertical integration, whereas Nigel Lawson had argued for restructuring. Gas was the most successful of all the nationalised industries and lobbied to be left whole. Its chair, Denis Rooke, was a giant of industry and a formidable opponent for the privatisers. In the end, the government decided that it needed to complete privatisation before the 1987 election, which meant that there was no time for restructuring.[12]

Electricity went next. It was a different order of magnitude in scale and complexity to gas, with net assets double the size of British Gas and the sale raising nearly triple the amount of the gas industry in net proceeds. The 1983 Energy Act attempted to introduce competition into gas and electricity by allowing independent parties to use the networks to sell to end consumers. However, this failed to lead to any significant new entrants. The privatisers learned from this and from the experience in gas. This time they would parcel up the industry as it was migrated into private ownership.[13]

The Electricity Act of 1989 divided the CEGB into four organisations: two generation companies (National Power and PowerGen); a nuclear company (kept in public ownership until 1996); and a transmission company (National Grid Company). The area boards were turned into twelve regional electricity companies (RECs) covering distribution and retail, which were sold off in 1990. Over the 1990s, these RECs were gradually split into distribution network operators (DNOs) and suppliers, and by 1998 all customers were free to choose their supplier. The Scottish electricity industry, however, was left in the hands of two vertically integrated companies, Scottish Power and Scottish Hydro Electric (now SSE). The British electricity industry still has the same basic structure today.

Privatisation was a messy process, but it can be distilled down to four pillars: private ownership, unbundling, competition in markets and independent regulation. The architects of privatisation were convinced that private ownership was inherently superior to state ownership. John Moore, the minister who became a spokesperson for privatisation, believed that the policy simply 'returned [assets] to where they belonged – the private sector'. The idea was that managers chasing the carrot of profits and fearing the stick of bankruptcy would drive efficiency. Private ownership would also reduce state interference, or the so-called 'dead hand of government', in industrial matters, or let 'managers manage, not government', as Littlechild put it.[14]

The privatisers were, in fact, somewhat confused as to whether they were for or against governmental control. In the early stages of privatisation, many took the view that the nationalised industries had far too much autonomy. In 1981 Geoffrey Howe, then chancellor, commented that the British nationalised corporations had 'a degree of autonomy which is probably unique in the Western World . . . and they are better shielded from Ministerial control than the complaints of Government interference may suggest'. Thatcher annotated a memorandum on the electricity industry with the underlined words 'The CEGB still seems *accountable to no one*.'[15]

It was widely acknowledged by economists that there was very little difference in productivity between state-owned and privately owned vertically integrated monopolies. The crucial innovation was unbundling: to separate the bits of the system that could be competitive from those that could not. Economists argued that the nationalised industries had falsely assumed the boundaries of the natural monopoly to cover every step in the value chain, as had been the assumption since the first gas undertakings in London in the 1810s.[16]

In practice, unbundling meant splitting the networks from the services supplied over those networks (generation and retail). Networks were split up even further into different components to drive specialisation (gas transmission, gas distribution, electricity transmission and electricity distribution). System operations, the balancing of supply and demand, were later formally separated from operating the physical network. A crucial assumption behind unbundling was that there were not any significant 'economies of scope' from vertical integration (that is, benefits from coordinating generation, networks and retail within the same firm). As we shall see, this assumption held only when the industry was in an asset-sweating phase. Unbundling was a crucial component of privatisation in another sense; it made it easier to sell off assets. The electricity industry was so massive that financial markets wouldn't have been able to absorb the whole of it in one go.[17]

The third feature was competition in markets. Separating ownership of the networks from the services offered *over* these networks allowed for competition between generators and between suppliers. If privatisation in a pure sense was about transferring ownership, the term 'liberalisation' was used to refer to subjecting utilities to market forces through unbundling. In practice, privatisation and liberalisation became intertwined. Arguably, private ownership was seen as more important than unbundling and competition. In 1985, a Conservative spokesman noted that it was government policy to return state-controlled industries to the private sector even where competition was not possible.[18]

As the economist David Newbery explained in a classic book in 1999, private ownership was seen as a necessary condition for getting the benefits of competition. An obsession with private ownership is evidenced by the fact that networks were moved into private ownership, even though competition was not possible (except in a few cases) and there was no evidence that privately owned networks were more efficient than state-owned ones. Like Littlechild, Newbery thought competition in the capital markets (for example, network companies competing for investment with other companies) would drive efficiency and get the networks out from under 'stifling Treasury rules', but he admitted that this theory could not explain the successes of EDF. Other economists disagreed. In an influential book in 1988, John Vickers and George Yarrow advised that 'we would not privatize the national transmission grid' nor the nuclear plants.[19]

A fourth feature of privatisation was 'independent regulation'. Instead of direct regulation by government, the privatised gas and electricity industries would be monitored by an intermediate layer of regulators. Initially there were two – the Office of Electricity Regulation (Offer) and the Office of Gas Supply (Ofgas) – but these were merged in 2000 to create the Office of Gas and Electricity Markets (Ofgem). These regulatory offices were headed by a director general appointed by the relevant secretary of state. Many regulators were academic economists, which created the impression that they were neutral and scientific.[20]

Government was still responsible for setting energy policy. The energy regulators' primary duty was to promote competition. They had secondary duties as well, things like protecting consumer interests, promoting research and development and driving efficiency in the networks. The ordering is revealing. As Dieter Helm explained, 'If the promotion of competition conflicted with consumer interests, competition should come first.'[21] The privatisers had a theory that the regulators would diminish in importance over time. Competition would provide the disciplining mechanism in retail and generation, and regulation would be confined to the networks. The 'independent regulators' became a defining feature of the new neoliberal state, a state that derived authority from generating competition between firms. Regulators became a kind of modern priesthood overseeing the majesty of the market. In a classic textbook on privatisation, regulators were assigned almost God-like powers: 'In an ideal world the regulator of a firm would be omniscient, benevolent, and have ample powers of pre-commitment.'[22]

The theory and practice of privatisation were often two different things. Sir John Baker, CEO of National Power, later reflected that 'we were dealing with new concepts, this is a real jump into . . . an unknown method of organising an electricity industry . . . it was absolutely exhausting'. In interviews, industry insiders have reflected on privatisation as a messy process, often driven by ad hoc problem-solving within huge time constraints. Interviewees' memories are often contradictory as well, highlighting the confusing nature of the events unfolding before them.[23]

The process in gas was particularly messy, involving many compromises. Privatisation was achieved only by leaving British Gas as a vertically integrated monopoly. In 1988, Sheffield Forgemasters, a large steel-making firm, complained about price manipulation. This set off a series of investigations that revealed that British Gas had abused its power and practised extensive discrimination in the pricing of gas contracts (hiking prices for customers who did not have alternatives). The Monopolies and Mergers Commission (MMC) found that British Gas's dual role as seller of gas and owner of the gas transportation system led to an inherent conflict of interest which reduced competition. Yet the 1993 MMC recommendations were a compromise: British Gas would have to separate its trading and transportation business, but it did not need to fully divest. The process of breaking up British Gas took several more years. Gas supply was not opened up until 1995, and British Gas was split into two companies (Centrica and BG plc) in 1997. It took until 2003 for the distribution and transmission networks to be fully separated.[24]

The privatisers ended up learning the same lesson that the nationalisers had in the 1940s: changing ownership was not a silver bullet. Competition and/or effective regulation was necessary. How should the privately held monopolies be regulated? Here the British privatisers could turn to the US for guidance. Unlike in Europe, energy utilities had remained in private ownership since the nineteenth century, operating as vertically integrated monopolies in a territory. Over the 1930s, a stable regulatory settlement had emerged known as 'rate-of-return' regulation. A utility was given a legal right to provide services to an area, and its assets were assigned a 'regulated asset value'. If the company expanded its asset base, for example, to extend service or improve reliability, it was permitted to collect the cost plus a rate of return from end consumers through 'rates'. The model represented a bargain between politicians and utilities;

vertical integration and monopoly were tolerated for control of prices and profits.[25]

The main drawback of rate-of-return regulation was that it involved a great deal of administration. The British Treasury called it a 'highly undesirable superstructure of regulation'. Regulators had to estimate the value of the assets, ensure that investments were necessary and cost-effective and agree a reasonable rate of return. British economists therefore saw the American process as costly and time-consuming. Another criticism was that rate-of-return regulation incentivised overbuilding because the easiest way for a utility to increase its profits was simply to spend more. This became known as the 'Averch-Johnson effect' after the two economists who came up with the concept in 1962.[26]

Whereas rate-of-return regulation emerged over decades through practice, the British regulatory model would be designed in a few years by academics more comfortable with theory. In 1982 Stephen Littlechild was asked to write a report on the best way to regulate the telecoms sector. The paper he produced in just ten weeks became known as the 'Littlechild Report', and it was a foundational text in the privatisation programme. Littlechild thought the model of privatisation in the US did not go far enough. He argued that the rate-of-return approach 'resulted in waste of investment', 'costly bureaucracy' and 'overcapitalization' (the Averch-Johnson effect).[27]

Rather than put a ceiling on profits, Littlechild argued for a ceiling on prices. The approach was called RPI-X. At the start of every 'price control period' (usually lasting three to five years) the regulator and utility would agree a starting price point that all customers would be charged. The utility was allowed to raise the price each year by no more than the increase in the retail price index minus an X factor. The larger the X factor, the more the business was obliged to increase efficiency or reduce profits.

Littlechild believed companies must have the opportunity to earn unlimited profits, as only this would push the industry to the frontier of efficiency. RPI-X was supposed to mimic the effects of a competitive market. If utilities beat the formula and made huge profits, they would merely reveal how much it cost to run the network and so set the price lower in the next price control period. The other idea was to compare the performance of the different regional units to drive the poor performers to catch up with the more efficient ones, called 'yardstick competition'. RPI-X came to be termed 'light-handed regulation', as Littlechild believed it avoided the need for detailed administrative proceedings. The regulator would 'not have to make any judgement or calculations with respect to capital, allocation of costs, rates of return, future movement of costs and demand, [and] desirable performance'.[28] This conclusion would turn out to be naïve.

Price regulation was focused on efficiency, but it came at the risk of excessive profits. This created another problem: What if the state or regulator decided to raid profits or renege on the deal? Customers of monopoly networks are trapped. If they are unhappy, they cannot exit so must use their voice through politics.[29] What if they elected politicians who clawed back excessive profits? The privatisers realised that the utilities needed a regulatory framework that assured them of a 'fair' rate of return on past investments regardless of the government. Or, as Newbery put it in his textbook, insulation from political interference.

The licensing regime was therefore crucial. The state could revoke a licence only if the company failed to meet certain licence obligations (like reliability). The initial licences had a term of thirty-five years and were legally enforceable contracts. Changes would have to go through complex and lengthy procedures and had to be agreed by the various licence holders. Disagreements between the regulator and licence holders could be referred to the Monopolies and Mergers Commission. In addition, there were various 'codes' that set the rules for markets and network access, which were very difficult to change without the agreement of the companies.[30]

Technologies: The fall of nuclear and the 'dash for gas'

The three British nuclear programmes between 1950 and 1979 were something of a successful failure; early successes had led to perpetuation of a policy that was not working very well. How might the privatised industry handle the nuclear conundrum? In the early years it seemed that Thatcher's government would continue the pattern of muddling on. In their 1979 election manifesto, the Conservatives had committed to the purchase of one pressurised water reactor (PWR). Thatcher's first energy secretary, David Howell, committed to a fleet of ten. His successor, Nigel Lawson, in a 1992 memoir wrote that nuclear would support 'emancipation from Arthur Scargill' (president of the National Union of Mineworkers). Yet Lawson watered down the commitment to just four PWRs. In 1989, just after Thatcher praised nuclear power as a solution to climate change at the UN, plans for a fleet were shelved. Only one PWR was constructed, Sizewell B, in 1995. It ended up costing £2 billion (£5.6 billion in 2024 prices) and was 35 per cent over budget.[31]

Privatisation brought the failures of the British nuclear programme to a head. The cross-subsidisation of nuclear by other parts of the electricity industry was exposed. When PowerGen and National Power were carved out from the CEGB, nuclear assets were not included in the deal. It was obvious to the new managers of these companies that nuclear power stations were much more expensive than the alternatives. The companies were also determined to avoid taking on the long-term decommissioning liabilities, fuel-processing costs and risk of cost overruns. National Power and PowerGen had a higher cost of borrowing than the state, and when this was applied it killed the case for nuclear. Unable to sell such unattractive assets, the government was forced to withdraw nuclear from privatisation and move the assets into two state-owned companies called Nuclear Electric and Scottish Nuclear.[32]

Then something unexpected happened. Between 1990 and 1996 nuclear underwent a remarkable turnaround. The publicly owned companies Nuclear Electric and Scottish Nuclear ended up being extremely successful. By focusing exclusively on nuclear, and with nowhere to hide losses, productivity improved dramatically. The workforce was cut from 13,000 to 9,500, and load factors (the percentage of the time plants were producing) improved. In March 1993 Nuclear Electric announced an average load factor of 73.9 per cent, which narrowly beat the 73.2 per cent achieved by the fleet of PWRs in the US.[33]

Yet the privatisers had no time for introspection. No one seriously considered whether the example indicated that private ownership was not the miracle cure it was being touted as, or that some of the benefits from unbundling were compatible with state ownership. Instead, the privatisers saw the success of nuclear as an invitation to have another go at selling it off. Nuclear Electric and Scottish Nuclear were merged under British Energy, which was privatised in 1996.

British Energy shares at first performed very well. Good operational performance translated into high payments to shareholders, but not adequate investment in the plants. This led to several unplanned outages. British Nuclear also fell foul of its grand ambitions. In the late 1990s it formed a joint venture to acquire nuclear plants in the US and tried to increase its market power by buying an energy retail business. It then moved into coal-fired generation in Britain and Canada. By 2002 the company was overstretched.

From 1999 nuclear plant performance began to decline, but British Energy continued to pay shareholders large dividends and took on debt to fund expansion. Falling power prices and the end of subsidies (the fossil fuel levy) ultimately led to financial collapse. British Energy was effectively renationalised between 2002 and 2004. In 2005 the Nuclear Decommissioning Authority took over the liabilities of the legacy plant and facilities. Excessive profits, overexpansion, mismanagement and a state bailout: there is an eery similarity to the story of Thames Water today.[34]

The state-owned nuclear giant EDF stepped in and acquired British Nuclear in 2009. This was seen as a sign of the vitality of the industry, but it also reflected that the French wanted an export market for their reactors. Between 2003 and 2007 a series of white papers flirted with nuclear, but the economics made it an unattractive option for new carbon-free generation. As we shall see in the next chapter, since 2010 nuclear has limped along in a zombie-like state.

While nuclear was struggling, gas was becoming more important in electricity generation. The 'dash for gas' started slowly. In the 1980s, gas-fired generation began to take off in the US, with manufacturers like Westinghouse and General Electric taking an early lead in the design and manufacture of combined-cycle gas turbines (CCGTs). By the late 1980s, European firms like ABB and Siemens had also entered the market. The rise of gas generation was in part due to environmental concerns about nuclear and the pollution impacts of coal-fired generation. From the late 1980s, environmental regulation aimed at reducing acid rain required coal plants be fitted with 'flue gas desulphurisation' equipment, which significantly increased the cost of coal generation. The most important trigger was the relaxation of restrictions on using gas to generate electricity in August 1990. Until then, an EC directive of 1975 had effectively banned the technology on the basis that gas was a 'premium fuel' to be used for cooking and heating.[35]

PowerGen and National Power made a pivot from coal to gas from the early 1990s. The CCGTs had a clear cost advantage over coal. The regional electricity companies also turned to the new technology, forming consortia and pooling their permitted 'self-generation' allowances. Foreign companies entered the fray as well. The American company Enron constructed one of the first large CCGTs in Teesside, the largest in the world at the time, before the company collapsed in disgrace in the early 2000s.

The new world of privatised energy was a high-stakes game for strategic positioning. The regional electricity companies were partly motivated by the desire to undermine the market power of the two large generation companies. The RECs were being opportunistic. As one executive put it, CCGTs were a 'way to get equity into a non-regulated business' with higher returns than were available in networks. This reflects the reality that the RECs seemed to have adapted to the new commercial world better than the large generation companies, which were more wedded to the CEGB culture.[36] Over the 1990s, Britain had one of the fastest booms in gas-fired generation in the world. In 1990, there was no gas-fired generation, but by 1998 there was 17 GW worth, or a quarter of national generation capacity. Between 1991 and 2005 there was a fiftyfold increase in gas use for power. The 'dash for gas' in turn triggered the collapse of the coal market and the closure of half the remaining deep pits by 1993.[37]

The CCGTs represented a very different kind of techno-economic system to that of nuclear or coal: less capital-intensive, smaller, modular and quicker to build. The technology was imported, and there was very little interest in building up domestic supply chains, as the CEGB had assiduously done for coal and nuclear. As one regional electricity company insider said, 'We are profit driven . . . The R&D is being done by the people who sell the kit, and they publicise their work widely – we don't have to be very proactive in monitoring technology advancements.' Another industry insider claimed that 'we were basically forced by the banks' to adopt imported technology.

This highlights the crucial role financial institutions played in the 'dash'. International loans were secured using future revenue as collateral. Enron's Teesside plant was financed through a fifteen-year £800 million syndicated loan from thirty international banks. The need to pay back these loans incentivised speed. The fact that private sector organisations had a higher cost of borrowing also favoured the CCGTs compared to coal and nuclear. As another industry insider explained:

> Pre-privatisation a CCGT would have always lost out because of the investment appraisal used. Private sector discount rates of

> 15% to 20% mean the economics swing from fuel to capital. CCGT plants are essentially modular . . . Ten years, the time needed to build an old CEGB plant . . . is a lifetime in the capital markets. We built Rooscote [a CCGT plant] in 24 months.[38]

The term 'dash for gas' is apt. The nuclear programme required patient capital and focused on building a foundation of engineering capabilities in Britain. The 'dash for gas' was driven by impatient capital. The technology was imported, and infrastructure was built for an economic life just long enough to pay back the loans. There was little consideration of the long-term consequences of shifting the generation mix away from nuclear to gas, even though Britain's own gas reserves were finite. In 1995 the trade union leader Rodney Bickerstaffe warned that 'Britain will become dependent on external fuel sources sooner than we would wish'.[39]

The 'dash for gas' is often heralded as an example of the kind of dynamic buccaneering capitalism that Thatcher installed in Britain. However, it was possible only because the nationalised industries had done a lot of the hard work laying the foundations for the privatised industry. Most of the new power stations were built on top of old coal-fired ones – a better term might have been a 'rush from coal'.[40] The new CCGTs were able to access gas through the transmission network that had been built in the 1970s. In a National Power advert from 1991, electricity pylons break free from their shackles and march across the landscape to admire a new CCGT power station. The advert implied that the 'dash' required a massive restructuring of the electricity network. However, between 1991 and 2005 capital spending on electricity networks was flat. The 'dash' was a sprint for the line, possible only because the electricity and gas networks were already there.

Would the 'dash for gas' have happened under nationalisation? Some industry leaders thought so. In 1990, the CEO of National Power said that his company was 'not burning gas as a consequence of being a private company . . . The CEGB would have . . . it did not because it was not available.'[41] In the early 1970s, the CEGB's chief engineer had taken a keen interest in gas-fired generation. T. G. N. Haldane also expressed an interest in the technology as early as 1949. Showing his genius, he spotted the role gas would end up playing as a way of balancing the electricity system as intermittent renewable forms of generation, like wind, came online. The main reason the CEGB never scaled gas was because the 1975 European directive prohibited it. Where privatisation was decisive was in incentivising the speed of the 'dash'. The CCGTs were a technology perfectly suited to the new dynamics of the industry: a quick, cheap bolt-on to the foundations that already existed.[42]

Markets, regulation and ownership

The speed of the 'dash for gas' was remarkable considering that, in parallel, the privatisers were entirely reconfiguring the way electricity was bought and sold. Electricity is a very peculiar commodity; it is extremely difficult to store and because it travels close to the speed of light, supply and demand must be matched at every moment or there is a risk of power outages. This was the major reason generation and transmission were typically integrated in a single firm. The nationalised industry had believed that a central coordinator was required to schedule and dispatch power stations, and to ensure that supply and demand were always in harmony. They feared that trusting this to a market of decentralised decision-makers would risk blackouts. Electricity's unsuitability as a commodity is one of the reasons why economists became so obsessed with making it one – doing so would be proof of the universal applicability of their discipline.

One fundamental concept in electricity economics is the 'merit order'. Imagine lining up all generating stations in order of their cost of producing a unit of electricity, from the least expensive to the most expensive. As you go down the line you add up the amount of electricity each plant can supply. At a certain point you will reach a level that is equal to the demand for electricity over a given period. The plant that gets to supply the final unit of electricity to meet aggregate demand is known as the 'marginal producer'. In economic theory the price for electricity at a given time should equal the cost of the marginal producer generating one additional unit. The concept of the merit order was well understood by the Central Electricity Generating Board and was the basis of the computer system that governed its power station dispatch, GOAL.[43]

Privatisation involved building a market for electricity around the merit order. In April 1990 the England and Wales Electricity Pooling and Settlement Agreement, or the 'Pool', opened for trading. It was the cornerstone of electricity privatisation. As with so many other aspects of energy policy, Stephen Littlechild, Eileen Marshall and Michael Beesley had a significant role in its design, as did economic and management consultants. The idea was that generators would compete to supply customers and this would reduce prices. The Pool had to be designed to solve two problems: efficient scheduling and sufficient capacity to meet peak demand. In technical terms, the Pool was a day-ahead sealed-bid market using 'pay as clear'. Each generator submitted sealed bids for each half-hour slot over the next day. These bids represented the price at which they would sell electricity.[44]

In theory, these bids would be equal to each station's 'short-run marginal cost' (the cost of producing one additional unit). The generators had to declare which of their stations would be available the next day and then provide prices. At the same time, all suppliers (regional electricity companies and from the late 1990s independent retailers) would estimate their demand at each of the time slots. The National Grid Company would take all this information and line up the generators in a merit order. The point along the line where the supply of power would match demand was the 'clearing price' or 'system marginal price'. All other stations that produced electricity in that time slot were paid the clearing price, hence the market was called 'pay as clear'. National Grid simply replicated the old computer model that the CEGB ran but used the bids from generators instead of estimates of each plant's short-run marginal cost. In addition to this day-ahead market, generators would be paid an availability payment to ensure that enough power stations remained operational to meet peak demand.

Once again, reality proved to be more fickle than theory. The Pool faced numerous issues. During the first three years the two large generation companies, PowerGen and National Power, set the price 90 per cent of the time. This duopoly would deliberately raise their bids and thus increase the revenue earned for all their plants (known as 'infra-marginal rent'). Power station managers would declare plant unavailable to increase the price and use other similar tactics. The very existence of the duopoly was something of a mistake. Many had argued that the CEGB should have been broken up into several companies. However, a group within government, including the prime minister, was concerned that this would mean that no company would be large enough to take on the nuclear power stations. By early 1988 the decision was made to go with two large companies, a decision that turned out to be pointless because by late 1989 it was clear that the duo would not take on nuclear anyway.[45]

Over the 1990s, there were repeated skirmishes between the regulator and the generation companies, with Offer desperately trying to reduce the market share of the two big generators. Offer found that PowerGen had abused its market power to gain an additional profit. Availability payments were also subject to gaming. The payments to generators should have fallen as more gas-fired capacity was built, but the reverse happened. In 1993 Offer (headed by Littlechild) threatened to take PowerGen and National Power to the Monopolies and Mergers Commission. In response, the companies backed down and agreed a cap on Pool prices for 1995–96 and to divest some of their assets. The largest regional electricity company, Eastern, bought these assets to become a major generator itself. By 1998 PowerGen and National Power still set the price two-thirds of the time, and by 2001 National Power had to be split up further.[46]

The shortcomings of the Pool should be understood in the context of just how novel the whole endeavour was. Britain was one of the first countries in the world to develop a national electricity market. There were undoubtedly issues with the Pool, but it was much more successful than similar efforts in other countries. For example, the creation of an electricity market in California in the late 1990s was a disaster, leading to rolling blackouts.

The Pool was not long for the world. For many economists it was not a pure enough market. One economist complained to the Institute for Economic Affairs that the CEGB's model 'GOAL morphed into super-GOAL'. In March 2001, England and Wales switched to the 'New Electricity Trading Arrangements' (NETA). The basic idea of NETA was to allow generators and suppliers to contract with each other directly – hence it became known as 'bilateral trading' as there was no centralised pool. The amount of electricity bought and sold might not coincide with the physical amounts needed, so there would be a balancing out of positions undertaken by the system operator, National Grid. It was Ofgem's most important reform and the culmination of the work of the market fundamentalists. A speaker at the Institute for Economic Affairs argued that the 'major virtue' of NETA was that it 'moves the electricity market much closer to that of a normal market'. Similarly, an Ofgem publication boasted that 'electricity is now being traded like any other commodity'. It was simply assumed that this was a good thing, and it never occurred to the market fundamentalists to question whether electricity is a commodity like apples or cat food.[47]

The New Electricity Trading Arrangements cost nearly half a billion pounds to implement and experienced numerous delays. It is unclear whether NETA was worth it versus a reformed Pool. The balancing mechanism was so complex it required hundreds of painfully negotiated modifications to function. Ofgem tried to claim that NETA led to a drop in electricity prices. Yet the price of electricity was falling before NETA was introduced. A parliamentary report in 2003 found that while prices fell from 2001 with the introduction of NETA, there were too many other factors at work to know what proportion of the reduction was because of NETA. NETA had made 'it harder for prices to be artificially inflated', but the 'prices that domestic consumers pay have not fallen much since NETA was introduced'. Finally, NETA was fantastically complex. For Dieter Helm it was 'introduced without much understanding from politicians and civil servants as to their radical effects'.[48]

Over the 1990s, energy retail was separated from the energy distribution network. It is worth noting just how unusual this was. In the US, networks were always privately owned but distribution and retail remained bundled together in most states. In Europe, it was more common for retail to be split off from distribution during the 2000s, but the networks remained overwhelmingly state-owned or in a mix of public-private ownership. Even the privatisers acknowledged that there was no evidence that publicly owned networks were less efficient than privately owned ones. Therefore, the burden fell entirely on the quality of regulation.[49]

The approach used to regulate the networks, RPI-X, was designed to drive efficiency. It had downsides that were understood and accepted from the outset; it created an incentive to underinvest and a risk of excessive profits. Indeed, for it to work the regulator had to err on the side of allowing above-average profits and so push networks to move to the 'frontier' of efficiency. RPI-X was also designed to be 'light touch', which Littlechild believed would obviate the need for the regulator to get involved in assessing the cost structure of companies or setting a rate of return.

RPI-X made more sense in theory than in practice. The first problem was that it created an incentive for network companies to overestimate their costs at the start of each price control period and then underspend. The companies would always know more about the state of their assets than the regulator could – what economists call the problem of asymmetric information.

The scale of the problem was huge. Between 1993 and 1996 National Grid Electricity Transmission persuaded the regulator that it needed £1.6 billion in capital spending – but it actually spent 45 per cent less than this. In effect, consumers were charged to finance £700 million of investments that were never made. Between 1994 and 1996 the British Gas Corporation asked to spend £3.1 billion but spent only £2.1 billion. The worst offenders were the regional electricity companies, which became pure distribution networks from 1998. In the run-up to privatisation the government had estimated that the RECs would need to spend £5 billion over the next five years. The companies ended up spending half that amount.[50]

Over the mid-1990s, there was a ludicrous 'cat-and-mouse' game, with the companies underspending and the regulator asking them to reforecast, only for them to overestimate then underspend again. Whenever underspending occurred, the management teams would respond with the same line, claiming that some unforeseen efficiency initiative was responsible. It is difficult to exaggerate the long-term negative effects of this pattern. It created a toxic relationship between the network companies and Ofgem and has led to systematic underinvestment over the last three decades.

That RPI-X incentivised underinvestment was well understood. The rationale was that the networks had been overbuilt under public ownership, so underinvestment would not really matter. Littlechild also feared that simple rate-of-return regulation would perpetuate overinvestment. This theory was merged with various more colloquial concepts such as 'gold plating' or 'rate padding'.

The Averch-Johnson effect became the monster that haunted the sleep of efficiency-obsessed regulators. There was just one problem: there was no evidence that the effect was real. The monster was a bogeyman. In 2005 the eminent energy economist Paul Joskow came to a devastating conclusion: there was so little evidence for the effect that searching for it for forty years had been a waste of time and effort. The effect disappears once you consider that the company-regulator 'game' has multiple rounds. If a company builds a bunch of dud assets the regulator is likely to find out. It will penalise the utility, either through disallowing addition of the expenditure to the asset base or by trimming the rate of return.[51]

Second, the Averch-Johnson effect assumes that capital and labour are easily substitutable and therefore networks can select a higher capital-to-labour ratio to make a larger profit. However, in energy networks capital and labour are not really substitutes and in many cases are complements. Finally, overcapitalisation is only an issue if the company ends up building useless assets. However, if there are plenty of useful things to build, then the real constraint is how much the regulators want to increase the customer bill. This critique of the Averch-Johnson effect was pointed out in the early 1970s.[52] In short, RPI-X was based on weak theoretical foundations.

The promise that RPI-X would be 'light touch' also turned out to be false, and the Treasury had warned as much in 1988. From the early 1990s, the network companies ended up generating massive profits. Littlechild was insistent that he should not intervene, believing that the best way to bear down on costs was to exploit the profit motive. He managed to fend off pressure to intervene in 1992. After the first regional electricity company 'price control' deal was announced in 1994, it became apparent that Littlechild had underestimated just how much profit these companies were set to make. The share price of the RECs increased dramatically. Under intense political pressure, Littlechild revisited the price cap in 1995 in response to public concern.[53]

A regulatory model that relied on restraint failed at the first hurdle. Excessive profits persisted throughout the 1990s. In 1995 Tony Blair, then leader of the opposition, stated that 'regulation of utilities will be one of the most important issues for the next Labour government' because of the 'evident discontent over levels of profit being reported and a perception that companies are being run only in the interest of shareholders and top executives'.[54] When New Labour was elected in 1997 it introduced a windfall tax. This was another failure for RPI-X on its own terms. It was a similar story in gas. After repeated conflicts with its regulator, Ofgas, British Gas *chose* to subject itself to an investigation by the Monopolies and Mergers Commission to break the deadlock. One of the central issues that the MMC had to address was setting transparent charges. This meant taking a view on the value of the regulated asset base and an appropriate rate of return.

A related flaw with RPI-X was its assumption that a company's existing price level was a reasonable starting point for the formulae. However, if the network company needed to do different things in one period to the next, the existing price level was useless. It was inevitable that the regulator would have to take a view on whether a company's forecasted costs were reasonable and if the associated work was necessary. The economists John Vickers and George Yarrow had pointed this out as early as 1988. By the mid-1990s, Ofgem was performing the same cost analysis as regulators in the US. And by the mid-2000s, Britain had one of the most complex and administratively burdensome systems in the world. This was the opposite of what the privatisers had said would happen.[55]

Privatisation was motivated by desire to move capital expenditure and borrowing off the state's balance sheet. This was presented as an exercise in fiscal responsibility. Britain would stop 'living beyond its means'. Ironically, privatisation led to an increase in debt levels and borrowing simply moved outside the state's control. Under public ownership, energy infrastructure was built on a 'pay-as-you-go basis', meaning that it was paid for from bills and transfers from general taxation. Under privatisation the model switched to 'pay when delivered'; investments were funded by taking on debt which would be paid off by future consumers. Debt levels can be measured using the 'gearing' ratio – the ratio of equity to debt. A low gearing means less indebtedness, and most companies were set up with very little or no debt at the point of privatisation.[56]

By 1998, National Grid Group had a gearing ratio of 24 per cent, Scottish Power 18 per cent, and Southern 4 per cent. Gearing increased significantly over the 2000s, which was a rational strategy in the context of low interest rates. The regulator, Offer, condoned the move. In 1998 it noted that a 'number of [companies] have credit ratings above the minimum investment grade level . . . [which] suggests that many . . . have the scope to increase gearing . . . Gearing levels of about 50 to 60 per cent would be consistent with an efficient capital structure.' By 2010 gearing had increased to these levels. Offer's rationale was that networks could take on debt to fund new infrastructure development. Yet the increase in gearing did not lead to a major expansion of the network. Capital spending was persistently lower in the 1990s compared to the period from 1948 to 1979, and most of it went on refurbishing the existing network rather than building new infrastructure. The additional debt was used for dividend payments to shareholders.[57]

In the early 1990s, the privatisers had carefully unbundled the energy system because they believed that the vertically integrated monopolies were inefficient. What they did not foresee was that the system would be stitched back together in a totally different configuration thanks to two decades of mergers and acquisitions.

One of the first events to give an indication of what was to come was when the property conglomerate Trafalgar House tried to buy Northern Electric (an REC) in 1994. Trafalgar offered a price that was four times what Northern Electric had been sold for. To defend itself, Northern Electric offered shareholders a payout revealing that it sat on a mountain of cash so large it could in effect offer its customers free electricity for a year. Other companies and banks quickly realised that the regional electricity companies were gold dust; they had little debt, lucrative price control deals and minimal investment requirements. At privatisation, dividends were projected to be ten pence per share, but a few years later were up to sixteen pence.[58]

The first wave of mega-deals involved the entry of American utilities. Between 1994 and 1997 there were twelve takeovers of regional electricity companies, eight of which were by US companies. The Americans also bought up generation assets, with Edison Mission Energy of California buying power stations from PowerGen in 1999. The American firm and the 'smartest guys in the room', Enron, were major investors in CCGTs. The architects of privatisation welcomed the takeovers and saw them as evidence that company management was being subjected to proper pressure from capital markets. Company executives also welcomed them, unsurprisingly, given takeovers increased the value of their share options. However, it was ironic that US utilities were buying up British utilities, since Littlechild's entire approach to regulation assumed that US energy companies were fat, lazy and little better than the CEGB. Yet here they were conquering Albion.[59]

The reason US utilities entered the British market was precisely because of Britain's extremely lucrative regulatory settlement. To ensure that network companies had sufficient income to invest in their assets, the regulator needed to estimate how much it would cost them to borrow money – the cost of capital. However, the estimated and real costs of capital might differ. This created an opportunity for financial arbitrage. The Americans' entry reflected the fact the cost of borrowing was lower for them in the US. This highlights another issue with Littlechild's regulatory approach. Utilities in the US were vertically integrated, with simple low-risk rate-of-return regulation. The British system became known as a 'high-powered' regime, meaning that there were strong incentives for efficiency. The downside was that the range of performance from the best to worst companies was larger than in the US, and there was a risk of state intervention in response to excess profits. This high-powered regime went hand in hand with a higher cost of capital.[60]

Unbundling the energy value chain into its constituent parts was the most radical element of privatisation. Yet victory was short-lived. From the late 1990s, vertical integration became the normal model to which all the big players aspired. The regional electricity companies diversified upstream into generation and horizontally into gas supply. Some even merged with water companies. Buying generation assets made the RECs both buyers and sellers of power. There were numerous concerns at the time that the prices negotiated with the independent CCGT consortia were therefore soft. The big power generation companies then started to buy RECs. PowerGen bought Eastern Electric in 1998, and Scottish Hydro bought Southern in 1998 to create Scottish and Southern Energy (SSE). The regulator objected to some mergers and acquisitions, but the laissez-faire attitude of successive secretaries of state and lobbying by the big companies won the day.

In Scotland unbundling was never applied. Under nationalisation the two Scottish electricity boards were the only ones in the country that were truly vertically integrated. In the late 1980s, the secretary of state for Scotland, Malcolm Rifkin, successfully argued that splitting the boards up would create companies that were too small to be financially viable. In many ways there was a separate privatisation programme in Scotland, with a separate white paper and legislation. The Scottish electricity companies also had £1.2 billion in debt written off, which was a huge sum (for comparison, the entire water industry had £6.5 billion written off). The soft version of privatisation in Scottish electricity would have profound long-term consequences, as it created two powerful companies that could influence government policy on renewable development.[61]

The case of Scotland highlights that while the system architects of privatisation loved unbundling and competition, the privatised companies hated it. Competition in generation and supply from 1998 made it riskier to do business in each area. The 'dash for gas' had brought about a squeeze on profits in generation. The solution was to hedge and buy companies at both ends of the value chain. Littlechild cited the fall in the share of generation made up by the big two generators (from 78 per cent in 1990 to 39 per cent in 1999) as evidence of increased competition. However, this was only because of the entry of the regional electricity companies – the biggest being Eastern, which had 10 per cent of the market. By 2000, 65 per cent of power generation was by companies that owned both generation and retail. By 2010 the Big Six suppliers controlled 99 per cent of the domestic retail market and all six owned generation assets.[62]

Over the early 2000s the Americans sold up and were replaced by a new set of entrants – European energy giants. These European companies came from countries that hadn't embraced unbundling as ferociously as Britain. It was fitting that the Europeans would introduce a new dynamic – the consolidation of generation, retail and networks. The French state-owned monopoly EDF bought London Electric in 1998, giving it stakes in both retail and distribution networks. It then expanded its ownership of electricity networks, and between 2002 and 2010 owned all the distribution networks in the South East, London and the East of England. In 2009 it bought the nuclear company British Energy, making it the largest power generator in the country as well.

German giants also entered. Eon bought PowerGen in 2000–1 and RWE bought Innogy (carved out from National Power) in 2002. RWE also owned Thames Water from 2001 to 2006. Eon became both a generator and supplier, and following further acquisitions also owned the electricity networks in the Midlands from 2004 to 2011. Consolidation also occurred in the networks. In 2002 National Grid Company bought Lattice, a gas network company which had been carved out from the old British Gas. This meant that National Grid owned the majority of electricity transmission, all gas transmission and most gas distribution.

The regulator, Ofgem, maintained its theoretical commitment to unbundling and created extremely complex rules to ensure 'business separation' between divisions. This approach went back to the Monopolies and Merger Commissions (MMC) investigation into British Gas in the early 1990s. The MMC did not require British Gas to divest its trading arm, just to separate business units in a way that would be 'viewed by competitors as virtually equivalent to divestment'. The Ofgas annual report emphasised that it would require 'extremely strict' mechanisms to ensure that 'confidentiality is sacrosanct'. This set a precedent for allowing consolidation if companies remained internally separated.[63]

Despite the strong language, these mergers contradicted the original logic of privatisation. The privatisers had argued that the electricity and gas industries were inefficient because all the components came under a single owner, the state. They claimed that having separate divisions and area boards in competition was not enough, that there had to be competition between multiple private firms in both energy and capital markets. The consolidation of firms over the 2000s made a mockery of this argument. Whereas Littlechild argued against mergers and acquisitions, Ofgem under Callum McCarthy (CEO from 1999 to 2003) was more positive (McCarthy would go on to be the regulator of the banking sector until 2008). Ofgem pointed to the economies of scale and lower cost of capital. No one asked the obvious question: Then what was so wrong with the CEGB and the area boards? Ofgem proved itself to be pro-business first, and pro-competition second. By 2010 the unbundling experiment had in effect come to an end.[64]

Government policy on these mergers and acquisitions was made up on the hoof. The wave of American entrants was a free-for-all. There was very little discussion of the appropriate level of debt financing or rules on corporate structures. Few questioned the fairness of it all; it was easy for US companies to buy up utilities in Britain, but it was much more difficult for British companies to do the same in the US. Even ardent

Thatcherites like the Tory MP John Redwood in 1996 said that it was 'a period of piecemeal decisions on bids and deals in the utilities without setting out any principles to make the policy intelligible'. Redwood had questioned the way the nationalised industries had borrowed foreign capital in the late 1970s, so may have been horrified by the ownership of the industry in 2010.[65]

Impacts of privatisation

Did the privatisation of energy work? For the privatisers there were five main objectives: improve efficiency, reduce prices, reduce the burden of regulation, broaden ownership and replace public with private sector investment. Did the system they created deliver on these objectives?

Did privatisation make the energy industry more productive? In the early years it seemed so. By 1995 it was estimated that 100,000 utility jobs (gas, electricity, water, telco) had been cut since privatisation. In 1989, the Central Electricity Generating Board employed 47,000 workers, but by 1996 the four successor companies employed just 21,000. The advocates of privatisation pointed to these massive layoffs as proof the plan was working.[66]

Economists measure productive efficiency – how much output is generated from inputs – using output per worker and total factor productivity (see the last chapter). Over the 1990s productive efficiency did improve in the gas and electricity industries, but it was less of a sharp break than a continuation of a longer-term trend. In electricity, output per worker grew steadily from 1950 to 1992 and then increased substantially from 1992 to 1997. The number of persons employed fell steadily from 1950 to 1992 and then more rapidly from 1992 to 1997. Average hours worked fell steadily throughout the period 1950 to 1997. In short, the productivity gains from privatisation came from accelerating workforce reductions. It was a slightly different story in gas. Labour productivity and real output ramped up very rapidly from 1970 to 1986, flatlined briefly, and then grew again from 1992. Labour inputs, measured by the number of persons employed and average hours worked, grew between 1950 and 1966 and then fell steadily to 1996. Essentially, the nationalised industries were improving productivity before being privatised thanks to a narrowing of their objectives and more stringent financial targets.[67]

The jump in productivity in the 1990s was also partially good luck and an endowment effect. Good luck because the initial transition from monopoly to competition took place in the context of abundant and cheap energy supply (especially North Sea natural gas). The privatised industry was able to take advantage of this abundance thanks to the endowment of assets inherited, especially the gas and electricity networks. This allowed managers to focus on cost cutting.[68]

The improvement in productivity in the 1990s was temporary, however, and since then productivity growth has been sluggish. This was clearly demonstrated in a study by a group of Cambridge economists commissioned by Ofgem in 2018. Over the period 1990–2020, the British gas, electricity and water sectors performed poorly when compared to the whole British economy and to other countries. There was thus a reversal of the pecking order from before privatisation. Britain's nationalised electricity industry had higher total factor productivity growth than the electricity industry in the US between 1950 and 1973, but lower growth from 1979 to 1997. Two economic historians concluded that the productivity record after privatisation was 'unremarkable relative to its own past experience', with no pronounced improvement. This conclusion is consistent with the experience in the water sector, where privatisation has had a negligible impact on productivity.[69]

Productivity growth was stronger in some parts of the value chain. Over the 1990s and 2000s, network operator costs fell and reliability improved. In the case of the distribution networks, it was only after 2008 that reliability was consistently better than the average from 1965 to 1980. Moreover, it is hard to tell whether the cost reductions were just the result of deferring capital expenditure for the future, and in any case other countries in Europe managed to generate similar improvements from 'yardstick competition' without privatising their networks.

In summary, privatisation did not deliver the miracle jump in productivity that was promised. It is hard to overstate how important this empirical finding is. Efficiency improvements were the cornerstone of the argument for privatisation. The British model was built on the idea that giving companies the ability to make abnormal profits was justifiable because it would lead to spectacular efficiency gains. As Dieter Helm summarised, the reality was 'too little investment, too high returns, and grossly excessive executive salaries . . . all this and no clear efficiency advances over most of the European public sector comparators'.[70]

What is perhaps surprising was that this was known even before privatisation. In their important book on privatisation in 1988, the economists John Vickers and George Yarrow noted, 'It can safely be concluded that the evidence does not establish the clear-cut superiority of private ownership in respect of cost-efficiency.' One explanation is that the state-owned gas and electricity industries that came before were not unproductive. Another explanation is that it was just easier to increase profitability by playing the regulations and using financial engineering. Improving efficiency was too much like hard work.[71]

Initially, it seemed that privatisation was having the desired effect on energy prices. When adjusting for inflation, the price of electricity for domestic consumers per kWh fell 10 per cent over the 1980s but 21 per cent in the 1990s. Gas prices rose in the 1980s but fell 22 per cent in the 1990s. Prices fell across all customer types, from very large industry to domestic households. It is worth noting, however, that Cecil Parkinson, energy minister from 1987 to 1989, put up prices just before privatisation, which created headroom for them to fall. This prompted

Private Eye to run a cover with the statement 'higher prices mean cheaper electricity for all'.[72]

Many triumphalist accounts of privatisation were written in the early 2000s just as prices bottomed out.[73] However, from 2000 to 2010 the price of electricity rose by 40 per cent, and rose especially dramatically for industrial users from 2004 to 2009. Britain had some of the highest industrial electricity prices of comparable economies, which contributed to its ongoing deindustrialisation. Industries had been given a subsidised price for electricity in the post-war period, but from the 1990s they had to pay the full marginal cost of electricity. Gas prices followed a similar pattern as electricity, falling in the 1990s, then rising by more than 89 per cent in the 2000s.[74]

What impact did privatisation have on these price trends? This is hard to test because it is difficult to separate the various components of privatisation from broader macroeconomic factors or changing input commodity prices. We cannot study a Britain in the 1990s and 2000s without privatised energy, nor know what would have happened if the networks had been kept in state ownership. The only way to really test the impact is to look at the results of various privatisation reforms in multiple countries over a long period of time.

In a landmark 2013 study, the economist Massimo Florio did just this. He found that when countries moved bits of the gas and electricity industries into private ownership, prices went *up*. When countries unbundled parts of the value chain the effect was negligible. Opening gas and electricity up to market competition had a more positive impact on driving down prices. But overall, the privatisation and market competition effects tended to cancel each other out.

This makes intuitive sense: private sector firms that are exposed to competition may be more efficient than public sector monopolies, but unlike public sector firms they need to make more profit. Florio concluded that after twenty years of reforms, 'this nearly zero-sum game in terms of consumers' welfare does not seem an impressive outcome'. Despite the great expectations, the benefits of privatisation for end consumers were zero to modest.[75]

The privatisers wanted to reduce the burden of rules and regulations. In 1995 a trade union leader astutely observed that 'we were told . . . that competition would make regulation unnecessary . . . but this hasn't happened. If anything, the utilities are more regulated today than they were a few years ago.'[76] In electricity generation the regulators repeatedly intervened to discipline companies and change market design. The 'Pool' lasted only a few years before Ofgem became convinced that another market was needed.

The New Electricity Trading Arrangement reforms of 2001 were only moderately successful, and another set of reforms was implemented in 2015 ('Electricity Market Reform'). In 2022 the state initiated another major market reform programme. This highlights a pattern. Energy markets do not function as economists intended, pressure builds to reform market design, new rules are implemented on the promise that this time it will work, only for the new reforms to disappoint, and the cycle starts again.

In the networks, the elegant simplicity of RPI-X was matched only by its naivety. Ofgem ended up undertaking all the activities that 'light-touch regulation' was supposed to avoid – cost estimation, assessing the cost of capital, estimating the value of the asset base. The problem was that the regulators could not help getting more involved. As the behaviour of the network companies fell short of expectations, Offer, Ofgas and Ofgem kept adding new performance metrics. Network service levels fell, so the regulators added 'standards of service' metrics in 1992. Companies stopped doing any research and development, so Ofgem added an 'innovation funding mechanism' from 2005. The network companies would consistently ask for funding to refurbish parts of the network and then not do the work, so

Ofgem added an 'information quality incentive' in 2005 to nudge companies into submitting more honest plans.

Around twenty new 'incentives and outputs' were added by 2010. In a sense this was a predictable outcome given human psychology; it is very easy to say one accepts a trade-off at the start of a process, but very difficult to accept the downside once the trade-off bites. The foundational principle of RPI-X was that by allowing companies to make a killing it would reveal the real cost of running the network. This was always foolish. Politicians were bound to get involved if profits were perceived as excessive.

Far from the regulators diminishing in importance, if anything they became more powerful. Stephen Littlechild and Clare Spottiswoode (director general of Ofgas, 1993–98) were as much public figures as Denis Rooke or Christopher Hinton. The perception emerged that regulation was heavily influenced by the personality or whims of these individuals.[77]

In a talk to the Institute for Public Policy Research (IPPR) in 1995, Tony Blair noted that the changes in decisions by Littlechild had 'left the credibility of the current [regulatory] system severely damaged' and that New Labour would need to address this 'highly personalised approach'. Managers came to suspect there was professional competition between Ofgas and Offer as to who could appear tougher on the companies. Over time the relationship between the regulators and companies became acrimonious. The 1993 Ofgas annual report complained that British Gas had been conducting 'megaphone diplomacy', a 'sustained media campaign' and making comments that were 'hysterical in tone and content'.[78]

The independent regulators were supposed to remove political considerations from the energy system. For Littlechild, 'The regulator is independent: he has to carry out the duties assigned to him by Parliament, not the orders of the Government of the day.' Spottiswoode put it more frankly: 'If a regulator is independent of government, he or she cannot be accountable to it . . . And a Select Committee can't compel a regulator to do anything.' She went on to assert that 'only the company and ourselves have the background information to prove we have made a good decision'. Giving independent regulators such power inevitably led to the accusation that those regulators were taking political decisions. One participant at the IPPR conference in 1995 summed it up: 'Regulators are non-elected officials who are effectively making policy on the hoof.' There was an element of truth to this. In an annual report, Ofgas commented that it believed 'that competition will also bring substantial long-term benefits to the UK economy as a whole'. This was either an irrelevant thing to write, given that it was already government policy, or dubious overreach into politics.[79]

Regulatory organisations are not immune from the same dynamics as for-profit companies. Managers try to acquire responsibilities and increase the size of teams to justify pay increases. Every regulatory intervention justified adding more people. Between 1993 and 2012 Ofgas and Offer grew from around 270 to 600 employees. Costs rose even more rapidly, in part thanks to the liberal use of consultants. Ironically, the privatisers had undergone the same process of administrative bloating that they had pilloried the nationalised industries for.[80]

The growing complexity of regulation directly benefited those experts that could navigate the tangled mess. Think-tanks, academic economists, economic consultants and management consultants did well. Littlechild even advised other countries that 'as regards types of staff, all regulators will probably want to use the skills of accountants, economists and financial analysts'. He didn't mention engineers. It is a stark contrast with the prominence given to consultant engineers like Merz, McLellan and Haldane in the days of CEB and CEGB.[81]

Over the 1990s and 2000s, individuals circulated in and out of the various state, private and regulatory bodies building up skills and knowledge in one part and carrying their capabilities to another. The revolving door between the regulators, companies and consultancies is so much of a feature of the industry that no one even questions it anymore. In the late 2000s, Ofgem even changed the titles of its senior leaders to match the terminology used in consultancies, with 'partners', 'senior partners' and 'associate partners'. Such titles were strange, given that Ofgem was not a partnership like a consultancy or law firm because there was no shared equity.

In Conservative ideology, privatisation was part of a new era of 'popular capitalism'. It was supposed to create a new class of British retail investors and incubate an 'entrepreneurial society'. Initially it seemed to work, with 10 million Britons taking the opportunity to become shareholders in the privatised industries. However, by 1997 only 2 million were actively participating owners and most of those shareholders ended up with a negligible value in shares.

'Tell Sid' was great marketing but was unrepresentative. Small investors were not the chief beneficiaries. The real transfer of assets was from the British state to foreign owners, asset managers, insurance companies and pension funds. The net beneficiaries of privatisation belonged to the wealthiest 20 per cent of the population. They gained a transfer from the Exchequer as purchasers of underpriced shares and additional returns on capital from the profits of the privatised firms.[82]

Financial institutions did particularly well out of energy privatisation. The City derived substantial revenue from underwriting and advisory fees, and banks also benefited from buying shares on their own books. Alongside legal firms and consultancies the banks were deeply embedded in the governmental machinery of privatisation. The accrued expertise was valuable. From the 1990s, the City turned to selling energy privatisation as a service to countries around the world.[83]

The other group of elite beneficiaries were the senior managers in the privatised firms, whose compensation increased dramatically. Average chief executive pay in the regional electricity companies increased threefold in the first two years of privatisation. Between 1984 and 1994 top-level executive pay increased eightfold in the British Gas Corporation and fivefold in PowerGen. The poorest 20 per cent of the population were the losers. They had to pay increased tariffs, and some lost their jobs. The trade unions in the energy industry were also significantly weakened.[84]

The privatisers were extremely successful at 'de-nationalising' the British energy system but not in the way they meant it. First came the Americans, then the continental Europeans, then the asset managers. By 2010 the British energy industry was overwhelmingly owned by foreign entities. Three of the major firms were EDF, Eon and RWE from France and Germany. In a sense the British energy industry had become an annex to the European one. There was a particular irony to the fact that one of the biggest beneficiaries of British privatisation was the French state-owned monolith EDF. As EDF was buying British Energy one reporter in the *Financial Times* warned to 'prepare for Gallic smugness'. By 2014 other major owners were Li Ka-shing, Hong Kong's richest man, the Australian asset manager Macquarie, the American multibillionaire Warren Buffet and the Pennsylvania Power and Light Company.[85]

In the 1980s there was little discussion about the prospect of non-British companies dominating the energy industry. There was an implicit assumption that British firms would outcompete less efficient state-owned monopolies. This never happened. The lack of political or regulatory interest in who was buying up British firms meant British interests were bypassed. As politicians in the New Labour government later recalled, the focus on price controls and competition became a fixation. The acquisitions by European players were not challenged because they were seen as a distraction or worse an irrelevance. As one MP later recalled, 'We didn't get a grip of the regulators . . . Why was it that we had to lose our nationalised industries in order to hand them over to nationalised industries from other countries?'[86]

At a deeper level, what had happened was a privatisation of tax. Before privatisation, energy infrastructure was paid for from a combination of bills and taxation. After privatisation, it would be paid for from bills. So, in effect, foreign companies, many of them state-owned, had won the right to extract tax from British citizens. In stripping the British state of its duty to make long-term plans the privatisers had not liberated citizens from planning, they had just made them subject to the plans of the likes of EDF and RWE.[87]

International trends reveal a clear connection between privatisation and levels of investment. In the 1990s and 2000s, countries with mature networks and sufficient generation capacity tended to adopt a model closer to the British one. Countries with less developed grids and higher demand growth tended to favour keeping public ownership because of the lower cost of capital. In Britain energy privatisation had a dramatic impact on reducing investment levels. Between 1950 and 1979 energy sector investment in fixed assets (or what economists call gross fixed capital formation) averaged 1.5 per cent of GDP. Between 1979 and 1990 in the transition to privatisation, this fell to 0.6 per cent, and since 1990 it has fallen even more to just 0.5 per cent.[88]

Privatisation led to a fall in investment for two reasons. First, privatisation raised the cost of capital. The higher the cost of capital, the more the future is discounted, and the more the firm makes short-term decisions. By the end of the 1990s, British energy companies had a high cost of capital compared to utilities in the US and continental Europe. High borrowing costs killed off investment in capital-intensive areas like nuclear and networks. Second, privatisation reduced investment levels because reducing capital spending increased profitability. In the networks, RPI-X regulation created an incentive to overestimate how much capital spending was needed and then underspend. This dynamic eroded trust between regulators and companies. Over the early 2000s, the companies asked to increase capital spending levels, but by this stage Ofgem didn't believe they were being honest.[89]

The fall in investment was somewhat predictable, given that the whole privatised system was designed to sweat the assets that had been built in the nationalised era. The downside was that the industry lost the capacity to build. It is now a common observation that British infrastructure costs are higher because of the absence of a 'stable pipeline of projects', a problem which goes back to privatisation. As capital spending fell, engineering jobs were cut, workforces reduced and supply chains offshored. Financial engineering became more important than real engineering. Private companies developed sophisticated techniques to rack up debt levels and extract dividends, but very little of this translated into physical infrastructure. Unbundling the industry made it more difficult to coordinate investment in different parts of the value chain – generation, transmission, distribution.

The nationalised energy system developed a simple and relatively benign form of 'fiscal mutualism'; the state mobilised capital and oversaw a virtuous circle that translated bills and tax into infrastructure. Privatisation came to resemble something entirely different – a kind of 'fiscal extractivism'. The investment cycle revolved around the private sector companies and financial institutions. The goal was not to turn bills into infrastructure; it was to turn bills into returns on capital with the infrastructure being a by-product – akin to a broken vending machine, where money in does not always mean products out. This may sound extreme, but consider what National Grid called its division responsible for building infrastructure: Capital Delivery.[90]

The privatisation of energy was the second state-directed reset in the history of the energy industries. It was a revolution of global significance. Delegations from various countries visited London think-tanks to 'obtain the new British cure', boasted Thatcher. Over the 1990s and 2000s, international institutions like the European Commission, the World Bank and International Monetary Fund became cheerleaders for the British model, instructing countries to adopt it. Much of this ended in failure. In 2004 the chief economist at the World Bank admitted that 'there was probably some irrational exuberance' over the benefits of the British privatised model. In 2017, a major World Bank study showed that many countries had reversed privatisation, meaning that privatisation joined the long list of failed British exports.[91]

Privatisation was a radical break made possible by nationalisation. The nationalisation acts of the late 1940s had amalgamated all the local supply undertakings. Once they had been aggregated, it was possible to break them up again by value chain segment. In contrast, the US never experienced nationalisation and its energy system remained organised around geographically fragmented and vertically integrated monopolies. This made British-style liberalisation very difficult, as it was very hard to break up so many organisations. Privatisation was born of nationalisation in another sense; the publicly owned electricity and gas industries had built an endowment of assets that the privatisers inherited. The 'dash for gas' was the only significant construction programme of the 1990s and early 2000s, and even this relied heavily on the existing asset base.

An outcome of the 'dash for gas' was that electricity and gas became fully intertwined. In 2000 the gas and electricity regulators were merged into a single entity, Ofgem. Markets also became increasingly interlinked, with the gas price setting the price of electricity. Tellingly, it was in the 1990s that people started to quote the price of gas in pence per kWh hour, as for electricity, rather than pence per therm. Regulation also converged. The network code for gas shippers, developed between 1995 and 1998, was modelled on the electricity Pool.

In 1991, gas generated just 1 per cent of the country's electricity, but by 2010 it was 46 per cent. With the 'dash for gas', the industries were now physically intertwined as well; gas flowed through a pipeline network into gas-fired power stations to generate electricity. The gas and electricity networks were now part of an indivisible system sustaining human life, like arteries and veins. Yet the carbon emissions produced by the same system posed an existential threat to all human life. The adaptability of the privatised system was about to be tested in ways few could have predicted in 1979.

5

The Idea of an Energy Revolution, 1988–2010

By the end of the 1980s, anthropogenic climate change was widely acknowledged by states, companies, universities, charities and international organisations.[1] In 1988 Margaret Thatcher, in a speech to the Royal Society, outlined the basic science of the greenhouse effect and issued a call to arms: 'Stable prosperity can be achieved throughout the world provided the environment is nurtured and safeguarded.'[2] A year later Thatcher gave an impassioned speech to the United Nations.

> What we are now doing to the world, by degrading the land surfaces, by polluting the waters and by adding greenhouse gases to the air at an unprecedented rate – all this is new in the experience of the earth. It is mankind and his activities which are changing the environment of our planet in damaging and dangerous ways.

Thatcher argued that the solution lay in international agreements and technology. 'I am thinking of the use of nuclear power which – despite the attitude of so-called greens – is the most environmentally safe form of energy.'[3]

Talk trumped action. In the months following Thatcher's speech, Britain's nuclear programme was effectively paused. This pattern of behaviour was then repeated across the energy system from 1988 to 2010 as Britain procrastinated on adapting energy policy to deal with climate change. When the shift was finally made in the late 2000s, it was done by grafting environmental policy onto the existing policy of privatisation. This created the conditions for the emergence of the dysfunctional zombie system that Britain is still living with today.

By the mid-1990s, nobody in the energy industry could reasonably claim that they did not understand what climate change was and why it was of existential importance. Despite Thatcher's clarion call, it is remarkable how little climate change featured in the thinking of the privatisers in the 1990s. There is almost nothing on the topic in the landmark publications on privatisation in the 1980s and 1990s: the Littlechild Report, the various Monopolies and Mergers Commission investigations, the 1986 Gas Act and 1989 Electricity Act. Perhaps there was also a lack of political pressure. In 1989 ministers in the Conservative government were asked to present options on reducing greenhouse gas emissions. The responses argued that it would be too costly and would not make a difference when compared to the emissions that would flow from China and India over the coming decades. A government memo concluded: 'There is little we can do at a national or even international level to prevent global warming.'[4] In 1997 Britain was one of the signatories to the Kyoto Protocol, which committed countries to reducing carbon emissions. Following Kyoto, Callum McCarthy was the CEO of Ofgem from 1999 to 2003. In talks in 2003 and 2009 reflecting on his time in charge, he barely mentioned climate change. For McCarthy, competition, markets and developing the frameworks bequeathed to him by Littlechild were the priority.[5]

The Conservative energy policy of privatisation was accompanied by some minor interventions to support renewables and increase energy efficiency. The 1989 Electricity Act included what was called a Non–Fossil Fuel Obligation. This instructed the regional electricity companies to buy a certain amount of electricity from non-fossil sources. In practice, it was a tax to support nuclear, which received 92 per cent of the revenue under the scheme. The impact on renewables was miniscule. Non-nuclear renewable generation was 1.8 per cent of the generation mix in 1990 and just 2.7 per cent in 2000.[6]

New Labour promised to be 'the first truly green government Britain has ever seen'. In the run-up to the 1997 general election, the party latched on to the ideas of the think-tank the Institute for Public Policy Research (IPPR) on utility reform. However, renationalisation was out of the question, as Blair made clear at an IPPR conference.[7] Instead, New Labour had three priorities: merge the gas and electricity regulators into one, adjust the RPI-X model and add a broader set of social and environmental objectives to the regulators' mandate. These priorities were later reflected in the 2000 Utilities Act.

New Labour's rhetoric was not matched with action. In 1998 the government placed a ban on new gas-fired power stations to protect the coal industry, even though coal generated far more emissions than gas. Peter Mandelson was tasked with justifying the decision retrospectively in a white paper that was masterful in saying nothing. The climate change levy, introduced in 2001, was a simple energy tax that did not take account of the carbon content of the energy consumed.

The New Labour government did make some progress on carbon pricing. The 1997 Kyoto conference had recommended a cap-and-trade mechanism for setting a carbon price. In Britain, an Emissions Trading Scheme was set up in 2002, but it was voluntary and achieved little. In 2005 the European Union set up its own Emissions Trading Scheme. The policy set a level of emissions that was allowed by various sectors. These targets were then converted into permits that could be traded (hence the term 'cap-and-trade'). The traded value was, in theory, the 'price' of carbon. Labour also introduced a Renewables Obligation scheme in 2002. This was an obligation on suppliers to buy a certain share of electricity from renewables, at least 10 per cent by 2010. The obligations could be traded as certificates, forming a second carbon price.[8]

While claiming to favour renewable electricity generation, New Labour did not see this initiative through. In parallel to various policies that supported renewables, the New Electricity

Trading Arrangements (NETA) were being implemented. Ofgem's priorities were competition and ensuring that prices reflected cost. Given that renewables were more costly, it was inevitable that they would be more expensive under NETA. The CEO of Ofgem, Callum McCarthy, took the view that environmental considerations were beyond his purview and unless told otherwise the NETA reforms would treat renewables like any other form of generation.[9] It was an early example of the incoherence that would define climate and energy policy.

What defined New Labour's approach was adding more objectives on top of the existing set that governed the energy system. This culminated in a 2003 white paper, *Our Energy Future: Creating a Low Carbon Economy.* The report said little of substance but cloaked itself in scientific precision by using complex statistical modelling (which turned out to be inaccurate). It outlined a plethora of technologies that could be scaled up by 2020 but gave little consideration to what changes would be required to institutions, policies or markets to bring this vision into being.[10]

Later, in 2009, McCarthy summarised the government's approach to climate change as

> setting out a long list of desiderata which they wished the regulator to take into account – without however giving any weighting to the various objectives set out in the list, and thereby not avoiding the need for the regulator to make judgments between items on the list, some of those items being mutually inconsistent.[11]

Another hallmark of New Labour's approach was the proliferation and growth of quangos like the Energy Savings Trust, Carbon Trust and Emission Trading Group. There was little clarity on how these entities were supposed to work with Ofgem.[12] Once created, each organisation adapted to defend itself, gain influence, grow and justify managerial pay increases.

Climate change decisively moved up the political and energy policy agenda with the 2008 Climate Change Act. This landmark legislation was passed by Parliament almost unanimously. The central pillar was a legally binding target to reduce carbon emissions by 80 per cent by 2050 versus a 1990 baseline. Using a baseline of 1990 made the target easier to hit because it was a recession year. The act also established a new institution, a Climate Change Committee (CCC), which was tasked with advising government on progress and drawing up a series of rolling five-year carbon budgets (the maximum emissions allowed to hit the target). An important decision by the CCC was to focus on territorial emissions (the emissions generated within the UK's borders). This took no account of the emissions that are generated by production of goods in another country and imported for British consumption.[13] The 2008 act had far-reaching consequences not foreseen at the time and made further government intervention in the energy system inevitable. To truly understand the rationale of 'carbon budgeting', it is important to understand the intellectual context in which it emerged.

The great market failure

Climate change emerged as an issue in the 1980s at the same time that countries were celebrating the virtues of markets and castigating the vices of public ownership. It is unsurprising, therefore, that governments turned to economists for answers. Climate change came to be defined as a market failure, indeed the greatest market failure in human history. The theory was simple. Generating greenhouse gas emissions in the present will cause harm in the future, but that cost is external to markets today. This leads to an overproduction of greenhouse gases.[14]

What was the solution to the market failure? For economists it was *more* markets. As a gaggle of Nobel Prize–winning economists argued at Kyoto in 1997, 'The most efficient approach to slowing climate change is through market-based policies.'[15] In effect, this meant making consumers today pay for the harm that carbon emissions would cause in the future. There were two ways to set a carbon price. One way was to create a market in permits to pollute. Another was to set a carbon price through a tax on emissions.

Calculating the right tax level required quantitative modelling by economists, and no economist had more influence on energy and climate change policy than the American William Nordhaus, who won a Nobel Prize in 2018. Nordhaus pioneered various modelling approaches to estimate the price of carbon based on the harm emissions would cause in the future. The tool he developed became known as an integrated assessment model (IAM), because it combined a model of the economy and a model of the geophysical climate system. An IAM allowed economists to calculate the 'optimal pathway' and the balance between reducing emissions now or at a slower rate.[16]

Nordhaus's modelling and the IAMs he spawned contained assumptions that had a significant impact on Britain's energy system. First, Nordhaus made a standard economic assumption that consumption in the present was more important than consumption in the future. How much more valuable was determined by the 'discount rate', the rate at which you discount the future. Second, Nordhaus also assumed that economies would continue to grow, and that technology would improve. These two assumptions led to a simple but compelling logic: societies should ration how much they pollute in the present, but they should not overdo it because consumption now was more important than later consumption. Future generations would be richer and have better technology anyway. This idea of the climate as a resource – a 'great mine in the sky' – to be rationed and priced became all-pervasive.[17]

There were numerous issues with the integrated assessment models. One economist noted that 'the models are so deeply flawed as to be close to useless as tools for policy analysis' and suggest a 'level of knowledge and precision that is simply illusory . . . and misleading'.[18] The relationship between climate change and reductions to gross domestic product in the future – the so-called 'damage function' – was impossible to quantify.[19] The IAMs also assumed a slowly rising carbon price, something which never materialised.[20]

The biggest debate was over whether Nordhaus had selected an unreasonably high discount rate. This was controversial because the dilemma is not merely whether to sacrifice consumption in the present but how to escape from extinction in the future.[21] In 2006 Chancellor Gordon Brown commissioned a report by the economist Nicholas Stern. Stern recommended using a 1.4 per cent discount rate, rather than the 6 per cent rate recommended by Nordhaus. Stern also pointed out that Nordhaus's modelling implied that the 'optimal' path would be to allow 3.5 to 4.0 degrees Celsius of warming because the well-being of future generations that would experience catastrophic ecological breakdown could be discounted.[22] Others, such as the philosopher Derek Parfit and the economist Tyler Cowen, argued that any discount rate was morally indefensible as the future impact of climate change will still occur.[23] Stern's advocacy of a low discount rate came from his appreciation of an older tradition of economic thinking from the 1930s to 1950s. This was the same tradition that influenced the nationalised energy industries, which focused on building endowments for the future and therefore used low discount rates.[24]

High discount rates encourage procrastination. Waiting until later crystallised in the concept of 'overshoot': too much heat was acceptable because it could be undone later with technology that cools the earth. Acceptance of 'overshoot' became prevalent between 2018 and 2022, but the logic flowed directly from the thinking of Nordhaus and assumptions about technological progress. If technology always gets better, it would make sense to allow more emissions in the short run and wait until technology emerged in the future that could remove carbon either from the production process or from the atmosphere.

This idea of 'overshoot' was embedded deep in the computer models used for Kyoto in 1997 and was explicitly part of the

Intergovernmental Panel on Climate Change modelling from 2007.[25] The 2005 IPCC report contained two relevant technologies, BECCS and CCS. BECCS, or 'bioenergy with carbon capture and storage', is planting trees which absorb carbon, harvesting them before they have shed their leaves, burning the matter (to make heat or electricity) and capturing the emissions. The process can operate like a pump for removing carbon emissions. Carbon capture and storage (CCS) involves capturing carbon from industrial processes and storing it in the ground, helpfully in the same depleted oil and gas reservoirs from whence the emissions came. These technologies were seductive because they would allow companies to keep burning fossil fuels and would preserve the value of fossil fuel assets.

A shift in the energy policy paradigm

Between 2008 and 2012 there was a discernible shift in focus for Britain's energy institutions. The Stern Report of 2006 had significantly raised the political profile of climate change.[26] Over the following several years numerous programmes across Ofgem, the Department for Energy and Climate Change and the Climate Change Committee brought climate issues to the fore.

The Climate Change Committee (CCC) was charged with turning the 2008 act into a pathway. Its first report was a tome over 500 pages long. There were a few key features. First, the CCC framed the issue primarily as a matter of advancing new technological solutions. It claimed that meeting the emission targets was possible because 'technologies are available or with appropriate support could be developed'. This rationale would become commonplace; any technology could liberally be described as 'feasible' so long as the right government support was made available (in the form of subsidies).

Second, the CCC argued that reducing emissions would be 'possible without sacrificing the benefits of economic growth and prosperity'. Third, the CCC asserted the primacy of the electricity system; wind, solar, tidal, electric vehicles and nuclear power were the most important technologies to develop. The committee also recommended the development of CCS technology and claimed that it was a 'technically feasible solution and best estimates suggest that it is likely to play a major role in a cost-efficient global abatement strategy'. This would turn out to be a bad prediction.

Fourth, the report argued that these technologies would not emerge without market reform. Of primary importance were the carbon markets, but the committee recognised that these had limitations. This was a response to the collapse of the Emission Trading Scheme carbon price between 2007 and 2009 during the Europe-wide recession. By 2010 the CCC was arguing for new long-term contracts for renewable generators (primarily wind and solar). Finally, the CCC noted that electricity markets needed to change to reflect the intermittency of wind and solar. Reforms should incentivise consumers to 'shift electricity demand from current peaks, bringing it closer into line with the natural pattern of low carbon supply'.[27]

Around the same time, Ofgem followed the wind and became very interested in climate change, after several years of being relatively uninterested in the matter. In the early 2000s, Ofgem was overwhelmingly focused on competition. In its 2000–1 annual plan environmental and social objectives were grouped in a single section. The report noted that the regulator was still trying to understand its role in tackling climate change. There was a minor allusion to 'reducing barriers to renewable generation'.[28] Ofgem's 2005 annual report was still overwhelmingly focused on competition. Going around Europe to campaign for the 'full liberalisation of energy markets' was given more space than climate change. The report noted the need to strike a balance 'between protecting customers' interests – our first priority – and other concerns such as ensuring there is adequate investment in the networks to cope with the growth of renewable generation'.[29]

The 2010 Ofgem annual report was radically different. 'Building a low carbon economy' was the top priority, placed above security of supply and value for consumers.[30] During 2009 and 2010, Ofgem undertook its first major investigation into the implications of climate change, the innocuous-sounding 'Project Discovery'. The year-long study arrived at the conclusion that significant investment would be required across all parts of the energy system to meet the 2008 commitments. The modelling suggested £200 billion of investment over ten years (around £290 billion in 2024 prices), with a particularly significant increase in electricity network expenditure.

Project Discovery signalled a shift in language from competition to 'investability'. Ofgem endorsed the CCC's position that markets would need major reform, because the volatility of the carbon price was deterring investment. Of more immediate concern, there was a risk of insufficient generation capacity because 'short term price signals at a time of system stress do not reflect the value that consumers place on security of supply'. Ofgem proposed several reforms, such as a carbon price, various demand-side response measures, a centralised renewables market and procurement of generation capacity.

Project Discovery ended up being swamped by the government-led Energy Market Reform programme. The two programmes were very similar, but remarkably they conducted totally separate modelling. In retrospect, Project Discovery was prescient in spotting that Britain was becoming heavily dependent on international gas imports and that this would almost certainly lead to price spikes. One of the scenarios Ofgem modelled even included an analysis of the impact of a war between Ukraine and Russia. Project Discovery is also interesting because it emphasised that in the short run end consumer bills would likely have to go up. Ofgem acknowledged that this might mean that some customers could not pay, or that businesses would be less competitive, and hinted that it was for government to address these trade-offs.[31]

Energy revolution

These reports highlight that by 2010 a consensus had emerged around the energy system and across the political spectrum about how Britain should reduce emissions. The strategy can be summed up as a 'double electrification': electrify demand and decarbonise generation. This would involve building infrastructure, deploying new technologies in homes and reforming markets. There was also a consensus that most of the funding would come from the private sector. The way to bring this forth was a combination of carbon pricing, subsidies, long-term price support mechanisms and other governmental measures.

In the early 2010s, the double electrification strategy was blended into various other concepts like an 'energy transition', 'transition to a low-carbon economy' or even an 'energy revolution'. The basic idea was that technology has developed in 'waves of innovation' over human history. Lord Nicholas Stern claimed that the 'energy revolution was merely the latest in a

Figure 5.1. A typical 'waves of innovation' graph

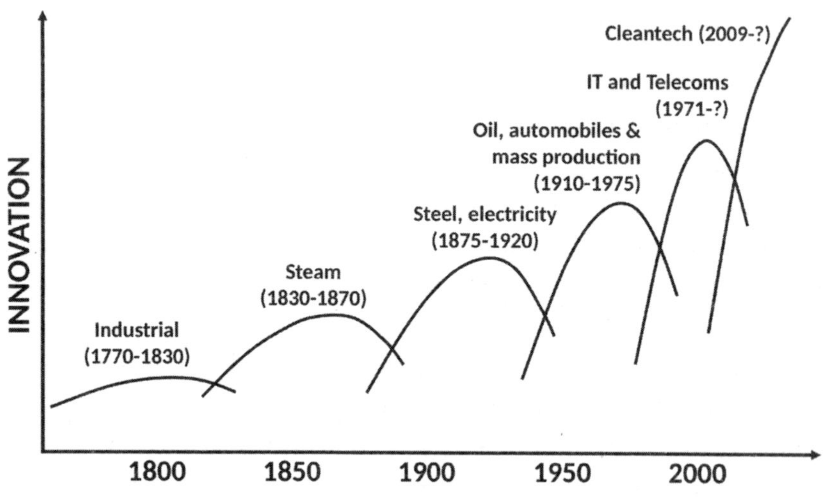

Source: Author, modelled on Nicholas Stern, 'Why Are We Waiting? The Logic, Urgency, and Promise of Tackling Climate Change', presentation, 3 June 2015.

series of waves of innovation in human history'.[32] Countless other reports by international organisations, government departments, think-tanks and consultancies would use the same basic technophilic idea.[33]

These waves had little historical coherence. However, the simple diagram of rolling waves was compelling and easy to digest. To set off a new technological wave required creating a 'system of innovation' that would lead to 'learning curves' and increasing returns to adoption. Various reports acknowledged that technology systems tended to have a strong path dependence, which could create lock-in. For example, it was difficult to replace boilers with heat pumps because boilers and the gas pipes that supply them are built into the fabric of buildings and streets. However, the argument went that with enough private sector investment and state support the 'same effects that created lock-in to high carbon systems offer the potential to decrease the cost and improve the commercial/consumer attractiveness of a low carbon system'. The low-carbon technology system would out-muscle the fossil fuel system.[34]

Lord Stern referred to the task in hand as 'nothing short of a new energy industrial revolution'.[35] This triumphal notion helped justify Britain acting in advance of other countries on reducing emissions, termed 'unilateralism'. Over the 1990s and early 2000s, the various international conferences on climate change had been largely a failure. European and British politicians decided to go it alone. There was a moral defence of such unilateralism. Britain is only 0.8 per cent of the world's population but has contributed about 4.4 per cent of the carbon emissions in the atmosphere. If a rich polluter like Britain cannot decarbonise, then other countries might not bother.

Unilateralism was, however, also justified on the assumption that going first would be good for economic growth. Britain would gain supremacy in various technologies.[36] With the economy in malaise, climate change presented an opportunity for the realisation of a new growth story.[37] Stern argued that the growth effects of a 'new energy industrial revolution . . . could be similar to or larger than those of the railways or electricity in earlier periods'.[38] The Climate Change Committee made a similar argument. Ofgem's Project Discovery was unusual in striking a more sober tone, arguing that consumer bills would increase significantly over the transition. Stern and the CCC's framing won out, unsurprisingly, as it was more palatable. Dieter Helm has characterised this logic as the 'miracle solution' that dissolves the problem of decarbonisation.[39]

The neo-Schumpeterian view that innovation would inevitably drive fossil fuel industries out of business triumphed. It was just a matter of when, not if. The flip side of this argument was that it encouraged procrastination. Citizens and politicians became convinced that there was no need to sacrifice consumption in the present to deal with climate change. One simply had to wait for the necessary technology to show up. Framing the mission as an 'energy transition' or 'new energy industrial revolution' was comforting, as it gave the impression Britain was undertaking something that had happened before (like switching from horses to cars).

The concept of an 'energy transition' avoided the need for wholesale change. If all that was required was to let technologies compete, then the defenders of privatisation could claim that the existing political economy of energy was, in theory, ideal. It might need some tweaks – some new markets or targeted subsidies here and there – but the basic principles of private ownership, unbundling, competition in markets and independent regulation could be left whole. It probably came as a relief for a generation of bureaucrats that they would not have to undo any of their hard work. Even better, grafting new markets and institutions onto the existing set would involve more work.

This fixation on technology was convenient for another reason, and it would lead Britain down the path of overshoot. By the early 2000s, the British North Sea was a 'mature field' long past the peak of its productive potential and the country was dependent on gas-fired power stations. Carbon capture and storage (CCS) seemed like a perfect fit; Britain could keep burning gas, pump the carbon emissions into depleted reservoirs and in the process become a global leader in the new technology. Both BECCS and CCS were included in the pathways modelled by the Climate Change Committee and Ofgem in Project Discovery. The 2008 CCC admitted that CCS was 'currently not a proven technology at full commercial scale'. Even this was an exaggeration. CCS was not a technology of any scale.[40]

Projecting activities far into the future as opposed to focusing on immediate actions required in the present: this is a description of procrastination that will resonate with most. The procrastinator's folly is to assume their future self is more disciplined than their current self. The same behaviour took hold of the energy industry from the late 2000s. The industry developed an obsession with complex quantitative forecasting and 'scenario modelling'. From 2011 the System Operator division of National Grid started to publish the annual Future Energy Scenarios (FES) report, with a range of scenarios covering the mix of technologies out to 2030, 2040 and even 2050. Every publication contained the same caveat at the start: the scenarios were not forecasts but did reflect a 'plausible range of outcomes'. This was a semantic distinction. The FES consistently said that electricity demand would go up when it consistently went down. In short, the scenarios did not reflect a plausible range. Yet no FES document contained an analysis of whether the prior year's FES was accurate.

In retrospect, it is curious that the concept of the 'energy transition' became so fixated on technology. The terms 'techno-optimist' and 'energy transition' boomed in popularity around the same time from 2008. However, it was unclear why any optimism was required. The 2008 Climate Change Committee report argued that the transition to a low-carbon economy was *not* actually a challenge in terms of technical feasibility, as all the technology existed or nearly existed. If the challenge was not technical feasibility, why think about the energy transition as being like the Industrial Revolution? The Industrial

Revolution involved the invention of all sorts of new technologies that would not have been seen as feasible (or even imagined) in the mid-eighteenth century. If the challenge was not technical feasibility, would it have been better to think of the energy transition as something else, like a social and political revolution?

A different school of thought argued that tackling climate change required a fundamental change to the political and economic model of neoliberal capitalism. A technocratic approach might have worked in the 1990s, but ongoing failure made the challenge too great and required a shift from moderate change in the economic system to a revolutionary overhaul.[41] There would need to be bans and prohibition of fossil fuels, not just 'technological innovation'. Fossil fuel companies would protect themselves from such disruption, and the state would likely defend them. Some of the institutions of capitalism seemed to agree with this framing. A 2020 report by J.P. Morgan argued that a global carbon tax 'is not going to happen' so 'we cannot rule out a catastrophic outcome where human life as we know it is threatened'. The only thing that would avert this was 'premature scrapping' of fossil fuel assets, but that was also deemed impossible.[42] The *Economist* noted that it would take the 'collapse of civilisation' to deliver the 1.5- to 2.0-degree target.[43] These are perfect examples of the philosophical insight that it is easier to imagine the end of the world than the end of capitalism.

In this 'new industrial energy revolution', the role of the state was to facilitate: to create markets and subsidise early-stage technologies.[44] As one pair of academics acknowledged, subsidies might be needed 'throughout the deployment and dissemination phase' rather than just stopping with R&D or demonstration projects. However, there was no suggestion that the state should also be an owner of energy infrastructure, as it had in the post-war period. Another role for the state was to remove barriers to investment by the private sector, which came down to reforming the planning system and dealing with the dreaded 'NIMBYs'.[45]

Public ownership was not even discussed in the landmark publications of the late 2000s. Neither the Stern Report nor the first Climate Change Committee report considered it. This is strange. What the nationalised energy industries achieved over the 1950s to 1970s was almost exactly what these reports were advocating: a massive infrastructure construction programme, the development and scaling of new technologies, and dramatic changes to consumer behaviours. This shows how comprehensively the privatisers had tarnished the reputation of the prior generation. The lack of interest in public ownership was also odd, given numerous economists highlighted that the cost of capital would be one of the biggest variables impacting the cost of the 'energy transition'. Stern highlighted the importance of development banks in lowering the cost of capital, but like so many others he remained wedded to the assumption that 'the big majority of the additional investment required to manage climate change will come from the private sector'. Even though he saw little risk of 'crowding out', the state's role was restricted to correcting market failures.[46]

The more fundamental market failure was that capital markets failed to price the future appropriately. As Martin Wolf explained in the *Financial Times*, the returns investors sought implied that 'the welfare of future human beings is close to irrelevant'. Wolf argued that the state must override this bias and set the cost of capital very low. This was the same dilemma that the post-war system builders had faced, and they had found public ownership an ideal tool.[47]

The logic of privatisation trumped all else. Climate change policies were merely grafted onto the political economy of energy created in the 1990s. The basic principles of private ownership, competition in markets, unbundling and independent regulation were left untouched. This had an unintended consequence: complexity. Sadly, this was only the beginning. Over the next fifteen years government intervention would create an energy system riddled with contradictions. It is to this process of zombification we now turn.

6

Zombie Privatisation, 2010–2024

In summer 2022 electricity networks hit the news. Britain was facing a housing crisis, but developers in London were told they had to delay their projects because of the time it would take to connect to the grid. The culprit? Battery storage projects and data centres were swallowing up all the potential capacity of the network. This was an uncomfortable experience for many in the industry, who were not used to being in the limelight.[1]

The delays to housebuilding were due to a problem that had snowballed over a decade, the Great British Electricity Connection Queue. Over the 2010s, the number of projects trying to connect – a mix of wind and solar generators, data centres and batteries – had steadily then rapidly grown. As of April 2022, these projects were hoping to add ~200 GW of capacity to the system. The entire system's capacity was only 112 GW at the time, and the networks were connecting several GW of new capacity every year. In the wake of the energy crisis the government had committed to weaning Britain off fossil fuels, so a 200 GW–long queue of renewable projects was bad press.[2]

The government made a predictable move and appointed an industry veteran with a fancy title. Nick Winser, a former National Grid executive, was made the 'electricity network commissioner' in July 2022. Winser did not have the power to commission any physical assets. He was there instead to write a very long report, like all good policy tsars. Meanwhile, the situation kept getting worse. By October 2023 the queue stood at a whopping ~450 GW. In that month, Claire Coutinho, then secretary of state for energy security and net zero, said that the government would set out a 'geo-spatial plan . . . to make sure we have an overall strategy for the country, which will immeasurably speed up the connection process'. It was a poor choice of words. The connection queue got measurably bigger. By April 2024 the queue was up to 700 GW.[3]

A term long used in the industry made its way into the mainstream: 'zombie connections'. These were projects that had applied for a connection without planning permission or adequate funding. Like zombies, the projects were already dead but lurched on, clogging up the queue. The rules of the electricity queue were simple: 'first come, first served'. If someone at the front delayed their connection date, everyone behind them was also delayed.

The other complication was that each connection might trigger the need for grid reinforcements. If a wind farm connected to the network in a field in East Anglia, more network capacity might be needed along the routes to London. Without reinforcement, the network would get congested, and the generator would have to turn down. In 2010 the government decided that the best way to deal with this problem was with a regime called 'connect and manage'. Projects could apply for a connection and would be given a date *ahead* of the completion of reinforcements. The network congestion would be managed by paying generators to turn off when the grid couldn't handle the power flows.

As the volume of applications increased, the connection dates being offered developers moved further out. The backlog of reinforcements mounted up, so the dates started moving *really* far out. The rational strategy was for developers to spread their bets and apply many times. This set off a spiral of further delays, more reinforcements and more applications.

By the early 2020s, the industry was in fervent agreement on the need for connection reform. Yet no one could agree what that meant. Some argued that the problem was that it was too easy to apply for a connection. The whole British energy system was designed around the principle of competition. Generators were merely acting on their competitive instincts. Raising barriers to entry might simply stimulate the creation of different strategies to acquire scarce connection slots. Others in the industry suggested a more radical solution. A central planner should take control of the queue and pick all the projects required to reach net zero. This would be tantamount to reintroducing the kind of central planning that privatisation removed in the 1980s. After much flip-flopping, central control was imposed in 2024. Yet neither set of reformers seemed to consider that what they were really suggesting was de-privatisation.[4]

Zombie projects were a direct consequence of privatisation, which was designed around competition and asset sweating. The connection queue was a result of competition for slots and underinvestment in the networks. The whole episode demonstrated that privatisation itself had become a zombie project. Over the period 2010 to 2023, many of the basic principles of privatisation were abandoned, yet the ideology lurched on. Like a zombie, Britain's energy system lost its sense of identity. Zombies are a bad hybrid; the destructive tendencies of the infection are blended with the advanced physical capabilities of the human host, but all morality and intelligence are extinguished. So it is with Britain's energy system: half privatised and half nationalised, with none of the benefits of either and all the costs of both. A zombie's only motivation is to feed. The energy industry feasts on state subsidies. Zombies are aggressive, highly durable and resistant to damage and rot despite their undead state. Similarly, there is nothing inevitable about Britain's energy system evolving; it could well limp along, protected by the political influence of vested interests (as Schumpeter warned).

The theory of zombification

One way to interpret the changes over these years is as a benign process of adaptation, or 'hybridisation'. In 2010 the defining features of the British energy model were private ownership, unbundling, competition and markets, and independent regulation. Over the next fifteen years these features were gradually eroded. Climate change introduced a new dynamic, and energy policy shifted focus to investment, security of supply and decarbonisation.[5] In an influential paper in 2012, the political scientist Andreas Goldthau argued that energy policy had decisively shifted towards state intervention. The new model was a hybrid system mixing 'state *dirigisme* and market liberalism'.[6] Energy economists also observed the emergence of new 'hybrid' market approaches for renewables, with long-term contracts between firms and governments alongside spot markets.[7] Other academics summarised the emerging paradigm for energy policy as 'new interventionism', a combination of state subsidies, renationalisation and direct government involvement in place of independent regulation.[8]

An alternative way of conceptualising the changes between 2010 and 2023 is as a more unintentional and malignant process. As discussed in chapter 5, over the early 2010s there emerged a consensus that addressing climate change would require a technological revolution but *not* any significant change to the basic principles of privatisation. Policy-makers and regulators gradually discovered that this approach was a mistake. From 2010 on, the energy system underwent waves of incremental reforms driven by both decarbonisation and the failures of the privatised model.

Each intervention seemed like a small step, but each led to unintended consequences, leading to more interventions resulting in greater complexity. To use a computer programming analogy, the changes were patches intended to fix bugs in the system. At a certain point, adding patches makes the programme perform worse, especially if the patch conflicts with some other piece of code.

All the interventions created a contradictory hybrid, like a zombie with two sets of DNA in conflict. The account in this chapter is similar to the historian Elizabeth Chatterjee's work on the Indian electricity system in the 1990s and 2000s. In

India, liberalisation involved the layering of new institutions, organisations, policies and programmes on top of the old statist system. Over time, layering grew more chaotic as old institutions were never shut down. The result was dysfunction. Excessive complexity made the industry incapable of coherent change, with new policies rarely turning out as planned. Lobbying and rent-seeking became the dominant business strategy. With accountability and decision-making powers spread so thin it also became impossible to apportion blame when things went wrong.[9]

Wind, gas and Electricity Market Reform

In 2010 renewables (wind, solar, hydro and bioenergy) represented only 6.8 per cent of electricity generation, with wind and solar just 3 per cent. The 2008 Climate Change Committee report argued that onshore and offshore wind would need to grow from around 3 GW of capacity in 2007 to nearly 28 GW by 2020, a 64 per cent growth per year. Over the early 2000s, government interventions did not have the desired impact and Britain had fallen behind Germany and the Nordics. The first major reform was to move from a hotchpotch of subsidies and support mechanisms to a single 'feed-in tariff' in 2010, whereby renewables were given a fixed price per unit of green electricity generated. This scheme was cut back by the new coalition government over 2011–12.[10]

Between 2010 and 2015 the government implemented more significant changes under a programme called Electricity Market Reform (or EMR). The objective was to 'transform the UK's electricity system to ensure that our future electricity supply is secure, low-carbon and affordable'.[11] More specifically, this meant reducing the risk of investing in renewables and at the same time ensuring that fossil fuel generation remained operational *until* renewables reached a certain scale. The logic was that wind and solar were cheaper and so would eventually drive out fossil fuels. This created an awkward timing issue. Many gas-fired plants were coming to their end of life and investors were entitled to shut them down.

There were two pillars to Electricity Market Reform. The first was the capacity market. This provided a regular payment to gas generators in return for being available when the electricity system was under stress. Capacity was procured through annual auctions looking one year and four years ahead. The capacity market was essentially an insurance policy against the risk of blackouts.[12]

The second pillar was the contract for difference (CfD) scheme, introduced in 2014. CfDs were designed to support investment in new low-carbon generation by fixing the power price. It was a long-term contract between an electricity generator and a state-owned body, the Low Carbon Contracts Company. The CfDs gave generators a stable price at an agreed level, the 'strike price', for the duration of the contract (fifteen years). Generators received revenue from selling electricity in the wholesale market. However, when the wholesale price was below the strike price the generator received a top-up payment. Conversely, if the wholesale price rose above the strike price, the generator paid back the difference. These contracts were also awarded in a series of competitive auctions.[13]

For its defenders, EMR was a necessary set of pragmatic reforms. It became obvious in the early 2000s that private companies would not deliberately engineer a situation of excess capacity above average expected demand because this would depress prices. The emergence of renewables with 'zero marginal costs' (meaning once built, a wind or solar farm can produce an additional unit of electricity at basically zero cost) that could undercut gas generators just made this problem more acute. The government had to step in.[14]

The reforms set off a boom in renewables. One wind sector consultancy said that the CfDs played 'the single most important role in the astonishingly rapid commercialisation of offshore wind technology'.[15] Solar and wind capacity grew by 30 GW from 2014 to 2023, outstripping the pace of the 'dash for gas'.

By guaranteeing developers a more stable revenue for fifteen years the CfDs removed a lot of risk and reduced the cost of borrowing. The CfDs are praised internationally and some claim they have become the 'instrument of choice for the energy transition' around the world. The cost per unit of electricity generated by offshore wind also fell by around 70 per cent between 2015 and 2022.[16]

Despite ongoing commitment to the rhetoric of privatisation, EMR was a complete reversal. One of the principles of privatisation was that the market should decide how much generation was needed, and contracts should be between private sector actors. EMR meant that the market was estimating no longer future demand, but government officials. The government would thus decide both capacity levels and the mix of technology. Almost all new power stations now came with a state-backed contract, making the state the customer. A tipping point was reached in 2019, when over half the generators on the system would be receiving some type of state support by 2024.[17] The old guard of privatisers looked on in horror. Stephen Littlechild called EMR a 'morass and nightmare', while Colin Robinson wrote that it was a 'retreat from liberalisation'.[18]

The contracts-for-difference (CfDs) and capacity market payments were basically subsidies for companies to do unprofitable things. The problem with subsidies is that it is difficult to wean companies off them. But getting subsidies to do an unprofitable activity is a lot easier than trying to make the activity profitable.

Some in the renewables industry try to claim that CfDs are not subsidies – they are instead 'price support mechanisms' or 'fixed-price contracts'. This is semantics. Even renewable companies recognise that a CfD is a subsidy in the language they use. A firm is given a guaranteed price by the state, and if the actual wholesale price ends up always being lower than the strike price, the state makes up the difference. This arrangement is what allows the investment to proceed.

The CfDs were intended to be a temporary measure, around just long enough to get renewables to the point of being competitive with fossil fuels. However, the renewables industry has aggressively lobbied against their removal, particularly following the government's 'Cost of Energy Review' in 2019 led by Dieter Helm. The CEO of Scottish Power, one of the country's leading wind developers, put it bluntly in 2017: 'If you think we would build a £2.5 billion offshore windfarm at market risk' (that is, without a guaranteed price), 'then you're bonkers, completely bonkers. It's just not going to happen.'[19]

Over the early 2020s, the renewables industry became dependent on these subsidies. In 2023 the government reduced the 'administrative strike price' for that year's offshore wind auction and the auction failed: there were no bids from offshore wind projects. The government had been hoping to add a further 4 GW of capacity, but increases to the cost of borrowing and inflation in the supply chain meant that the target administrative strike price was unprofitable. A wind farm consultancy noted that the government had 'squeezed the margins of the industry and the supply chain to the point where investing in offshore wind is simply not attractive enough in comparison to other sectors. Capital will always flow where there are returns, and government would do well to remember this.'[20]

In 2024 there were bids but only because the government raised the price support level (the strike price). Wind boosters said it was a 'turning point' for the industry but also argued that the 2025 round would be a success only if the subsidies kept flowing. There is a similar pattern in other countries. In December 2024 the Danish wind tender for 3 GW was supposed to be the first without state subsidies. It failed to attract any bids.[21]

As Brett Christophers highlights in *The Price Is Wrong*, the persistence of subsidies is a puzzle. Renewables are supposed to be cheap. Fossil fuels are commodities that become more expensive over the life cycle of a mine or reservoir. Renewables are manufactured goods, so production costs should fall with scale and experience. The renewables industry constantly informs the public that renewables are cheap, but if this is the case why do they need subsidies to outcompete gas-fired generators?

One explanation is that the cheapness of renewables, and especially offshore wind, is overstated. The metric often used by the renewable industry is the levelised cost of electricity (LCOE). This is the projected total cost of a generation project over its lifetime divided by the projected electricity output. There are many flaws with the LCOE metric. It really reflects the partial cost of each additional electron from a renewable plant – not the total system cost of renewables, as it ignores network reinforcements, congestion costs and backup storage costs. Moreover, the metrics relies on discounting all costs to the present. This does not reflect the different risk profile of something with high upfront costs versus costs spread over a longer period. Many financial institutions, the organisations that must finance renewables in a privatised system, are particularly sceptical of LCOE. A J.P. Morgan banker has described the metric as 'practically irrelevant'.[22] Yet government departments are still fixated on chasing the technologies with the lowest LCOE.

A second explanation for the persistence of subsidies is that price and LCOE are the wrong metrics. Profit is a better measure for explaining how capitalist economies work. Renewables may be cheaper than fossil fuels, but if they are less profitable, capitalists will be reluctant to invest, and subsidies will be required to juice up profits. A report commissioned by the government in 2024 highlighted the profitability problem facing renewables. The report estimated the 'hurdle rate' for various electricity generation technologies. This metric is the minimum required return for an investment in a given technology to go ahead, given the risks associated with that technology. The report calculated the hurdle rate for each technology both with and without state support measures (like CfDs). The analysis shows that without state support, solar and offshore wind have the highest hurdle rates of all the technologies considered. This reflects some of the risks that Brett Christophers has identified (high upfront costs, price cannibalisation). However, when state support measures are factored in, the hurdle rate of solar and offshore wind falls dramatically to lower than or equal to gas-fired generation.[23]

Why are rates of return low for renewables? Wind and solar farms are often located away from population centres because that is where land is cheaper. This means paying for expensive grid connections and potentially for grid reinforcements. Another factor is high levels of competition for the low-risk, subsidised returns on offer. As we have seen, in Britain the electricity connection queue is heavily oversubscribed. However, the most important factor is price volatility and 'cannibalisation'. Windy and sunny periods over the day tend to benefit numerous renewable generators simultaneously. This means there is an excess of electricity supply over demand. Wholesale prices fall to very low and even *negative* levels. Subsidies like the contracts-for-difference provide generators with protection against extreme price fluctuations and negative prices, which props up profitability. Ultimately, the costs of these subsidies are collected from billpayers.

Christophers is not alone in making the argument that renewables have a profitability problem. In a 2023 report, the management consultancy Bain noted that 55 per cent of executives in the energy sector cited 'lack of return on investment' as the most significant obstacle to renewables. In September 2024 another consultancy, the Boston Consulting Group, argued that electricity prices will continue to become more volatile as renewable penetration increases. The report argued that policy-makers would inevitably need to augment market mechanisms with capacity markets and contracts-for-difference for the foreseeable future. An International Energy Agency report in 2024 found that globally more than 80 per cent of all large-scale renewable capacity in the pipeline to 2030 had some form of government support.[24]

In a sense, this is unsurprising; making a profit from a 'free' flow resource like the wind or sun requires deliberately creating scarcity. Companies would want to make renewables more like fossil fuels. It was common for politicians and business leaders to claim that they wanted to make Britain the 'Saudi Arabia of wind'. Building a small number of vast wind farms offshore, rather than many small ones onshore, and then creating scarcity in the subsidies regime so only large firms can compete for access: these are highly effective ways of engineering scarcity out of that which is abundant.[25]

A route not taken was establishing a state-owned enterprise to develop, own and operate renewables, relaxing the need for profit. This would have avoided ploughing subsidies into the renewables industry to make it more profitable for investors. Yet policy-makers were so blinkered by the notion that private ownership was superior that no one seriously considered this option. This was strange, given that other countries established state-owned renewables companies that ended up being highly successful in the British market, most notably Orsted (Danish) and Vattenfall (Swedish). In hindsight, a state-owned renewable developer would have made it easier to develop an onshore supply chain, reducing Britain's reliance on imported technology.

The Electricity Market Reform programme had another downside: the reforms created market distortions that are still causing issues today. The fixed-price nature of the contract-for-difference meant that renewable assets were not fully exposed to price signals. A lack of real-time market exposure reduced the incentives for plants to operate more flexibly where possible. The generator would get paid a fixed price only if it generated, so there was an incentive to bid at very low prices. This sent the electricity markets haywire and meant that the system operator had to unpick trades in the 'balancing mechanism'.

Generators also had limited incentive to locate their assets where the grid had capacity, as they would receive the same fixed price regardless. Large-scale renewables tended to locate where wind and land were plentiful, and where it was easier to get planning consent. This was often at the edges of the electricity network and far away from demand centres. From 2015 the Conservative government placed a de facto ban on onshore wind in England, which pushed developers to build onshore wind in Scotland. The majority of the very large offshore wind farms ended up being concentrated in the North Sea off the coasts of Scotland and East Anglia.

The electricity network can only move so much power through its circuits without breaching 'thermal constraints'. One way of managing this problem is to build more network reinforcements, but this is expensive and time-consuming. The alternative is to pay renewable generators in one part of the network to turn down (the wind farm is turned off, or brakes are applied and it is slowed down) while paying other generators (usually gas) elsewhere on the network to turn up. These payments are called 'constraint costs'. Both grid reinforcement and constraint costs are socialised, meaning that the costs are divided up and spread over all end consumers.

In 2010 the government decided to put off dealing with the issue of constraint costs. The 'connect and manage' regime meant delaying network upgrades and paying renewable generators to switch off when the grid was congested. The decision was based on the advice of an economic consultancy that said constraint costs would max out at £420 million by 2020. This proved to be a bad projection.

Constraint costs instead exploded, rising from £170 million in 2010 to £1.3 billion in 2022, an eightfold increase. This represents a staggering waste of electricity. Over 2022, curtailed electricity could have powered 1 million homes. Since then, the problem has only got worse; in 2025 constraint costs were £1.8 billion. The approach is also unfair. The companies that cause network congestion do not bear the cost; end consumers do.[26]

The absurdity of constraint payments is illustrated by the case of the Shetland Islands. The citizens have some of the highest energy bills in the country. Yet the isles host the largest onshore wind farm in the country, Viking (owned by SSE). Viking was paid £20 million in curtailment payments over 2024 and 2025, and in 2025 it was curtailed for around 60 per cent of the time it could have been generating.[27]

Britain's fragmented state exaggerated the problem. The Scottish Crown Estate went further and faster than the English Crown Estate in releasing offshore seabed leases. Companies encouraged this via trade organisations like RenewableUK. Scottish Power and SSE stood to gain the most from the emerging imbalance in the geography of power. These two giants could get paid to build wind farms in Scotland, backed with subsidies. They would also get paid to switch those generators off when the grid was congested. SSE would also get paid to turn on its gas-fired generators to stabilise the grid. The icing on the cake was that because they were also the two transmission operators in Scotland, with a monopoly on their patch, they would eventually get paid to build the transmission lines down to England – transmission infrastructure that was necessitated by them. It was a genius, if cynical, multi-decade strategy.[28]

In response to these issues, in April 2022 the government initiated another market reform programme, the Review of Electricity Market Arrangements (REMA). The initial publication argued that 'we do not consider that existing market arrangements are likely to deliver our ambition for a decarbonised and secure electricity system by 2035'. Despite the seriousness of the diagnosis, urgency was distinctly lacking. The consultation and policy development phase were scheduled to last until mid-2025. At the outset a broad range of options were on the table, but all the radical options were killed off, leaving a set of compromises. After three years of torturous debate the government decided to stick with the existing market design, with some small adjustments.[29]

The nuclear renaissance that never was

In 2002 the reputation of nuclear power was at an all-time low following the collapse of British Energy. Privatisation had decimated the prospects of nuclear in Britain. Over 2005 to 2008, however, Prime Minister Tony Blair and other senior ministers became convinced of the need for the technology. The 2008

Climate Change Act effectively committed Britain to another nuclear programme. The 2008 report of the Climate Change Committee argued that staying within the carbon budgets was possible only with a 'significant shift towards renewable and nuclear power generation'. In the foreword to a white paper in 2008, Gordon Brown announced that 'we have therefore decided that the electricity industry should, from now on, be allowed to build and operate nuclear power stations'.[30]

The Climate Change Committee was reflecting a bullish mood on nuclear in the late 2000s, with industry leaders talking of a 'nuclear renaissance'. After a multiyear torturous dance to find a buyer of British Energy, EDF acquired the company for £12.4 billion in 2009. The British firm Centrica had backed out as a sole bidder. Only the state-owned and vertically integrated EDF had the balance sheet to do the deal. The French energy model had once again outmuscled the British. For a brief period, the British nuclear industry was in good spirits, believing that the acquisition showed its quality. Initially EDF was able to improve the performance of the stations it had acquired. In its 2008 results, EDF spoke gushingly of a 'global nuclear revival'.[31]

By the time Ed Miliband, then secretary of state for energy and climate change, left office in 2010 the official target was 16 GW of new nuclear by 2025. The coalition government entered office in 2010 and promised to be the 'Greenest Government Ever'. The 2010 National Infrastructure Plan argued that the private sector had the appetite to invest in nuclear. The government just needed to channel the flow of capital and remove barriers, 'cut red tape' and reform the planning system. Hopped up on free market ideology and self-imposed government austerity, the coalition government insisted that there would be no billpayer or taxpayer money committed to building new nukes.[32]

The 2011 Fukushima disaster in Japan damaged the reputation of nuclear power. EDF's share price tanked, and its partner, Centrica, got cold feet and pulled out of Hinkley Point C in 2013. Financially weakened, EDF needed another partner to come in on the project. Around the same time EDF started to argue for more support from the British government. In 2013 negotiations between the state and EDF intensified. EDF was requesting a contract for difference (CfD) to reach its target rate of return.

After some tense discussions the government capitulated. It gave EDF a £92.50 per MWh strike price in a thirty-five-year CfD. This was twice the upper end of the £30 to £44 per MWh range that a report commissioned by the government had advised, and twice the average wholesale electricity price in the country that year. Moreover, the deal was inflation-linked, so the price would ratchet up. The government also agreed to guarantee a portion of the loans raised by the project company, albeit through a very complex corporate structure. This insulated investors from some of the project risk, but if EDF defaulted the British taxpayer would have to pay creditors. This was on top of the support the state was already providing by underwriting all the decommissioning and waste-removal costs of existing plants. The coalition government had to completely abandon its commitment to no public subsidies.[33] Hinkley Point C received planning consent in March 2013.

As with wind and gas, the deal for Hinkley reflected an acceptance of the increased role of the state. The subsidies were a violation of the principles of the privatised model. Having abandoned nuclear to the private sector, even though between 1990 and 1996 it had been run extremely well under public ownership, the British state had very little negotiating power. By the mid-2010s Britain had started a pattern of extending the lives of the nuclear plants that the CEGB had built and EDF now owned. This cycle would continue until today. EDF did well out of the Hinkley deal, with a thirty-five-year guaranteed power price. In 2016 it was estimated that EDF had received £58 billion in subsidies. The state's debt guarantee also increased the returns for EDF. One City analyst concluded that EDF was getting a return on equity of between 20 and 35 per cent.[34]

EDF's financial difficulties meant it needed another partner. The British government then courted the Chinese and secured an investment by China General Nuclear Power Corporation in 2015. This meant that in the home of energy privatisation, British nuclear was effectively owned by the French and Chinese states.

Despite the fact that EDF had most of what it wanted, Hinkley Point C was a car crash, with delays and cost overruns. EDF's choice of the European pressurised water reactor (EPR) made sense initially, as it was going to be deployed in other countries before Britain. However, all plants suffered multiyear delays and cost overruns, such that by the time it came to Hinkley the case for the EPR was significantly weaker. The cost overruns for Hinkley Point C are well documented. It is currently projected to be completed by 2030 at a cost of £46 billion, making it the most expensive nuclear plant in the world.[35]

The pattern of the state propping up nuclear continued. By 2019 the government decided to move nuclear power over to a regulated asset base model, which meant the state would provide a guaranteed rate of return for investors. In his final two weeks in office, Prime Minister Boris Johnson announced a £700 million package of funding for another reactor, Sizewell C (estimated to cost £25 billion).[36]

In 2022 the chair of the Nuclear Industry Association compared the decisiveness of the nationalised era with the 'prevarication, naïve assumptions, and the curse of caution' in the 2010s. The story of nuclear highlighted the 'limits to markets and inescapable obligations of every government'. Hunterston B and Hinkley Point B retired in 2022 with no replacements. Britain had gone from being an advanced nuclear nation to having less nuclear capacity than Sweden, Spain, Belgium and the US state of South Carolina. The story of nuclear over these years illustrates the dysfunctional nature of zombie privatisation; numerous governmental bodies said it was a must, but the system lacked the ability to convert intention into reality. The only reason Hinkley Point C will (eventually) exist is because the state intervened with subsidies, thus abandoning one of the core principles of the privatised model.[37]

Molecular miracles

The story of both hydrogen and carbon capture and storage (CCS) since 2010 is like that of nuclear: the technologies were deemed necessary but then fell short. The 2008 Climate Change Committee report included coal CCS into its projections for 2020. The 2011 Future Energy Scenarios (FES) report by National Grid assumed that coal CCS would be operational from 2016 and gas CCS from 2022. But CCS consistently disappointed. Every year targets were scaled back or pushed further out. The 2016 version of FES contained a scenario with 8.8 terawatt hours (TWh) of electricity generation by power stations with CCS by 2030, rising to 80 TWh by 2040. By the 2024 FES the projection for 2030 was just 4.6 TWh, but this rose to 60 TWh by 2040. The 2024 FES now included another miracle molecule – hydrogen – with a projection of 20 TWh of hydrogen-fuelled generation by 2040. But as of 2024 there wasn't a single commercial CCS facility in Britain, and the estimated cost of building CCS had remained stubbornly high for decades.[38]

One of the benefits of CCS and of hydrogen is that they allow fossil fuel companies to argue that their assets have long-term value. As a 2005 report to Parliament on CCS made clear, the objective was 'lengthening the life of the North Sea oil fields, as well as releasing stranded oil assets'.[39] As long as hydrogen and CCS are kept as options, governments and companies can avoid dealing with the consequences of writing off the value of oil and gas assets. This is one of the greatest failures of 'climate capitalism' – an inability to face up to the issue of stranded assets.

The problem is that hydrogen and CCS are not profitable. This is normal for early-maturity technologies. Since the early 2000s, oil and gas companies have pushed for government support measures. As one hydrogen CEO let slip, 'There is a lot of money to be made in layering all the different subsidies.'[40] But to date these have been largely unsuccessful. CCS projects collapsed in 2015 when the Treasury pulled funding. After a brief revival in 2023, a consortium of investors pulled out of Britain's first major carbon capture project in the Humber. That same year, the government's first hydrogen electrolyser procurement rounds only met half its target.[41]

As in the case of renewables, the energy system has remained trapped by the ideological commitment to private ownership. If CCS and hydrogen were so essential to Britain's decarbonisation strategy but the private sector could not provide them, why not set up a state-owned entity to develop these technologies? This was what the gas industry had done to develop oil-to-gas and LNG technology in the 1960s. It is also what many European countries had done for offshore wind. Instead, Britain chose the path of perpetual subsidies.

Price caps

Privatisation involved the gradual introduction of competition into energy retail. This was perhaps the most radical part of the programme, and one that few countries outside Europe followed. Stephen Littlechild had campaigned very hard for retail competition in the face of opposition from the big generators and distributors. In 2002 Ofgem deemed that competition was now effective across all social groups and methods of payment and removed the price cap. Ofgem was the first regulator to decide that competition was sufficiently advanced for retail price regulation to be abolished. It had won the race with telecoms, which was surely a source of professional pride for a generation of regulators.

The dream of pure competition was, however, always something of a fiction. The incumbent organisations that made up the nationalised energy industry were allowed to enter the retail market. Many customers stuck with the supplier they were with when the market was opened. British Gas was the big winner. It cross-sold electricity to its nationwide book of gas customers. Eon and Npower were the retail arms of Powergen and National Power after they bought up regional electricity companies. SSE and Scottish Power were the old Scots boards, which were left as vertically integrated regional companies. For the most part, the 'Big Six' inherited customers.

In 2008 the Big Six energy suppliers were 99 per cent of the retailer market and prices for end consumers had started to consistently rise. Between 2008 and 2017 Ofgem made a series of interventions to try to introduce more competition and drive down prices. The problem was that customer switching rates between suppliers were very low. This of course benefited the incumbents, especially British Gas as the largest supplier. Problems persisted, and in its 2013 Retail Market Review Ofgem blamed low levels of switching on the complex pricing structures. There followed some reforms to make tariffs simpler. This and other measures lowered the barriers to entry and attracted some challenger brands, most notably OVO (founded 2009) and Octopus Energy (founded in 2015).[42]

By 2014 switching rates were still very low, and Ofgem referred the matter to the Competition and Markets Authority (CMA). Customers on standard variable tariffs who did not switch were being charged far more than more active customers. The 'loyalty penalty', as it became known, had created a two-tier market. The CMA argued:

> the Six Large Energy Firms enjoy a position of unilateral market power over their inactive customer base and have the ability to exploit such a position through pricing their standard variable tariffs materially above a level that can be justified by cost differences from their non-standard tariffs.[43]

The CMA concluded that the retail market lacked sufficient levels of competition; 70 per cent of customers had stayed on standard variable tariffs rather than moving to cheaper ones, costing them on average £1.4 billion a year more. The two-tier system was in effect a kind of cross-subsidisation. The fixed-term tariffs were priced low to attract customers. The standard variable tariffs were then made extremely expensive to cover the loss. It was a 'tease and squeeze' strategy. New suppliers struggled to compete, which pushed them to adopt unsustainably low prices. The CMA recommended a price cap, but only for customers on prepayment meters. However, government ministers warmed to the idea of a more comprehensive cap in the face of pressure to deliver cost-of-living improvements. In 2019 Theresa May's government introduced a 'Default Tariff Cap'.[44]

As with EMR, the ex-regulators were irritated. Eileen Marshall and Colin Robinson complained that Ofgem was trying to bypass the competitive process, and that the price cap was the latest attempt at 'replacing the competitive energy market of the early 2000s by an increasingly dirigiste centralised policy that involves constant ministerial meddling'. In 2017 five ex-regulators wrote a long letter to Ofgem that defended the profit levels of incumbent suppliers and argued that there was sufficient competition. Their central point was that it was all the fault of customers. 'Less engaged customers are not being exploited . . . a customer that chooses to be more active could get a better price.' The tone revealed their frustration. The system architects were watching the house they had built being renovated in a way they disliked.[45]

Over the late 2010s and early 2020s, many other obligations were imposed on suppliers, creating monstrous complexity. Some think-tanks, like the ex-regulators, have argued that the retail market just needs to be returned to a pure, unrestricted form of competition. This overlooks the necessity of the price cap, which has protected 'sticky customers' with a low propensity to switch from rising prices. As of 2024, 90 per cent of customers are under the protection of the cap. There are distributional benefits as well. The poorest 10 per cent of customers have benefited from savings six times those of the wealthiest 10 per cent. The fear that the cap would kill competition and reduce switching rates has not been borne out. The price cap has also encouraged companies to be more efficient and improve customer service as a way of differentiating themselves.[46]

Debates about the price cap are often conflated with debates about the energy crisis from 2021 to 2023. In the years prior to the price cap there was an explosion in the number of small challenger suppliers, which peaked at seventy in 2018. Russia's invasion of Ukraine in 2022 set off a dramatic increase in gas prices and electricity prices. Suppliers were put under stress, and many ended up folding. At the height of the crisis, in late 2021 to mid-2022, twenty-eight suppliers exited the market. Some blamed low barriers to entry. A former government official complained, 'You could set up an energy company standing in a shopping aisle on your phone.'[47] Others argued that the price cap was to blame because it constrained what suppliers could charge customers. This is equivalent to arguing that citizens and customers should have borne the brunt of the energy crisis. As of 2026, the energy price cap remains in place as a safeguard for consumers, yet it represents a significant departure from the pure market-led vision of the architects of privatisation.

Regulating networks

In the early 2010s, there was widespread recognition that electricity networks were critical for decarbonisation. Wind and solar farms needed to connect to a reliable grid to sell their power. This would create a bow wave of work to connect these generators and reinforce the network. In addition, many parts of the network needed replacing and refurbishing, given that the last major build-out was in the 1950s and 1960s. The Stern Report in 2006, the Climate Change Committee's 2008–10 reports and Ofgem's Project Discovery report in 2010 all recommended increasing expenditure on networks.

The problem was that the regulatory framework from the 1990s, RPI-X, was made for sweating assets. The formulae incentivised it. As we have seen, the networks would repeatedly ask for expenditure to pay for investment, not do the work, then pocket the difference as profit. By the early 2000s, there was a recognition that RPI-X had severe limits. Regulation needed to be redesigned to limit excessive profits and ensure that companies didn't underinvest. Ofgem conducted a series of investigations, all with opaque titles like the 'Information and Incentives Project' and 'RPI-X@20'. These concluded that the regulator needed to shift its focus to how networks were performing on outcomes like reliability and network capacity. 'Outcomes-based' regulation was born. If the regulator could track the outcomes it was 'buying', companies could not then underspend without an alternative way to deliver those outcomes. Littlechild's RPI-X model assumed that the regulator could never know more than the companies, so involving the regulator in setting detailed outcomes was a change in philosophy. Another idea was to implement a sharing mechanism so that companies had to share a portion of any underspend with end consumers. Limitations on profits would move Britain close to the rate-of-return approach used in the US. Outcomes-based regulation would therefore unwind both the simplicity of RPI-X and the principle that unrestricted profiteering was good.[48]

In 2013 Ofgem launched the new regulatory model, called RIIO. RIIO stood for Revenue = Incentives + Innovation + Outputs (a spectacular example of the energy industry's ability to create meaningless acronyms). At the start of a five- or eight-year period, companies would estimate how much money they needed to deliver certain network outcomes. Ofgem would then conduct a rigorous interrogation of their plans and approve an expenditure level, or 'baseline allowance'. Ofgem even set up an 'Engineering Hub' to scrutinise what the networks were planning to build (the kind of inefficient duplication that the CEGB was supposed to have been guilty of). Network companies would add capital expenditures (CapEx) to their regulated asset base, and they would earn a predefined rate of return on the value of the asset base. RIIO had a clever mechanism, colloquially known as 'the TIM' or 'Totex incentive mechanism' (Totex = CapEx + OpEx, or total spending = capital + operational spending). If a network spent less than the allowances it could keep some of the difference, but a proportion would be given back to end consumers. A final element was 'uncertainty

Table 6.1. Electricity networks' actual expenditure versus approved (%)

Electricity transmission

Regulatory period	Network growth CapEx	Network replacement CapEx
2008–13	73%	89%
2014–21	80%	67%
2022–25	82%	75%

Electricity distribution

Regulatory period	Network growth CapEx	Network replacement CapEx
2011–15	80%	97%
2016–23	73%	86%
2024–25	65%	86%

Source: Ofgem, DPCR 5 Performance Report, 2010–2015 data tables; Ofgem, 'Transmission Networks: Report on the Performance of the Transmission Owners During Regulatory Periods TPCR4 and TPCR4RO 2007–08 to 2012–13', 21 March 2014; Ofgem, 'RIIO-ET1 Supplementary Data File 2020–21', 28 September 2022; Ofgem, 'RIIO-2 Electricity Transmission Annual Report 2024–25', 15 January 2026; Ofgem, 'RIIO-1 Electricity Distribution Summary Annual Report: 2022–23', 8 August 2025; Ofgem, 'RIIO-2 Electricity Distribution Summary Annual Report: 2024–25', 15 January 2026.

mechanisms'. If it was unclear whether infrastructure was needed or how much it would cost, Ofgem would provisionally agree to some funding but the network company could always come back to ask for more.

For all its complexity, RIIO did nothing to reverse the patterns of poor behaviour that went back to the 1990s. The Totex incentive mechanism was too tempting. Networks continued to ask for money and then not spend it. Table 6.1 shows how powerful the incentive was. Between 2008 and 2025 the network companies spent between 65 and 97 pence of every £1 of CapEx they asked for. Network replacement CapEx did not face any planning system restrictions, meaning the culprit was not NIMBYs or environmental regulations. The companies had repeatedly claimed their networks were keeling over and needed investment, only to underspend.

In response, the regulator tried to get smarter. It was very hard for Ofgem to prove the networks were underinvesting. Monitoring reliability was insufficient because it would take a long time for underinvestment to show up in poor reliability scores. In 2013 Ofgem came up with what seemed like a bright idea: a very complicated statistical model called NOMs, which stood for Network Output Measures (later updated to NARMs, Network Asset Risk Measures). Every major asset on the network would be assigned a 'probability of failure' score, reflecting things like condition and age, and a 'consequence of failure' score expressed in *monetary terms*. Loss of life, loss of load, loss of an arm, buildings burning, airports getting shut down: all eventualities were given a monetary value. The probability of failure was multiplied by the consequence of failure and out the other end popped a 'monetarised risk' level. Armed with NOMs, Ofgem thought it finally had a way to determine whether networks were spending too little. At the start of every regulatory period, the companies would agree to a particular percentage reduction in the monetarised risk level, which would translate into a certain volume of assets being replaced with an associated cost.[49]

NOMs turned out to be flawed. The networks controlled the model and all the spreadsheets that went into it. The idea that NOMs might reduce the asymmetry of information between regulator and company was naïve. Before NOMs, Ofgem could not really know whether a network needed to spend money on replacing old assets. After NOMs, Ofgem still could not know but now had to interrogate very complicated statistical information. The NOMs model just created a more elaborate type of game playing. The companies could adjust the probability of failure scores to reduce the risk level or swap more costly replacements with cheaper ones to hit the same risk reduction. Over time Ofgem came to mistrust the whole NOMs and then NARMs methodology. This was one of the reasons for the creation of an Engineering Hub in Ofgem in the mid-2010s. This group examined millions of images of rusty equipment to double-check the plans submitted by the companies.

The network companies continued to underspend their allowances. For example, from 2013 to 2021 National Grid Electricity

Transmission spent 40 per cent less than it was approved to spend on network replacement CapEx, some £2.5 billion of underspend. Ofgem reported that this was due to 'a revised understanding of the asset condition, extension of asset lives and more targeted asset replacement'.[50] Over 2021–24 the electricity transmission network companies underspent their asset replacement CapEx by £500 million as compared to the [£2 billion] they had requested. In 2024 the electricity distribution networks underspent in this area by £290 million versus the £1.3 billion requested.[51]

One of the objectives of RIIO was to unlock investment to support the decarbonisation of the energy system. In 2013 the grid companies were committed to building 30 GW of capacity by 2021 but ended up falling 9.3 GW short. The 'uncertainty mechanisms' were poorly named. A better term would have been 'certainty mechanisms', inasmuch as expenditure would only be approved once the need for infrastructure was certain. Rather than invest in a big network upgrade in anticipation of some demand that *might* emerge, Ofgem would push the project into an uncertainty mechanism and wait until things became clearer. By the time the demand materialised, it was of course too late. The Great British Connection Queue was born out of this muddled thinking.[52]

One of the principles of privatisation was unbundling, splitting up bits of the energy system. Over the early 2000s and 2010s, regulators and policy-makers remained zealously committed to the principle. The installation of smart meters was critical for the modernisation of the networks. Unlike in most other countries, Britain decided to split the programme off from the distribution networks and give it to suppliers. In many European countries, the distribution networks simply installed the meters street by street in one continuous programme. In Britain this did not happen. As of 2022, only 56 per cent of households had smart meters, compared to more than 90 per cent in France, Spain, Italy, the Netherlands and the Nordic countries.[53] At the other end of the network, offshore electricity transmission infrastructure was split off from the onshore transmission companies.

This led to a disorganised series of binary links to the shore, rather than an integrated network as in the Netherlands and Denmark (where state-owned transmission operators are responsible for both onshore and offshore).[54]

RIIO left one of the principles of privatisation in place: networks were completely in control of their balance sheets. The hope was that companies would take advantage of very low interest rates in the wake of the financial crash to fund new infrastructure, but this was never mandated in regulation. In the late 1990s gearing levels were between 10 per cent and 30 per cent.[55] By the early 2020s gearing levels were up at 50 per cent to 70 per cent.

Gearing was supposed to unleash a wave of construction. Yet most of the capital expenditure over these years was on replacing and refurbishing existing assets. Where did that debt go if not to build new infrastructure? In short, dividends. Financial engineering trumped real engineering. Sadly, debt levels are now a major issue for many companies as they need to build again but have used up their ability to borrow. Another issue is that in the early 2010s Ofgem decided to extend the time frame over which customers would pay networks back. This had the advantage of keeping bills flat but now means that future generations will likely face steep bill increases.[56]

Privatisation was designed to promote asset sweating. In the 1990s and 2000s, the British networks got good at it. As the industry moved into an asset-building phase, Ofgem and policy-makers made the mistake of trying to retrofit the old regulatory system with patches. RIIO was a very complex patch that did not work. Ongoing game playing created a deep mistrust between the regulator and the companies. Today, Ofgem is suspicious that it is having the wool pulled over its eyes, and the companies are suspicious that Ofgem will continue to add more regulatory complexity. Network regulation is now so complicated it is impossible to understand all the interactions.

There was a route not taken: renationalisation. There were voices that suggested precisely this. In 2008 the *Financial Times* journalist Martin Wolf argued, 'It seems obvious that the finance of assets is a suitable function for the public sector, which has one huge advantage – the ability to borrow cheaply.' Wolf suggested a neat division of labour: the state could own and finance the networks, with the private sector competing to construct and operate the assets. In 2009 even the right-leaning think-tank Policy Exchange acknowledged that when it came to the networks, 'the private sector will not deliver the optimal system'.[57] The Labour Party manifestos of 2017 and 2019 included a commitment to the renationalisation of networks, which was bitterly opposed by the vast majority of the energy industry.

As shown in earlier chapters, there is substantial evidence that the nationalised networks of the 1930s, 1950s and 1970s were simply better at building network infrastructure. Nationalisation would have also helped address the issue of regulatory complexity. Regulation existed only to stop privately owned networks from making excessive profits. If the networks were not-for-profit entities, most of the regulatory architecture could have been scrapped.

Tellingly, there are only a handful of countries in the world (Britain, Chile and Portugal) that have privatised all their energy networks. Most European countries have a mixed public-private ownership model, and many countries in the Global South have renationalised networks they were told to privatise by the IMF and World Bank.[58] Since 2023 the Germans have been trying to renationalise parts of their electricity transmission network.[59] However, in Britain any suggestion of nationalisation is shrugged off by the industry as antiquated and unnecessary.

The National Energy System Operator

By 2020 it was obvious that infrastructure was not getting built quickly enough and the constant back-and-forth between Ofgem and the network companies was part of the problem. There were complaints about the lack of 'coordination' and 'whole system thinking'. Few pointed out that this was a consequence of privatisation: the industry was incapable of coordination because it had been split up into silos in the 1990s. There was also confusion within the machinery of government. Decarbonisation policies had created immense interdepartmental complexity. This favoured established players with sufficient resources to navigate the mess and influence policy.[60]

Reading these signs in 2022, the Conservative government initiated the most significant restructuring of the energy system since 1986. In a spectacular case of irony, the party of Thatcher announced it would renationalise one part of National Grid plc and turn it into the National Energy System Operator (NESO). In summer 2024 the NESO launched as 'an independent, public corporation responsible for planning Britain's electricity and gas networks and operating the electricity system'.[61]

NESO was tasked with formulating a series of grand plans. Its annual 'Future Energy Scenarios' would become 'Future Energy Pathways' that specified the mix of generation and demand needed. These pathways would be converted into a 'Strategic Spatial Energy Plan' that would define the optimal location of generation and storage. In addition, a 'Central Strategic Network Plan' would define all electricity transmission investments needed for the next twenty-five years. Central plans would be accompanied by 'Regional Energy Strategic Plans'.

It would be a planning bonanza. For its defenders, the National Energy System Operator represented a shift back to the central planning of the post-war period. In fact, the NESO has adopted a form of extremist central planning that even the CEGB would have thought preposterous. The CEGB planned in five- to seven-year waves. Its leadership thought trying to pick all power station locations and lines for even a decade ahead would be 'impractical' and 'deceptive'.[62]

The renationalisation of system planning was an acknowledgement that privatisation was defunct. Conservative politicians argued that to reach net zero Britain needed a central planner '*in public ownership, in a way which ensures it is truly and properly independent . . . of asset ownership and other commercial energy interests*'.[63] For forty years the British public had been fed the line that the best way to manage the energy system was for private companies to plan everything while animated by the profit motive. The establishment of the NESO has shown that this was profoundly wrong. Rather than private companies planning the system motivated by profit, planning would move to a not-for-profit governmental body. Rather than the market dictating the mix and location of generation and demand, the NESO would. Rather than unbundled utilities specialising in one part of the value chain, the NESO would build a 'whole system plan' across gas, electricity, hydrogen and carbon capture.[64]

Like so many reforms of the last twenty years, the NESO only added more complexity. Rather than three layers (the state, Ofgem, companies), there were now four. Confusingly, NESO is owned by the government but regulated by Ofgem, even though Ofgem also reports to government. To make matters more complex, NESO has an advisory role back into government. Network companies will have to speak to Ofgem about investments to replace and refurbish the existing network, but to the NESO about building new infrastructure. Or to both in the case of a project that might address both objectives.[65] The NESO will write spatial plans dictating the mix and location of various technologies, but a government department (the Department for Energy Security and Net Zero) controls the subsidies that determine whether anything gets built, and Ofgem sets the network charges for those generators to try to nudge them to locate where they are supposed to go. There is significant scope for confusion and contradiction.

One of the mistakes made by policy-makers and regulators since 2010 was to add responsibilities without removing others. By mid-2025 it was clear that the NESO was overloaded and that a series of high-profile projects had come at the expense of its day-to-day activities.[66] The focus on central planning in the NESO was contradictory to some of the electricity market reform options being considered by the Department for Energy Security and Net Zero. No one bothered to tidy up the incoherence. Government just asked the various organisations for 'coordination' and 'joined-up thinking'.

The regional energy strategic planners (RESPs) are another example of the confusion caused by adding coordination layers. The RESPs have been tasked with comparing the plans of local authorities, gas and electricity networks and other 'stakeholders' to reveal inconsistencies. However, the RESPs don't have any powers to enforce consistency. Getting to a unified plan isn't just a technical modelling exercise. There will be many decarbonisation pathways for any one area, and different groups will have different preferences. The regional planners will be stuck in the middle, with no power to override decisions made by other actors.[67]

In November 2023 Ofgem said that it would 'introduce a governance mechanism for regional planners that embeds democratic representation and accountability in the process', but it couldn't say what this mechanism would be. By November 2024 there was still little clarity on what the RESPs were supposed to do. One industry expert put it marvellously: 'Ofgem's efforts to describe the RESP role reminds me of the mediaeval painters who attempted to depict wild animals they had never seen but had heard tales about.' Another commentator pointed out that NESO was creating a 'parallel universe' of planning and 'all it's going to do is make things more complicated'.[68]

Unlike the great energy institutions of the past, the National Energy System Operator is a central planner without any power to deliver its plan. It cannot raise capital and will not have any direct role in building infrastructure. There is also a risk that it becomes portrayed as an unelected bureaucracy, the bastion of the 'Net Zero Elite'. NESO's only tool for generating social consent will be interminable 'consultations' and 'stakeholder engagement'. There is a sense of déjà vu here. Regulators emerged in the 1990s as independent from governments. This allowed politicians to outsource decision-making. Yet the regulators were soon seen as too powerful, and regulation was perceived to be personalised, unclear and arbitrary.

Once again, the British energy system has opted for half-measures. If 'whole system' thinking is so important, why not reintegrate the different bits of the industry that have been split up? The NESO represents a very restrictive view that 'whole system thinking' should only be allowed to happen in one place. There are more radical options. In the Netherlands, gas and electricity distribution are grouped together. In many countries in the world, retail and distribution are combined. In China, transmission and distribution networks are in the same organisation. If the central planner must be independent of commercial interests, why are for-profit companies the ones to deliver the plan? If the consent of 'stakeholders' is so important, why not go beyond consultations and directly involve local and national-level elected politicians?

In a world of central planning, what is an appropriate return for private companies? The NESO will basically decide what generation and networks are required. This is very far from the idea that under capitalism businesses decide how to invest their money and make a return in exchange for the risk they are taking. In the British energy system, many infrastructure companies (especially the networks) don't really decide what to do, nor take any risk, but they still get to make a profit as if they did.

Dysfunction and zombie reforms

One of the hallmarks of zombie privatisation from 2010 was the proliferation of organisations. Policies focused on decarbonisation, security of supply and digitalisation were overlaid on the legacy arrangements. As new policies were introduced, new bodies cropped up. Coordinating something as complex as decarbonisation was challenging, and it was tempting to think that setting up new organisations that could act as 'integrators' would help. In 2009 there were three separate governmental bodies responsible for supporting infrastructure financing: the Treasury Infrastructure Financial Unit, the Infrastructure Planning Commission and Infrastructure UK, all founded between 2008 all 2009. In 2015 the think-tank Policy Exchange identified thirty bodies involved in administering the rules governing the energy industry. The report claimed that they were adding £500 million of cost every year. By 2023 the situation was even more complex.[69]

One winner from the complexity was trade associations. It was difficult for individual companies, especially smaller ones, to keep up with all the consultations coming out of government departments and Ofgem. Trade associations were formed to engage with the state on behalf of member companies and lobby. This reduced the administrative burden on any one company. Organisations like Energy UK, RenewableUK, the Energy Networks Association and Regen flourished.

As the complexity of the system increased, more people were employed just to manage all the interactions. Between 2003 and 2021 Ofgem's staff grew from 300 to 1,200. The new National Energy System Operator had 1,433 employees as of 2024, up from 688 in 2020. Complexity also created confusion and institutional rivalries. In 2024 rumours swirled that Ofgem and the NESO were blaming each other for high-profile issues like the connection queue. In a report on the NESO in September 2024, Ofgem noted that performance was lower than expected, 'primarily due to lack of alignment' between various activities. Ofgem argued that the NESO's work on market reform 'needed to better align with strategic network planning and connections reform', and that the market reform teams 'seemed to be working independently from other areas'. The criticism was somewhat unfair, given that NESO was not responsible for market reform; the Department for Energy Security and Net Zero was.[70]

Complexity made it very difficult to change anything. Reforms were frustrated by the vast number of interdependencies that needed to be considered and actors that needed to be consulted. Since 2010, numerous programmes and initiatives have failed or faced repeated delays. There have been at least five reviews of electricity transmission network charges and access arrangements over the last twenty-five years. Ofgem launched a 'Code Governance Review' in 2007 to simplify the codes (the technical rules governing system use) and improve consistency. It took three years to conclude and simply led to a second phase which ran until 2013. Switching the reference in the codes from fax to email took a year and a half.[71] By 2018 another 'Significant Code Review' launched that went on until mid-2022. One of the reasons why code changes are so torturously difficult is because of the influence companies have over 'code governance'. Whereas in many other countries a regulator sets the codes, in Britain the companies have much more of a say over these rules.

In March 2023 Ofgem launched an initiative that was supposed to fundamentally rethink network regulation, but after a few years it decided to stick with the existing model. The Review of Electricity Market Arrangements (REMA) kicked off in April 2022. There were multiple rounds of consultation, modelling and delays. The NESO was created in parallel, meaning that the civil service needed to try to reconcile the two programmes (with limited success). REMA concluded in July 2025 with the government dropping any significant changes.[72]

One of the documents produced by the civil service team working on REMA illustrated how complexity is a barrier to change. Buried underneath hundreds of pages of analysis were spiderweb-like diagrams that were supposed to make things easier to understand. Each one took an option like 'retain existing CfD' or 'retain the existing wholesale market' and worked through the various first-order and second-order effects. Each page ended up covered in interlinking boxes, with text so dense it was impossible to read. The diagrams illustrate the immense cognitive strain placed on civil servants and people in the energy industry. It is almost impossible to work out how making a change in one bit of the system might impact the rest.[73]

Even simple ideas floundered as they collided with other initiatives and became more difficult to implement. In 2023 Nick Winser, the electricity network commissioner, recommended compensating individuals and communities impacted by new electricity transmission lines. Before the recommendations had been implemented Winser was arguing that the plan should be extended to lower-voltage distribution lines. However, by September 2024 the new Labour government indicated that it was 'going back to the drawing board', dubbing the 'pounds for pylons' scheme 'tokenistic'. Since Winser's report, a new set of policies had been brought in that interacted with the original proposals, particularly the establishment of Great British Energy (a publicly owned energy company announced at the Labour Party conference in 2022). This pattern of behaviour leaves people inside the industry in a perpetual state of paralysis; it seems pointless to come up with any ideas until you have figured out what everyone else might be doing.[74]

A related reason why reforms fail is because of an unwillingness to move beyond certain principles of privatisation. A good example is the attempt to simplify the way levies are collected to support environmental and social initiatives. Over the last two decades governments have implemented dozens of subsidies for low-carbon technologies, paid for from levies on end-consumer electricity bills.

Unfortunately, this made electricity more expensive relative to gas, hence disincentivising electrification of transport and heat. There have been many attempts to fix the problem, but it is difficult to transfer the levies to somewhere else. A report by the innovation charity Nesta in 2024 argued that the best option would be for the levies to move to general taxation, as this would be 'fairer, more progressive' and would eliminate the disincentive to electrify. However, the report also discounted the option because policy-makers have an aversion to paying for energy infrastructure from general taxation.

This is a good example of zombie system thinking; whether citizens pay for levies through tax or bills, it is the same population paying, the only difference being how the costs are shared. Nesta was highlighting how the energy industry is trapped in a suboptimal state because one of the principles of privatisation, that energy infrastructure must be paid for from bills not taxation, is treated as inviolable.[75]

In the face of complexity, fragmentation and dysfunction, a reoccurring idea was to impose centralisation from the top down. The logic was that adding a 'task force', 'mission board' or 'transformation committee' that could break down 'siloed thinking' and drive 'cross-functional' collaboration would fix things.

In 2019 a report by a group of energy academics attempted to lay out a bold vision for the 'governance' of the future energy system. The paper ended up concluding that coordination across disparate departments and agencies required an Energy Transformation Commission. This was simply a new layer sitting in between the existing layers. A few years later, the CEO of Energy System Catapult came up with a similar idea. The prime minister should chair a 'Net Zero Cabinet subcommittee' or 'Mission Board', and underneath this should be an Energy System Transformation Office.[76] Neither recommended the removal of any existing institutions or policies, a good example of institutional layering. Both reports also reflected the triumph of management-consultancy-style thinking; everything involves a transformation.

Energy crisis

On 4 April 2024, the *Guardian* energy correspondent gingerly asked, 'Is Europe's energy crisis over?' European gas prices had finally fallen to €22 per MWh, a level comparable with the years 2016 to 2021. At the peak of the energy crisis in August 2022, the cost of gas was a staggering €339 per MWh. The journalist warned against complacency, noting that the fall in price concealed wider problems that still lurked beneath the surface.[77]

The energy crisis demonstrated that the British energy system was fragile, fragmented, comically complicated, lacking clear accountability, overwhelmingly dependent on markets and vulnerable to gas price shocks.

Energy prices rose for two main reasons. First, the global economy recovered faster than expected from COVID-19. Second, Putin's invasion of Ukraine in February 2022 led to severe supply restrictions. As the crisis started to unfold in summer 2021, commentators rightly spotted that these hikes would feed through to end consumers, both directly through energy bills and indirectly in the price of most goods and services.

Who was responsible for dealing with the problem? Ofgem was powerless when it came to rising wholesale prices. As part of its duties, Ofgem 'must have regard' for the need to secure 'all reasonable demands' for gas. Ofgem periodically reset the price cap for energy retailers, the maximum amount they can charge customers, and would need to factor in the increase in wholesale cost. The problem was the six-month lag between when costs rose and when retailers could increase their prices. As discussed, many smaller energy suppliers would end up going bust as they waited for the cap to increase. In June 2022 there were forty-nine suppliers, but by April 2023 there were only twenty-two.[78]

What about the energy suppliers? In June 2022 the retailer Centrica signed a major contract with the Norwegian oil and gas major Equinor for 1 billion cubic metres of gas. The government minister Kwasi Kwarteng celebrated this, claiming that it would 'underpin British energy security over the next few years'. But the deal was worth only 1 per cent of Britain's total gas demand. Government restarted discussions with Centrica on reopening the Rough gas storage facility, shut in 2017, but this would do little to address the immediate crisis. Britain still has some of the lowest gas storage levels in Europe.[79]

Energy suppliers could sign contracts for a particular volume of gas, but they couldn't really do anything about the price. In an interview, Greg Jackson, founder and CEO of Octopus Energy, revealed the logic of the system with clarity:

> I think energy companies can cope. We're fighting here because customers won't be able to, and we know just how bad this is because we have to buy the energy in the wholesale market. In the global gas market, these are the prices we faced to buy the energy for our customers. We just know that the level of increases is going to be unmanageable for so many without the right support from the government. And it's beyond what any one company can do.[80]

What about the system operators that were responsible for balancing supply and demand? The Gas System Operator, formerly part of National Grid but sold off to Macquarie in 2022, also had little control over the situation. In October 2021 it conceded that 'the underlying market arrangements in the UK are predicated on the basis that the market will provide'. Looking ahead to the next year the System Operator noted that 'a positive price differential to both Global and European markets will be required for . . . supply to direct flow into GB'.[81] In short, the gas might arrive but only if Britain was prepared to pay up.

Ultimately, in the British system the market alone was responsible for security of supply. The state could not influence the price of gas, and suppliers would have to pass the cost on to consumers (if they didn't go bust). There was nothing that Ofgem, the suppliers or the System Operator could do. Over the course of the crisis some commentators rightly asked why the price of gas should impact the price of electricity, especially given that more electricity was being generated from supposedly 'free' sources like wind and solar. The reason was because gas generators are the marginal price setters, and under the 'pay as clear' rules of the market every other generator is paid that price. In a documentary on Channel 4, Guy Martin tried to wrap his head around it as follows: 'Whoever is the dearest, they all just jump on the bandwagon . . . it is a ridiculous system, how can they get away with that?'[82]

Over summer 2022, calls for government intervention reached fever pitch. In August 2022 the money-saving guru Martin

Lewis warned that 'this is a national crisis on the scale of the covid pandemic' and that 'government alone' was responsible. The government decided to leave the market rules unchanged but increased support levels for end consumers.[83]

In October 2022 Ofgem announced a steep rise in the retail price cap to £3,549 per year. Government stepped in and capped energy bills at £2,500. Known as the 'Energy Price Guarantee Scheme', essentially the taxpayer made up the difference. Without the cap, end consumers would have faced eye-watering bills of £4,279 from January 2023.[84] The government flirted with the idea of going around the energy retailers and directly buying gas itself. However, the price tag was too great, and, as the *Financial Times* observed, negotiations were 'complicated as most energy companies are in the private sector, making it more challenging to secure long-term deals'.[85]

In hindsight, it is hard to see what else the state could have done. Energy is a basic requirement to live. One of the few innovative actions taken during the crisis was the 'Demand Side Flexibility' scheme designed by the National Grid Electricity System Operator and Octopus Energy. This scheme paid consumers small sums of money for turning down their demand at critical times when the grid was under stress. One million households registered to participate, and the trial generated an average demand reduction of 18 per cent among those participating. Posts on social media indicated that people participated both for the money and out of a sense of duty. Perhaps it was also a way to feel as if they had some degree of control over the energy system.[86]

The crisis led to immediate calls for fundamental reform. In April 2022 the minister responsible for energy, Kwasi Kwarteng, initiated the Review of Electricity Market Arrangements, which ran for three years before the government decided against making any radical changes. Another idea was to impose a windfall tax on the renewable generators who had made significant profits. Policy-makers discovered that this would be difficult because of all the various government support mechanisms. In May 2022

Rishi Sunak announced that he would impose a windfall tax, but a year later the idea was watered down, with an official stating, 'It was proving too complicated.'[87]

Companies across the energy industry look set to do very well out of the crisis. The tumultuous events of 2022 and 2023 have provided cover, masking the deeper problems with privatisation. The industry could unite around the claim that there was nothing fundamentally wrong with the system, it was just that an unexpected 'shock' had led to extreme price increases. This ignored that prices were rising before the crisis and that Ofgem had modelled the impact of a war in Ukraine as early as 2009. The crisis also provided the perfect justification for increasing the flow of subsidies: 'energy security' is now used to justify expanding every part of the system.

Evaluation

To many in the energy industry the period since 2010 is considered something of a golden age: years in which renewables flourished, emissions fell and the industry was swept by a wave of innovation. There have undoubtedly been some successes, but the picture presented in this chapter is more sobering.

Since the 2008 Climate Change Act was passed, Britain has met all its emission-reduction targets, having stayed within its 'carbon budgets'. In March 2024, the ailing Conservative government triumphantly announced that the UK was 'halfway to net zero', as territorial greenhouse gas emissions had fallen by 53 per cent between 1990 and 2023. This made the UK the first major economy to halve its emissions. However, this milestone is less impressive when you consider that since 1990 energy demand has fallen, in part due to deindustrialisation. Car production moved to Asia, petrochemicals to the US and steel shut down. Ironically, the last steel production facility, in Port Talbot, closed at the moment Britain's demand for steel to build energy infrastructure was going to go up.[88] Between 2000 and 2019, before the energy crisis, electricity demand per capita fell by 22 per cent. The only countries that experienced a greater decline in demand per capita between those years were Yemen, Zimbabwe, Jamaica, Tajikistan and Syria. One common response to falling electricity demand is to point out that Britain has not been actively trying to increase electricity demand but has rather been trying to increase the electrification level (the share of final energy demand serviced by electricity). However, even on this metric Britain's performance is mediocre. The electrification level was 18.4 per cent in 2000 and 20.4 per cent in 2019. Around the globe there are ninety countries that increased their electrification level by more over these years.

Did Britain simply outsource its emissions to other countries? One measure of this is trade-adjusted emissions, which take account of the carbon that is emitted in the production of goods that are exported or imported. Britain's trade-adjusted emissions fell by 27 per cent between 1990 and 2023, which is much less than the halving of territorial emissions. Another factor was the switch from coal to gas, as burning natural gas is much less carbon-intensive than burning coal. Between 2010 and 2023, the power sector has cut emissions by 76 per cent; demand reduction accounted for 37 per cent, and coal-to-gas switching was 21 per cent. Only 21 per cent came from renewables deployment. The carbon intensity of the grid (the carbon emissions per unit of electricity generated) fell 4.5 per cent per annum between 2010 and 2023 (although in 2025 it went up for the first time since 2021). This was an acceleration of a long-term trend going back to 1950. In short, the energy system has contributed to falling emissions, but the reductions are not as impressive as is often claimed.[89]

Energy bills rose between 2010 and 2023. Surprisingly, it is difficult to say by exactly how much. One would think that this simple, all-important data point would be tracked by Ofgem. It is not. On its data portal Ofgem has had a data series covering 2009 to 2020, but nothing before or since. There have been repeated efforts to address this gap to no avail. What the incomplete data does show is that the rise in energy bills over the last thirteen years was not just because of the energy crisis. Ofgem estimated that between 2009 and 2020 the average household gas and electricity bill increased by 9 per cent even after controlling for changes in consumption and inflation.[90]

Changes in electricity prices for domestic consumers (inclusive of grid charges, levies and taxes) tell a similar story. Over the nationalised period and the first decade of privatisation, electricity and gas prices fell but then started to rise from the early 2000s. Between 2010 and 2019 electricity prices rose by on average 2.3 per cent per annum, while gas prices fell by 0.2 per cent per annum.[91] Since 2020, bills have increased even more dramatically due to the energy crisis. Britain's reliance on imported gas and the dominance of gas as the electricity price setter, plus escalating network and subsidy costs, meant that by the end of 2023 electricity prices were higher than in any other European country. As of mid-2025 household electricity bills are 20 per cent above the average for major European economies, and industrial bills are 90 per cent higher.[92] The International Energy Agency tracks residential electricity prices for a group of fifty-seven countries. Only Australia and South Africa experienced a bigger price hike over these years (when adjusting for inflation). There is a human cost to this: fuel poverty and citizens having to choose between eating and heating. Renewable generation capacity may have risen, but households are not feeling the benefits of so-called 'cheap' renewables.[93]

How effectively did the energy system scale up low-carbon technologies? The picture on the generation side is mixed. Offshore wind has developed rapidly; between 2010 and 2023 capacity grew elevenfold. This was largely due to generous subsidies, which faltered in 2022 to 2023. In July 2024 the Climate Change Committee (CCC) noted that offshore wind was off track and that capacity would need to triple by 2030. Another issue is that the locational development of offshore wind has come at a huge cost. Wind farms are paid vast sums of money to turn off because the grid cannot handle the power transfers.

The decline in the use of coal for power generation is a notable success. In 2012 coal was 40 per cent of the generation mix, but this shrank to 2 per cent in 2019. In October 2024 the final coal power station, Ratcliffe-on-Soar, was closed.[94]

In other areas of generation, the picture is mixed. Onshore wind and solar were designated 'off track' by the CCC in 2024. To get back on track, onshore wind installation rates 'will need to double and solar installation rates will need to increase five times'. Nuclear has been plagued by delays and cost overruns. Hinkley Point C was only developed thanks to state subsidies. Carbon capture and storage and hydrogen have both spectacularly failed, without a single meaningful project up and running as of 2025.[95]

On the demand side the picture is also mixed. Electric vehicle sales have been a success, growing from less than 1 per cent of new vehicle sales in 2010 to 16.5 per cent in 2023. Electric vehicle penetration has consistently beaten the CCC's targets. In contrast, heat pump deployment has been significantly off track. Installations grew from 27,000 to 60,000 between 2018 and 2023, but this is far below the CCC's target of 130,000 installations, and a very long way off the government target of 600,000 a year by 2028.[96] By comparison, currently 1.7 million methane boilers are installed every year.

Underinvestment has been particularly acute in networks. Between 2010 and 2020 electricity network investment averaged around £4 billion per annum. Between 2025 and 2040 some have projected that this must rise significantly to between £8 billion and £14 billion per annum. This massive bow wave is a direct consequence of decades of underinvestment. Unfortunately, Britain's network companies have regressed in their ability to build and have some of the highest costs in Europe.[97]

The popular impression in the energy industry and the media is that the last decade has been a period of unprecedented investment in the energy system. This is an illusion. Gross fixed capital formation by the energy industry as a percentage of gross domestic product was at a historic low from 2010 to 2023.[98]

Underinvestment has led to a situation where the energy system is fragile, lacking resilience to change in an uncertain world. The energy crisis might be over, but geopolitical tensions are higher than ever, and Britain is still dangerously dependent on liquified natural gas arriving by ship. Long-term storage facilities like Rough have been degraded, so the country lacks a strategic reserve of gas; gas storage levels are at historic lows.[99] The electricity interconnectors provide some resilience, but there is no guarantee that these assets will be secure. Chinese-registered ships have been suspected of cutting undersea cables by deliberately dragging their anchors along the seabed. In 2023 Norway amended its Energy Act to make clear that the state can prevent exports to Britain if it is experiencing 'domestic stress'.[100] The complex statistical models that the energy industry uses to forecast the future are often based on absurdly optimistic assumptions: that LNG will always arrive, assets will always work despite being old, the interconnectors will always flow. After four decades of asset sweating there simply is not enough fat left in the system for it to be resilient to uncertain change.

Energy privatisation was a core part of a neoliberal programme that was supposed to lead to a retreat of the state from various areas of social and economic life. Yet over the 1990s and 2000s regulation proliferated across many sectors to correct various market failures and to protect the returns of private sector actors. After the financial crash of 2008, neoliberalism entered a zombie state. The organising categories were no longer trusted to function on their own without being propped up by various types of contingent political intervention. Since 2008 sluggish growth has led to repeated state interventions in the economy, especially in the guise of industrial strategy.[101]

What happened in the energy sector from 2010 was a microcosm of the slow death of neoliberalism. By the mid-2020s the process of zombification had created an incoherent mess. The industry became a strange and dysfunctional hybrid that combined the worst elements of statism and privatisation.[102] State central planning had been grafted onto the privatised model. Subsidies permeated every part of the industry. Retail and network regulation had changed beyond recognition. With the renationalisation of system planning in 2022 the privatised model was truly dead. However, one principle of privatisation was left untouched and sacrosanct: private ownership. Regulators and politicians demonstrated a quixotic commitment to private ownership. The industry enthusiastically supported greater levels of state intervention because it served to protect private sector profits. The unintended consequence of all these interventions was to set off a self-reinforcing spiral of complexity and dysfunction.

In 1976 the American sociologist Daniel Bell, looking at the nationalised industries of Europe, noted that this 'system of state capitalism could easily be transformed into a corporate state', a 'cumbersome, bureaucratic monstrosity, wrenched in all directions by the clamour for subsidies and entitlements by various corporate and communal groups, yet gorging itself on increased governmental appropriations to become a Leviathan in its own right'.[103] This is a remarkably accurate portrayal of Britain's zombie energy system today. The industry has entered what Antonio Gramsci termed an 'interregnum', a period when the old is dying but the new cannot fully be born. As Gramsci observed, in an interregnum it is common to find a great variety of morbid symptoms as the awkward hybrid limps along burdened by contradictions.[104]

The energy industry's obsession with decarbonisation as a technological problem represents a kind of loss of nerve. People have stopped believing in the capacity of society to develop new forms of economic and political organisation. The institutions and ownership models from the 1990s were not meant to deal with challenges like climate change and energy security; they were made for a world of asset sweating, not asset building. We must redesign the system around a new set of principles. This may sound radical, but it is what the Labour Party did in the late 1940s, and what the Conservatives did in the 1980s and 1990s. The nationalised energy system lasted about forty years. The privatised one has lasted about forty years. It is time to develop a new system.[105]

7

The Future of British Energy

Before turning to the future, let us briefly recap on the argument through one case study. In the North East of England, just outside Newcastle, is a coastal town called Whitley Bay. Along the seafront are ten well-preserved gas lamps installed between 1900 and 1910. No longer functioning, these objects once provided street lighting to the popular seaside resort. The lamps were designed to use sewer gas as a fuel source but ended up being fired by town gas from the nearby Minton gas works in North Shields. The Minton works was owned by the local Tynemouth Gas Company which manufactured gas from the 'black gold' the region was famous for.

The Tynemouth Gas Company faced many technological changes and political pressures over the years. The town council considered taking the company into municipal ownership in the 1890s, only deciding against it after winning concessions on reduced rates and improved service. In 1901 the council built its own electricity generator, big enough to power 15,000 lamps and the new electric tramway in the town. This forced the Tynemouth Gas Company to expand into new areas like heating and cooking. The council's electricity undertaking also faced competition, and in 1906 the operation was effectively taken over by the North Eastern Electric Supply Company (NESCo). The local capitalists and engineers who built NESCo would go on to play a crucial role in the massive expansion of the British electricity system under public ownership.[1]

Just twenty minutes up the road from Whitley Bay is Blyth. Just off the coast, Great Britain's first offshore wind farm was completed in 2000, the largest in the world at the time. The turbines were made by the Danish manufacturer Vestas, and the project was owned and operated by the French state-owned giant EDF and the German utility Eon. In 2021 Tenaga Nasional, the Malaysian majority-state-owned utility, took a stake in the project. Just down the coast from Whitley Bay in Teesside is a larger offshore wind farm constructed in 2013 for £200 million. It is also owned by EDF, and the turbines are German, having been manufactured by Siemens.

Offshore wind farms now generate the electricity needed to light Britain's streetlamps. In September 2024 Britain shut down its last coal-fired power station. Gas is still used to heat homes and generate electricity, but it is increasingly imported as liquified natural gas from the US and Qatar. Town gas was phased out in the 1970s, but the Minton gas works in North Shields wasn't fully dismantled until 2016. In its lifetime the works had moved from private into public ownership in the 1940s and then back again in the 1980s. The demolition was undertaken by Northern Gas Networks, owned by CK Infrastructure Holdings of Hong Kong, which also owned London's electricity network (until 2026).

The gas lamps and wind farms of the North East are testimony to the substantial changes to Britain's energy system since the early nineteenth century. Most histories of energy focus on how and why energy technologies change. The characters are inanimate objects – coal, gas, turbines, solar panels, batteries. This book has tried to show that changes in patterns of ownership have been just as dramatic. In the early twentieth century, public and private ownership co-mingled. Most companies were owned by British capitalists. From the 1940s to late 1970s, the British state owned and controlled the electricity and gas industries, building the foundations of the system today. In the 1980s and 1990s, the industry was radically restructured, sliced and diced into chunks and sold off to private investors. Today private ownership and foreign capital are totally dominant.

The argument of this book can be summarised in two words: ownership matters. Who owned and controlled the means of making, moving and selling energy shaped which technologies were developed, what infrastructure got built and the extent to which citizens and consumers benefited. Technology and political economy were locked in a two-way relationship. Technological forces often ran ahead of institutions and policy, leading to periods of procrastination and then dramatic change. State-directed resets, like those in the 1930s, 1940s and 1980s, also unleashed new technological dynamics. Public ownership gave Britain the electricity grid, the nuclear programme, liquified natural gas, natural gas conversion and hydroelectric power. Privatisation gave Britain the 'dash for gas', asset sweating in networks and wind farms paid to turn off.

The fifth phase in energy history?

Across the globe countries are attempting to transform their energy systems. This energy transition boils down to two things: the electrification of demand and decarbonisation of electricity generation. The pace, extent and motivations for the transition vary greatly across nations. Regardless, all nations are united in facing a common monstrous fate. If greenhouse gas emissions do not fall, then human life will be immeasurably worse in the future.

As in other countries, in Britain the energy transition came to be defined as a kind of new industrial revolution. From at least 2008 there was a broad consensus as to what was required. Policy-makers, economists and energy insiders convinced themselves that transformation could be accomplished within the established principles of the privatised system: private ownership, unbundling, competition and markets and independent regulation. However, as in the 1910s and the 1970s, technological change outstripped changes to political economy. Gradually, politicians and regulators found that they had to make significant policy changes that were contradictory to the key principles of the privatised model. This led to a process of zombification that has left the energy industry a dysfunctional hybrid.

As in the 1920s, 1940s and the 1980s, Britain stands on the precipice of another reset to the political economy of energy. It could be a gale of creative destruction or a further ossification of the privatised model. Sadly, the industry is poorly prepared for the former kind of transformation. Over the last decade the obsession with technology has obscured important discussions about ownership and institutions. And the frantic nature of constant adjustments to policy has left many trapped in incremental thinking.

As an example, take the industry's fascination with China. Numerous consultancy and think-tank reports fawn over the pace at which China is building its energy system. Some have even argued that China is the world's first 'electrostate' in contrast with 'petrostates' like Russia, Saudi Arabia and the US. That Britain's energy elite are in awe of China represents a reversal of roles. It used to be other countries marvelling at the 'British experiment'. Yet the fascination is superficial; analysts allow themselves to experience awe (and fear) of China, but not to learn from China. It is rare for industry experts in the West to acknowledge that the leading force in the global build-out of renewables has an energy system that cannot be classified as 'liberalised' or 'privatised'. Indeed, the Chinese energy system today shares many characteristics with the energy system that Britain had in the 1950s and 1960s. State-owned generation dominates. The entire electricity network is under the control of two state-owned companies, China Southern Power Grid Company and State Grid Corporation of China. The latter is the third largest company in the world by revenue. By contrast in Britain, which has a power system just 3 per cent the size of China's, there are ten network companies and all are in private ownership. Unlike in Britain, in China retail and distribution are integrated in single regionalised state-owned firms. China is ostensibly committed to certain aspects of liberalisation – particularly the creation of spot markets. Yet, tellingly, it has not pursued these policies in the asset-building phase it has been in for the last twenty years and there is no indication China will privatise its networks.[2]

Will Britain evolve or stagnate? In what follows I sketch two purely speculative visions of the future.

The Central Return Generating Board

In this scenario the state centrally plans private sector capital allocation. Given the extremely weak position of the British economy, the government goes to great lengths to protect the profits of companies and financial institutions. What companies and individuals want to achieve increasingly comes to depend on the state's sanction and support. Consequently, different groups jostle for the state's attention, seeking to appropriate it altogether.[3] 'De-risking', removing 'red tape' and 'ensuring investability' become the order of the day. Citizens do not see the benefits, and a political party is elected that walks away from Britain's climate commitments. This is the path that Britain is on: a system governed by a Central Return Generating Board.

The logic of a Central Return Generating Board begins with the idea that the state must jump-start the stagnant economy, and that decarbonisation provides a kind of totem for this endeavour. The Labour Party won the election in 2024 and committed to being a 'mission-driven' government focused on 'ambitious, measurable, long-term objectives that provide a driving sense of purpose for the country'. Tellingly, the top two 'missions' are to 'kickstart economic growth' and 'make Britain a clean energy superpower'. As in other countries, the energy sector has thus become a crucial pillar of state-directed industrial strategy – evidence of a return to mercantilism and perhaps even economic nationalism.[4]

The centrepiece of Labour's energy strategy is to build a 'Clean Power' electricity system by 2030, five years ahead of the prior government's target of 2035.[5] Before the election, one energy consultancy described both targets as near impossible. In summer 2024 the government appointed the former head of the Climate Change Committee, Chris Stark, to lead a 'Mission

Control' centre. Mission Control swiftly asked the National Energy System Operator to figure out if the target was feasible, and an 'Action Plan' was published in December 2024. The plan said that over the next five years the capacity of the electricity system would need to double. This would involve tripling offshore wind, tripling solar and doubling onshore wind. In addition, Britain might need to add 70 per cent more long-duration energy storage capacity, five and a half times more battery capacity and 30 per cent more subsea interconnector capacity. On the demand side, Britain would need four and a half times more flexible consumer demand. It might be possible to reduce the scale of the renewable build-out, but only if untested 'first-of-a-kind' technologies like carbon capture and storage and hydrogen can be developed.[6]

As well as building new infrastructure, the plan requires keeping all the existing gas-fired power stations operational. In addition to finishing Hinkley Point C, EDF will need to extend the lives of four of the nuclear reactors constructed by the Central Electricity Generating Board. The electricity networks will also need a complete overhaul and 'around twice as much new transmission network infrastructure will be needed in Great Britain by 2030 as has been delivered in the past decade'. The 'Clean Power' plan comes with an estimated price tag of just over £40 billion of investment every year between 2025 and 2030, which is nearly four times more than the average over the last five years.

This construction bonanza could continue even after 2030. Based on the National Energy System Operator's estimates, between 2030 and 2050 the generation capacity of the electricity system might need to double. Nuclear capacity could need to increase sevenfold. Hydrogen power generation capacity might have to increase from zero today to a staggering 30 GW by 2050 – significantly more than the 'dash for gas' of 1990 to 1998. This might also trigger the need for a first-of-its-kind hydrogen pipeline network of 1,500 kilometres that could cost £22 billion.[7]

In the face of the infrastructure boom, central planning has been grafted onto the privatised system. In April 2024, the Conservative energy minister bemoaned the 'net zero Leviathan of central planning'. Ironically, the Leviathan referred to was created under the Conservatives. The newly nationalised National Energy System Operator will develop various national and regional spatial energy plans with twenty-five-year-plus horizons. Via these plans and various subsidies, the state will effectively dictate the mix and location of different types of electricity generation.[8] In fact, subsidy regimes have been given a new lease of life by geopolitical tensions. It is notable that energy companies are increasingly branding their activities as critical to national security. Few point out that if offshore wind farms and electricity networks are security assets, it would then be logically consistent to bring them into public ownership like the military and to pay for them via general taxation.

The many attempts to reform the connection queue have failed. In September 2024 Ofgem announced that the NESO would essentially choose which projects get connections based on whether they fit with the Strategic Spatial Energy Plan and the Clean Power 2030 Action Plan. By December 2025 the new reformed queue was confirmed, a noteworthy success given that the queue has been a major issue for years. However, it is likely that there will be a string of legal challenges to the new queue, and any project that makes it into the grand plan will have significant bargaining power.[9]

Some in the energy industry look at these developments in horror, and none more so than the architects of privatisation. They argue that replacing markets with central planning is doomed. Some have even likened the new mechanisms of planning to the Soviet Gosplan. Yet the energy industry has for the most part celebrated the change. Defenders of the new status quo point out that the privatised system remains intact, with markets and competition in some parts, but the pendulum has rightly been swung back to long-term planning. Many present the new arrangements as a kind of a 'Goldilocks' system with the right balance of planning and markets. It is worth emphasising that this is based on a flawed understanding of post-war central planning. It also ignores the other things that made the Central Electricity Generating Board capable of delivering on its plans: vertical integration, operational responsibility, public ownership, paying for infrastructure from general taxation as well as bills, borrowing at the state's cost of capital, a supply chain that was entirely onshore.

The modern British state is in fact adopting a much more extreme approach to central planning than was ever undertaken by the nationalised energy industries. We are not tiptoeing back towards an older institution, we are sprinting towards something totally new: a centrally planned system designed around private sector companies, financial institutions and their returns, with the state liberally de-risking investments. This explains why the energy industry has been so approving of the way in which many of the principles of privatisation have been eroded or jettisoned entirely. The industry has supported state intervention because it has been in the service of protecting private sector profits. Target setting and central planning have become effective mechanisms for justifying subsidies and pushing costs and risk onto citizens.[10]

The coming construction bonanza will require lots of capital. The last time anything like this occurred was in the 1950s to 1970s, when Britain had high domestic savings levels, unlike today. It seems likely that the Labour government will therefore continue the pattern of the last thirty years and ask the private sector and foreign investors to finance most of this new infrastructure, with costs recovered from consumer bills. It did not have to be this way. In the run-up to the 2024 election, it seemed that the Labour Party was committed to the state picking up more of the cost. However, in a sliding-doors moment lobbying intervened. The chief executive of the Green Finance Institute, a quango, convinced the shadow chancellor, Rachel Reeves, to drop the pledge of £28 billion of state funding on the basis that it would 'crowd out' private sector investors who wanted to 'pour money into big green projects'. What this executive was really arguing was that it would be more profitable for investors if spending was recovered from bills and not taxation.[11]

This reflects an all-pervasive logic that there is a win-win deal to be done between financial institutions and governments. In 2024 Larry Fink, the CEO of BlackRock, the world's largest asset manager, argued that 'the global need for infrastructure combined with high deficits constraining government spending creates unprecedented opportunity for private capital'. The influence of asset managers has grown over the last decade. Electricity and gas networks are particularly attractive investments for these organisations because there is no competition; millions of customers have no choice but to use and no option but to pay. Many in the energy industry argue that Britain should sever its dependence on international oil and gas markets. In place of Shell and BP, Britain could just become dependent on BlackRock and Macquarie. The asset managers might end up replacing the oil and gas supermajors as the custodians of the energy system.[12]

For decades the industry has repeated the same mantra: there is a 'wall of capital' dying to get into the British energy system. This may be true, but it all depends on the returns on offer. One of the most important metrics in the energy transition is the cost of capital, or how much it costs to borrow money across equity or debt. Renewables and electricity networks have high upfront costs but then low ongoing running costs. How much it costs to borrow money to pay for the upfront construction has a big impact on the lifetime cost of the project and how much revenue companies need to make a profit. Figure 7.1 illustrates the profound shift in the cost stack; capital investment costs could go from less than 10 per cent of the total electricity system cost today to around 70 per cent by 2050. Even a slight increase in the cost of capital today will have a large impact on the cost of electricity many years from now, reverberating into the future.[13]

Figure 7.1. Forecast share of electricity system cost by type, Great Britain

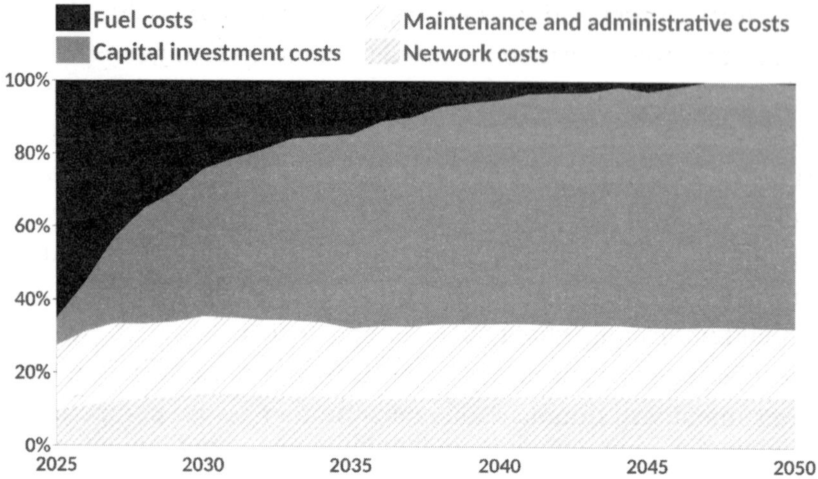

Source: Jonathan Marshall and Emily Fry, *Electric Dreams* (Resolution Foundation, 2024), p. 13.

One way to reduce the cost of capital is to load up on debt because it is less expensive than equity. Since the global financial crisis in 2008, Britain has had incredibly low interest rates. Energy companies could reduce the cost of borrowing by increasing the ratio of debt to equity, called gearing. Unfortunately, increasing gearing is no longer an easy option as interest rates have risen. Many of the largest energy companies have exhausted their balance sheets and will need to turn to raising fresh equity before they can load up on more debt. There is a risk that some go the way of Thames Water and Southern Water, with unsustainable debt piles leading to collapse.

An alternative lever for reducing the cost of capital is to make the investment less risky. In this model, the state's role is to ensure 'investability' by de-risking projects. Central planning is complementary to this strategy; the role of the central plan becomes to ensure that investors have greater certainty on their returns. The first National Infrastructure Plan in 2010 set the tone, arguing that the state must 'create the optimum environment for investment', 'reducing the levels of risk transfer to the private sector' and offering 'relatively certain economic returns'. The government created the UK Infrastructure Bank in 2020 to 'crowd in' private capital and 'manage risk'. In early 2024 Chris Stark argued that the government needed to make investing in Britain's energy system more 'exciting' to compete with the massive subsidies on offer in the US under the Inflation Reduction Act.[14] Another lever that can have the same effect as a subsidy is to reduce the exposure of companies to competition. In the 2010s Ofgem was highly committed to introducing more competition into onshore energy networks. However, over the early 2020s it has all but given up that goal.[15]

At the time of writing (summer 2025), it looks as if the Labour government will double down on a 'state-investor partnership' strategy, trying to reduce the cost of capital by de-risking investment. In practice, this means perpetual subsidies. In January 2025, £22 billion of subsidies was committed to carbon capture and storage even though some of the plants hadn't even been designed.[16] That same year the government lengthened the contracts-for-difference for offshore wind, so that developers have a guaranteed price for a longer period. By setting such a stretching target as 'clean power by 2030', the offshore wind industry knows that it has the government over a barrel and will need to raise the guaranteed price level.[17]

In the rush to build infrastructure various foundational reforms are being abandoned. In July 2025 the government made the decision to stick with the existing electricity market arrangements, following years of intense lobbying by generators and network companies against a change to 'locational marginal pricing' (or 'zonal pricing'). The minister in charge, Ed Miliband, celebrated that the decision gave 'certainty to investors'. This throws out the window the supposed principle of capitalism that investors earn their returns from taking a risk.

One of Labour's flagship policies was to establish GB Energy, a publicly owned energy company. The founding statement was bold, arguing that 'the British people should have a right to own and benefit from our natural resources . . . [which] should be harnessed for the common good'.[18] However, in practice the organisation has been allocated a relatively small sum of capital (£8.4 billion over four years). GB Energy has also been consumed by the logic of the Central Return Generating Board. In July 2024, a consultancy report paid for by the lobbying group RenewableUK argued that 'GBE's biggest value add is to minimise the development risk of projects'. The CEO of RenewableUK then went on to become the CEO of GB Energy. The organisation's focus seems to have shifted to 'crowding in' investment by de-risking. This is a reheated version of the failed Green Investment Bank, launched in 2012. Hydrogen and carbon capture lobbyists were quick to jump onto the gravy train, arguing that their sectors should be included in scope. Perhaps GB Energy will thrive, or perhaps it will go the way of the Green Investment Bank, which was sold to Macquarie in 2017 for £2.3 billion.[19]

In this new world of central planning and de-risking the critical infrastructure required for social existence ends up being perpetually reconfigured specifically to generate dependable financial returns for investors. Britain has placed so much of its critical national infrastructure in the hands of private companies, banks and asset managers that these institutions now have us at their mercy. Investor dissatisfaction in one industry spills over into another. Over 2024 the water companies were locked in a battle with their regulator, Ofwat, over bill increases. In September a major infrastructure investor warned that failing to keep the 'investment community on side' would 'put wider infrastructure investment at risk, beyond just water'. A Barclays banker put it more bluntly: the 'need for capital has gone through the roof', but international investors 'frankly can get better returns elsewhere for lower risk'.[20]

The focus on de-risking as the primary lever for economic growth narrows the scope for a more ambitious green developmental state. After decades of handing over responsibilities to the private sector, the British state is now so hobbled it may well be totally incapable of bold action.[21] Desperation for foreign capital could lead to more undignified behaviour. Businesses are likely to reposition themselves to focus on 'farming' subsidies. Lobbying is extremely intense in energy, and Britain's lobbying industry is the third largest in the world. In the new world of central planning and subsidies, lobbying will become only more valuable for companies. Reciprocally, politicians are becoming more willing to openly court financial institutions. In October 2024 the Labour government arranged an 'investment summit' for financiers, with ministers cosying up to the likes of Larry Fink of BlackRock.[22]

Maybe Labour pulls it off: infrastructure gets built on time and within budget, bills fall, growth returns. Or perhaps various headwinds scupper the best-laid plans being concocted by the National Energy System Operator and Mission Control. In September 2024 the head of Mission Control argued that 'making a plan is our central organising principle'. But making the plan is the easy bit. The government may discover (as the Soviets did) that the more all-encompassing the plan, the more the planning process cannot accommodate informational lags and omissions (no matter how good your computers are). This has already started to happen, with the NESO having to rework various interlocking plans to reflect new policies. Only a few months after the 2030 plan was produced it had to be updated on account of using 'out of date' assumptions.[23] The National Energy System Operator conceded that the Clean Power 2030 plan does not have *any* room for error. 'Several elements must deliver at the limit of what is feasible', and 'failure in any single area – generation, flexibility, networks – will lead to failure overall'. By June 2025 it was clear that some of the transmission grid projects were already delayed and that system costs could increase dramatically as a result.[24]

Labour force and equipment shortages could cause delays and cost overruns. It is not just the electricity sector that is undertaking a massive construction programme. After decades of underinvestment there are similar programmes in housing, airports, water, prisons, rail and road. Not since the 1950s and 1960s has the country seen such a steep increase in infrastructure spending across multiple sectors simultaneously. In electricity, Britain is dependent on imports for most of the physical equipment required. A government report highlighted very significant risks in offshore wind, electricity transmission and distribution, and solar. The severity of these potential bottlenecks is concerning. Demand could outstrip supply in multiple categories of equipment and services for the next five to ten years. In some cases, the imbalances are enormous.[25]

The situation is particularly bad in electricity networks. In April 2025 one of the major transmission projects needed to deliver the 'Clean Power 2030' plan was delayed by sixteen months because of supply chain issues. The British energy system is highly unbundled, which means that companies are competing for the same equipment, pushing up prices. Onshoring supply chains might help in the long run but would take time to develop and would likely increase costs in the medium term.[26]

Managing these supply chain constraints while holding down bills will be very challenging. In the run-up to the 2024 election, Labour promised that its flagship energy policy, GB Energy, would reduce bills by £300. This is only the latest promise. For at least a decade British citizens have been told that the energy transition is a win-win; emissions and bills would fall because renewables are cheaper than fossil fuels. That has not happened. The reasons why are debated ad nauseam. For end consumers the reasons are irrelevant. Support for decarbonisation is still high in Britain compared to other countries, but polling shows that support significantly falls if there is a financial penalty.

Concerningly, bills could increase in the near to medium term. Britain is betting heavily on offshore wind, which has stopped getting cheaper and whose cost has actually started to ratchet up. Network costs are likely to increase dramatically. Ironically, gas network costs are also set to increase, even though demand for gas is falling, due to the age and condition of the network and the need to pay back investors the accrued value of the assets.[27] The cost of balancing the system and constraint costs is also likely to increase. If subsidies for carbon capture and storage, nuclear, large industrial users and hydrogen continue to be paid from end customer bills, this could also put more upward pressure on bills. There should be cost savings from switching from gas-fired generation to renewables, but this may not be enough to offset cost increases elsewhere.

A nightmare scenario is one where bills remain high and infrastructure projects fail to deliver on time and within budget. Against a backdrop of continued economic malaise, citizens will undoubtedly ask, what is the point? Currently, roughly half of the population thinks net zero should be a top priority for government, but 63 per cent think that it will be too difficult to achieve.[28]

Across Europe there was a backlash against decarbonisation policies in 2023 and 2024 with many anti–net zero parties gaining votes in elections. In the US, Donald Trump has committed to an energy policy of 'Drill Baby Drill'. Trying to predict developments in British politics would be foolish, given the volatility in recent years, but the politics of energy are certainly changing. Nigel Farage's Reform party has already committed to scrapping net zero. The Conservative leader Kemi Badenoch has said that the target is 'impossible' and cannot be achieved 'without a serious drop in our living standards or bankrupting us'. Perhaps Labour will in response bow to the headwinds and walk back on some of its targets.

Mutualised energy

The 'Central Return Generating Board' scenario is the path Britain is currently on. Energy is an industry that strongly exhibits path dependency: the past constrains the present and future. This is true in both a technological sense and an institutional sense; policies, rules and regulations, and institutions tend to persist and shape what can be created. You can think of the energy system as being like a train on a set of tracks. In the 1990s a set of decisions was made that have sent us down a particular path. To change direction will require a dramatic upheaval to switch the system over to a new set of tracks – a state-directed reset like the ones in the 1920s, 1940s and the 1980s.[29]

The first step in the journey is to give up the delusion that Britain's institutional framework in energy is 'supreme' or 'world-beating'. Regulatory complexity is not something to be admired. Many countries around the world have embraced and subsequently unwound aspects of privatisation. We can learn from the countries that we once lectured. For example, in 2025 Mexico halted the long march of privatisation it had been on since the 1990s. The government implemented major reforms that stabilised the role of state-owned enterprises, replaced independent with direct governmental regulation and established a new hierarchy of public planning.[30]

A related requirement is accepting that we cannot retreat to older incarnations of the energy system. We cannot go back down the rabbit hole of 1990s-style privatisation. The twin challenges of decarbonisation and energy security have inevitably drawn the state deeper into energy. Energy prices are 'systemically significant', with knock-on impacts across the economy. It is naïve to imagine that we can reverse this. Equally, a 1940s-style nationalisation of the entire energy industry is untenable. Today there aren't the same economies of scale as in the coal- and nuclear-dominated world of the CEGB. There are areas of the system where competition between private firms is functional if not fully effective (in retail, EV charging, household solar and batteries, and in some parts of generation).

How might we go about developing a new system? One approach is incrementalism. Making a narrow series of small tweaks here and there, with the ambition of scaling these up gradually. This often underdelivers, with interminable pilots and consultations petering out. It will probably only make things worse. The addition of new policies, organisations and institutions will just make the energy system more complex. Another approach is 'big bang' change: making broad wholesale change in one move. This usually involves a long 'design phase' (with all manner of organisations consulted), followed by an 'implementation phase' dogged by delays. In fact, Britain has been trying both approaches in parallel since the late 2000s. It is not working.

An alternative is a stepwise approach: making a series of widespread changes to whole parts of the system in stages, or 'crossing the river by touching the stones', in the words of the Chinese politician Deng Xiaoping.[31] This approach builds off what exists and does not require a fully defined view of the end state.

Privatisation was the result of stepwise change. Stephen Littlechild's famous essay 'Ten Steps to Denationalisation' outlined a series of major changes in several areas that would put Britain on a trajectory to a new system. But the principles of privatisation were figured out along the journey. Gas went first, and mistakes were made. The system architects learned from these. By the time electricity privatisation occurred the model had been refined. The following steps to deprivatisation could be taken in parallel or sequentially.

Step 1: Dismantle the regulatory state

The state is the only entity that can undertake the kind of comprehensive rewiring of energy capitalism that is required. This must begin with an act of self-medication. The state should take a sledgehammer to the institutions that are incentivised to keep the system complicated. One simple reform would be to replace the 'outcomes-based' regulation of networks with a simple cap on profits. This would dramatically reduce the workload (and headcount) of Ofgem.

A more significant reform would be to dissolve the strange triangular relationship between DESNZ, the NESO and Ofgem. The current arrangement creates what Dan Davies calls 'accountability sinks': the delegation of decision-making to rulebooks and the breakdown of feedback loops that expose the rule-makers to the consequences of their decisions.[32] These accountability sinks allow each member of the triumvirate to pass the buck to the other two. Consolidating these institutions into a new Ministry for Fuel and Power and a slimmed-down NESO (focused on balancing the system) would make it easier to implement large-scale change. It would reduce confusion, duplication and complexity. It would also prevent companies playing each organisation off against the other.

Step 2: Establish public corporations

New forms of ownership could emerge with the institutional ground cleared. Britain must give up on its obsession with private ownership. Markets, competition and prices are not inextricably bound to private ownership. The energy system in the US is proof. It has the longest tradition of private ownership, but competition is limited and markets are partial. There are whole regions of the US South and Northwest dominated by vertically integrated monopolies in private hands.

State ownership in some parts of the system is entirely compatible with promoting markets and competition. The Nordic countries embraced competition in generation and retail soon after Britain in the 1990s, but have retained widespread public ownership in generation, networks and even retail. More recently, the Chinese energy system is demonstrating at a massive scale that public ownership and markets are compatible.

Renewables, nuclear and networks are highly capital-intensive. The state can borrow money at a lower rate than private companies, and this will translate into lower bills. The main reason companies were given responsibility for energy infrastructure from the 1980s was an ideological belief that private firms were better at allocating capital than the state. Even if this were true, it is of no relevance for today's zombie system, in which the state dictates where companies should allocate capital. Indeed, many within the renewable industry claim they have no choice over where to locate their projects.

It is a common misconception that public ownership means giving the civil service responsibility for running companies. In

British history the more common form of public ownership was the public corporation. This model was a pillar of the interwar and post-war energy systems. Public corporations were owned by the state but were highly independent commercial organisations that were granted the autonomy to build infrastructure at scale and pace. Another advantage to this model is that it combines public accountability with private financing. The Central Electricity Board raised all the capital needed to build the first National Grid on its own. Although it had the option of a Treasury guarantee, it was never actually used. In 1900, municipal bonds for gas, electricity and water companies were 50 per cent of the market for government debt. Today that figure is just 4.7 per cent.

Creating public corporations that directly raise capital would minimise the impact on central government borrowing. It would also ensure that the same organisations are fully responsible for both financing and building infrastructure. This reform would merely bring Britain into line with other European countries, which have many public corporations that issue debt for specific projects and are paid back by market sources of revenue, not tax. The liabilities of government-controlled entities outside general government as a percentage of GDP are 86.5 per cent in Germany, 79.5 per cent in the Netherlands and 68 per cent in France. The figure is just 2.2 per cent in Great Britain.[33]

Public ownership is a mechanism for reducing bills. Continuing to fund the energy transition through customer bills is regressive. Moving various policy costs and levies from electricity bills to general taxation is one lever. A second is to have the state fund some infrastructure from a combination of bills and general taxation, as it did from the 1950s to 1970s. This would also make the energy system fairer, with the rich paying a higher share, bringing energy more into line with how we fund roads, hospitals, schools and the military.

Public ownership should be applied only to parts of the industry that meet some or all of the following conditions: areas that are capital-intensive, monopolistic, dependent on subsidies and with wider externalities.

The first candidate for nationalisation would be the existing fleet of gas-fired generators. These need to be kept operational as a 'strategic reserve', but this will not be commercially viable without perpetual subsidies (in the form of capacity market payments) or allowing excessively high prices at times of system stress. Over the last decade, bill payers have paid £12.5 billion in capacity payments to fossil fuel generators. On top of this, the current owners hike prices when the electricity system supply is tight. On 8 January 2025, the electricity system was close to catastrophe. The system operator had to pay VPI's Rye House plant £5,750 per MWh, while Uniper's Connah Quay facility demanded £2,900 per MWh. At the time the actual cost of gas was around £40 per MWh. VPI is an arm of Vitol, one of the most profitable trading companies in the world. It generated staggering annual net profits averaging more than $12 billion over the past three years.[34] Ironically, some of these power stations are already state-owned, just not by the British state. Uniper (German), ESB (Irish) and Equinor (Norwegian) are fully or partly nationalised entities that own gas power stations in Britain.

The state should take these assets into full or partial state ownership, paying the owners a fair price that reflects the capital they have invested to date. This would reduce bills by ending the capacity payments. If, as the mantra goes, the problem with Britain's power system is that gas sets the electricity price more than 90 per cent of the time, the state can then intervene to control the price of generating from gas. The system operator (NESO) would be able to call on the generators when required, but at cost.[35]

The gas networks have served Britain well, but to decarbonise how we heat our homes these networks must be wound down. This is not as simple as just switching off the gas. For safety reasons the networks must be properly decommissioned.

Some form of state ownership is essential to ensure a cost-effective, managed decline and decommissioning programme. Without this intervention, private companies will continue to peddle untested technologies, like hydrogen for heating, to protect the value of their existing asset base. The state is going to end up paying the bill for the decommissioning of these networks (as was the case with nuclear waste), so it might as well get involved now.

Nationalising the electricity networks would simply bring Great Britain into line with most countries in the world. This would reduce the cost of capital for one of the most capital-intensive parts of the system, resulting in lower bills. Building more electricity network capacity will inevitably have a significant impact on Britain's landscape and environment. Public ownership would likely increase social and democratic consent for new infrastructure, as communities would be less suspicious that the profit motive was dictating the design of projects. Private ownership is only effective where there is competition. Electricity transmission networks are pure natural monopolies, and Ofgem has given up on any meaningful forms of competition. Over the last twelve years, every attempt at introducing competition for onshore transmission has been blocked by fear that it would negatively impact the incumbent networks. Ironically, state ownership would likely enable more competition because the state could auction off the construction and operation of projects without fear of blowback from the incumbents. A good use-case to start to introduce competition would be connections to the grid for data centres.

Electricity generation is the largest part of the industry in terms of asset value and annual investment. The state is already taking an ownership stake in new nuclear plants and is deeply involved in dictating the mix of technologies through subsidies. Rather than providing perpetual subsidies to pad private sector returns, the state could simply take an ownership stake, lowering the required rate of return.

Expanding state ownership to the entirety of generation would be politically unfeasible and unwarranted where there is meaningful competition (for example, in batteries, some solar and some wind). A more targeted approach would be for the state to take an equity stake plus own and operate specific renewable projects, mainly offshore wind and long-duration energy storage. In GB Energy and the Welsh publicly owned developer Trydan Gwyrdd Cymru the state has the institutional vehicles it needs. This would make the state a more informed agent when awarding subsidies to other companies, as it would have a yardstick to measure them against, without all the asymmetries of information that come from arm's-length regulation.

It is a common misconception that taking assets into public ownership would inevitably be expensive. If valuation of the assets is based on the book value (total assets minus total liabilities), then the state would spend £1 to buy an asset worth £1. If the valuation is based on the enterprise value of a company (what the market thinks it is worth), the price tag will be greater than the book value. However, in today's zombie system the enterprise value of many companies is based on business models totally dependent on state subsidies. The state controls the enterprise value indirectly and thus has significant negotiating power. The upfront cost of paying the current owners and investors a fair price for their assets would be somewhat offset by an enduring lower level of subsidies and a lower overall energy system cost.

Bringing energy infrastructure into state ownership offers an intangible value: sovereign control. Nationalisation has become increasingly normalised in recent years, exemplified by the German state acquiring Uniper in 2022 and the French state's buy-back of the remaining stake in EDF the same year. In 2025 the US federal government bought a 10 per cent stake in Intel on the basis that computer chips are of vital national importance. In a climate of rising geopolitical tension and increased military expenditure, direct control over energy infrastructure could become a critical pillar of national defence.

Resilience and optionality necessitate a degree of redundancy. Such safety buffers carry a cost that under a private model would inevitably push up consumer bills. Consequently, the state is best positioned to manage assets that may not be commercially viable due to infrequent use – like gas storage or gas-fired power stations.

Step 3: Decentralise

Throughout this book I have tried to show that technology and political economy are bound together in a dialectical relationship. From the 1920s to the early 2000s the techno-economics of the energy system exhibited strong economies of scale. In electricity, the system was built around large coal and nuclear power plants connected by high-voltage electricity networks. This centralised system went hand in hand with large national-level institutions like the Central Electricity Board and the Central Electricity Generating Board.

Over the last decade the technological building blocks of the system have changed. With solar and onshore wind, electricity generation has dispersed, with more electricity being generated and self-consumed by households and businesses or fed into the lower-voltage distribution system. Improvements in battery technology make it easier than ever to store electricity. When combined, these technologies should allow Britain to move electricity production and consumption closer together in space and time.

The falling cost of solar, onshore wind and battery equipment creates an opportunity to broaden the ownership of energy assets. This would give households, cooperatives and local authorities the means of electricity production. Citizens would retain more of the profits that currently go to executives and investors. Community energy schemes are already starting to flourish, with around 500 in existence today. Local authorities could take ownership stakes in these schemes. Surveys show that local support for energy infrastructure increases when projects are community as opposed to privately owned. With the right funding and some imagination this movement can grow. There is of course historical precedent: the 'golden age of municipal energy' in the early twentieth century.

Citizens will not support decarbonisation unless they feel that it improves their lives in the near term. Successive governments have prioritised producers over consumers, capital over citizens. The purpose of the energy system should not be to build wind farms, it should be to provide citizens with heat, light and motion. For many end consumers, a light bulb powered by wind is no different to a light bulb powered by gas – the only thing that matters is the price of the electricity input.

The electrification of demand, mainly for transport and heat, benefits consumers in a more immediate way; electric vehicles and heat pumps are cheaper to run than internal combustion engine vehicles and boilers because they are more efficient (although the benefits are entirely dependent on the price of electricity relative to fossil fuels). A huge amount of energy is lost in the process of burning things. Electrification would also reduce Britain's severe and worsening dependence on imported oil and gas.[36]

Policy needs to shift focus from subsidising producers to citizens. The post-war generation benefited from subsidised electricity and the gas conversion programme, which transformed homes with new appliances and central heating. It is time for this generation to undertake a similar effort, with the state paying a much higher share of the cost for the mass deployment of low-carbon technology in every home and business.

Decentralisation of physical infrastructure is complementary to decentralisation of decision-making. Today most of the population has no say in energy policy, leading to an absurd situation where unelected bureaucrats can effectively take decisions to sign the country up to spending hundreds of billions without a vote being cast. Polling indicates that half of people feel that the energy transition is happening to them and that nearly 70 per cent expect it to increase their cost of living in the short term.[37]

This will only lead to a popular backlash, as is happening in Europe and the US. It is also bad planning. As Hayek so presciently realised, the vanity of central planners leads them to believe they possess all relevant information. Decentralisation of planning to many separate persons and organisations is the only way to harness that society 'knows' far more than the central planner ever can. Prices and markets are just one potential mechanism for decentralisation.[38] Creating community- and municipal-owned firms is another. Britain is one of the most centralised states in the world. Local authorities have been decimated over the last thirty years and now have a negligible tax base and limited influence over decarbonisation other than the ability to obstruct. As is common in Europe, local authorities could be given a share in the ownership of the electricity generation assets, electricity and gas networks and heat networks. This would give councils a steady income stream and an incentive to drive decarbonisation.

Step 4: Use markets

Prices are an effective way to send signals to consumers and their devices when the wind is blowing, the sun is shining or the electricity grid is congested. With growing renewable penetration there will be times in the day when prices are negative, meaning consumers would be paid to use electricity. To ensure that prices reflect the true cost of electricity in each region, Britain should follow other countries and adopt something called 'locational marginal pricing'.

With locational marginal pricing we would stop paying wind farms to turn off, as they would have to sell their power at a lower price to reflect local demand. Locational pricing is especially important to unlock one of the most important weapons in Britain's arsenal: demand-side flexibility. With a relatively modest improvement in demand-side flexibility, society would waste less renewable power and electricity prices would be less volatile. In the long run an entirely new approach will be required. In an electricity system where renewables dominate, the marginal cost of electricity will be close to zero. In this world, marginal cost-based pricing will make little sense. It would be simpler to move renewables onto a fixed-return-based model.[39]

The 'energy transition' is taking place at the same time as another revolution, digitalisation. For 150 years the electricity system was balanced by toggling up and down fossil fuel power stations. The alternative is to flexibly shift around demand. Before the digital revolution this was very hard to do. With sensors, algorithms and smart devices it has never been easier. Electric vehicles, heat pumps and thermal storage technologies can 'follow the wind', operating as giant sponges for green electrons. This will require citizens to be able to trust the organisations controlling devices.

During Britain's energy crisis, more than 2 million businesses and households signed up to the 'demand flexibility service' to help avoid turning on coal plants at times of grid stress. Surveys show that participants were motivated by a sense of social responsibility as much as financial reward. This spirit of community can be harnessed.

What name should we give the new energy system that these steps would lead to? It is neither a nationalised nor a privatised system. These old terms won't do. I propose the term 'mutualised energy'. This term encapsulates the principle that the new system would be built around a set of mutually beneficial relationships between capital, citizens and the state. The new system would also be built around decentralisation of ownership and decision-making. Mutuals, or cooperatives, are a type of economic organisation that are neither private sector firms nor the state. They combine the benefits of not-for-profit collective ownership with variation and competition. In the Victorian period thousands of working class 'mutual' organisations blossomed – retail cooperatives, friendly societies, building societies and working men's clubs – to tackle the challenges that sprang from industrialisation. We can take inspiration and rebuild the energy system around the principles of mutualism.

It is time for Britain to break free from the relentless spiral it is in. We must shut down the zombie system. Today we have a centralised energy system organised around planning and private ownership, with the overarching objective of generating returns for capital. We need mutualised energy: a decentralised system organised around public ownership and prices that serves the citizens of Britain.

Notes

Introduction

1. Brett Christophers, *The Price Is Wrong: Why Capitalism Won't Save the Planet* (Verso, 2024).
2. Marc Bloch, *The Historian's Craft* (Vintage, 1953), p. 66.
3. David Parker, *The Official History of Privatisation*, vol. 2, *Popular Capitalism, 1987–1997* (Routledge, 2012), pp. 504–14.
4. National Gas Transmission, *Gas Winter Outlook, 2021/22* (National Grid House, 2021).
5. Gregor Semieniuk et al., 'Distributional Implications and Share Ownership of Record Oil and Gas Profits', PERI Working Paper, November 2024.
6. For example, Vaclav Smil, *Energy Transitions: History, Requirements, Prospects* (Praeger, 2010); Timothy Mitchell, *Carbon Democracy: Political Power in the Age of Oil* (Verso, 2013); Andreas Malm, *Fossil Capital: The Rise of Steam Power and the Roots of Global Warming* (Verso, 2016).
7. Chris Freedman, *As Time Goes By: From the Industrial Revolutions to the Information Revolution* (Oxford University Press, 2002); Nicholas Stern, *Why Are We Waiting? The Logic, Urgency, and Promise of Tackling Climate Change* (MIT Press, 2015), pp. 33–7.
8. W. Brian Arthur, *The Nature of Technology: What It Is and How It Evolves* (Penguin, 2010).
9. Jean-Baptiste Fressoz, *More and More and More: An All-Consuming History of Energy* (Allen Lane, 2024); Smil, *Energy Transitions*, pp. 63–5; Roger Fouquet, 'Historical Energy Transitions: Speed, Prices and System Transformation', *Energy Research and Social Science* 22 (December 2016), pp. 7–12.
10. Carlota Perez, *Technological Revolutions and Financial Capital: The Dynamics of Bubbles and Golden Ages* (Edward Elgar, 2003).

11. Joseph Schumpeter, *Capitalism, Socialism and Democracy* (HarperCollins, 1950), p. 87.
12. Adapted from James Foreman-Peck and Robert Millward, *Public and Private Ownership of British Industry 1820–1990* (Clarendon, 1994).
13. Christopher Hinton and William Holford, 'Power Production and Transmission in the Countryside: Preserving Amenities', *Journal of the Royal Society of Arts* 108, no. 5043 (February 1960), p. 186.
14. Elizabeth Chatterjee, 'Underpowered: Electricity Policy and the State in India, 1991–2014', DPhil thesis (Oxford University, 2015).
15. Written in summer 2025.
16. Mark Fisher, *Capitalist Realism: Is There No Alternative?* (Zero Books, 2022).
17. James C. Scott, *Against the Grain: A Deep History of the Earliest States* (Yale University Press, 2017), pp. 3–5.
18. Ben Southwood, Samuel Hughes and Sam Bowman, 'Foundations: Why Britain Has Stagnated', ukfoundations.co.uk, 2024; Torsten Bell, *Great Britain? How We Get Our Future Back* (Bodley Head, 2024), p. 16.
19. 'Volume Index Capital Services (VICS), Annual, UK', Office for National Statistics, 7 November 2024, ons.gov.uk; 'Annual Gross Fixed Capital Formation by Industry and Asset: 1997 to 2023', Office for National Statistics, 1 November 2024, ons.gov.uk.
20. Sam Freedman, *Failed State: Why Nothing Works and How We Fix It* (Pan Macmillan, 2024); Abby Innes, *Late Soviet Britain: Why Materialist Utopias Fail* (Cambridge University Press, 2023).
21. Mariana Mazzucato, *The Entrepreneurial State: Debunking Public vs. Private Sector Myths* (Anthem, 2013).
22. Hannah Richie, *Not the End of the World: How We Can Be the First Generation to Build a Sustainable Planet* (Chatto & Windus, 2024); Christina Figueres and Tom Rivett-Carnac, *The Future We Choose: The Stubborn Optimist's Guide to the Climate Crisis* (Manilla Press, 2020); Chris Goodhall, *Possible: Ways to Net Zero* (Profile, 2024); Akshat Rathi, *Climate Capitalism: Winning the Global Race to Zero Emissions* (John Murray, 2023).
23. Naomi Klein, *This Changes Everything: Capitalism vs the Climate* (Penguin, 2015); Matt Huber and Leigh Phillips, 'Kohei Saito's "Start from Scratch" Degrowth Communism', *Jacobin*, 9 March 2024; Andreas Malm, *How to Blow Up a Pipeline* (Verso, 2021).
24. International Energy Agency, *Renewables 2024: Analysis and Forecast to 2030* (IEA, 2024), p. 70.

25. Kohei Saito, *Slow Down: The Degrowth Manifesto* (Astra House, 2024).
26. Aaron Bastani, *Fully Automated Luxury Communism* (Verso, 2019).
27. Using the Bank of England's GDP deflator method.

1. Localised Energy, 1810–1920

1. Russell Thomas, *A History of the Gas Industry in London* (National Grid House, 2025); Leslie Tomory, *Progressive Enlightenment: The Origins of the Gaslight Industry, 1780–1820* (MIT Press, 2012).
2. R. Fouquet, 'Divergences in Long Run Trends in the Prices of Energy and Energy Services', *Review of Environmental Economics and Policy* 5, no. 2 (Summer 2011), pp. 196–218.
3. Danny Lawrence and Helen Lawrence, *Growing Up with Gas: A History of the Gas Industry* (Brewin Books, 2023), p. 38; *Imperial Continental Gas Association, 1824–1974* (London, 1974); Trevor Williams, *A History of the British Gas Industry* (Oxford University Press, 1981), p. 10.
4. Electricity Council, *Electricity Supply in the United Kingdom: A Chronology – From the Beginnings of the Industry to 31 December 1985*, 4th ed. (Electricity Council, 1987), pp. 16–17.
5. M. A. C. Horne, 'London Area Power Supply: A Survey of London's Electric Lighting and Power Stations', Metadyne, 2012, metadyne.co.uk; Thomas Hughes, *Networks of Power: Electrification in Western Society, 1880–1930* (Johns Hopkins University Press, 1983), pp. 50–5.
6. I. C. R. Byatt, 'The British Electrical Industry, 1875–1914', DPhil thesis (Oxford University, 1962).
7. G. T. Bloomfield, 'Yorkshire Electricity Board Area', British Electricity History, p. 13, britelechist.uoguelph.ca; Thomas Parker Hughes, 'British Electrical Industry Lag: 1882–1888', *Technology and Culture* 3, no. 1 (Winter 1962), pp. 27–44; Hughes, *Networks of Power*, pp. 77, 127–9; R. H. Parsons, *The Early Days of the Power Station Industry* (Cambridge, 1940), pp. 136–7.
8. P. Strange, 'Early Electricity Supply in Britain: Chesterfield and Godalming', *Proceedings of the Institution of Electrical Engineers* 126, no. 9 (1979); Brian Bowers, *A History of Electric Light and Power* (Peter Peregrinus, 1982); John F. Wasik, *The Merchant of Power: Sam Insull, Thomas Edison, and the Creation of the*

Modern Metropolis (St. Martin's Griffin, 2008); Hughes, *Networks of Power*, p. 211.

9. Parsons, *Early Days of the Power Station Industry*, pp. 52–65, 95, 138–9; G. T. Bloomfield, 'The North of Scotland Hydro-Electric Board Area', British Electricity History, p. 8, britelechist.uoguelph.ca.
10. Parsons, *Early Days of the Power Station Industry*, pp. 21–3; John F. Wilson, 'Ferranti, Sebastian Ziani de (1864–1930)', *Oxford Dictionary of National Biography*, 23 September 2004, oxforddnb.com; Hughes, *Networks of Power*, pp. 96–8, 238–42; Electricity Council, *Electricity Supply*, pp. 5–8.
11. Byatt, 'British Electrical Industry', p. 60.
12. Hughes, *Networks of Power*, pp. 29–35; Parsons, *Early Days of the Power Station Industry*, pp. 105, 185.
13. Everard Stirling, *The History of the Gas Light and Coke Company, 1812–1949* (A. & C. Black, 1992).
14. Williams, *History of the British Gas Industry*, p. 41.
15. Edwin Chadwick, 'Results of Different Principles of Legislation and Administration in Europe; of Competition for the Field, as Compared with Competition Within the Field, of Service', *Journal of the Statistical Society of London* 22, no. 3 (September 1859), pp. 381–420.
16. James Foreman-Peck and Robert Millward, *Public and Private Ownership of British Industry 1820–1990* (Clarendon, 1994), p. 4.
17. Lawrence and Lawrence, *Growing Up with Gas*, p. 56.
18. Derek Matthews, 'Laissez-Faire and the London Gas Industry in the Nineteenth Century: Another Look', *Economic History Review* 29, no. 2 (May 1986), pp. 244–56.
19. Ibid., p. 260.
20. Foreman-Peck and Millward, *Public and Private Ownership*.
21. J. W. Spark, 'Western Centre: Chairman's Address: "The Legislature and the Electricity Supply Industry"', *Journal of the Institution of Electrical Engineers* 80, no. 481 (1937), p. 26.
22. Foreman-Peck and Millward, *Public and Private Ownership*, p. 164; Robert Millward, *Private and Public Enterprise in Europe: Energy, Telecommunications and Transport, 1830–1990* (Cambridge University Press, 2005), pp. 18, 77–8.
23. Foreman-Peck and Millward, *Public and Private Ownership*, pp. 164–7.
24. John Stuart Mill, 'Public Agency v. Trading Companies: The Economical and Administrative Principles of Water-Supply for the Metropolis', 1 January 1851, available at jstor.org.

25. Tom Crewe, 'The Strange Death of Municipal England', *London Review of Books* 38, no. 24 (15 December 2016).
26. Millward, *Private and Public Enterprise*, pp. 8–9.
27. Foreman-Peck and Millward, *Public and Private Ownership*, pp. 178–89; Orren C. Hormell, 'Ownership and Regulation of Electric Utilities in Great Britain', *Annals of the American Academy of Political and Social Science* 159 (January 1932).
28. Avner Offer, *Property and Politics, 1870–1914: Landownership, Law and Urban Development in England* (Cambridge University Press, 1981), pp. 236–7.
29. C. Ashmore Baker, *Public Versus Private Electricity Supply* (Fabian Society, 1913).
30. Armen Alchian, 'Some Economics of Property Rights', *Il politico* 30, no. 4 (December 1965), pp. 816–29.
31. Eugene Fama, 'Agency Problems and the Theory of the Firm', *Journal of Political Economy* 88, no. 2 (April 1980), pp. 288–307.
32. Foreman-Peck and Millward, *Public and Private Ownership*, pp. 128, 137; Emile Garcke (ed.), *Manual of Electrical Undertakings and Directory of Officials*, vol. 23, *1919–1920* (Electrical Press, 1920), pp. 4–5.
33. Garcke, *Manual of Electrical Undertakings*, p. 9.
34. Baker, *Public Versus Private.*
35. Foreman-Peck and Millward, *Public and Private Ownership*, pp. 128–39.
36. Carlota Perez, *Technological Revolutions and Financial Capital: The Dynamics of Bubbles and Golden Ages* (Edward Elgar, 2003).
37. Fouquet, 'Divergences in Long Run Trends'.
38. Jeremy Paxman, *Black Gold: The History of How Coal Made Britain* (William Collins, 2021), p. 259.
39. G. T. Bloomfield, 'The North Eastern Electricity Board Area', British Electricity History, p. 12, britelechist.uoguelph.ca.
40. Marianna Dudley, *Electric Wind: An Energy History of Modern Britain* (Manchester University Press, 2025).
41. Leslie Hannah, *Electricity Before Nationalisation: A Study of the Development of the Electricity Supply Industry in Britain to 1948* (Johns Hopkins University Press, 1979), pp. 400–30.
42. Charles Klapper, *The Golden Age of Tramways* (Routledge and Kegan Paul, 1962); G. T. Bloomfield, British Electricity History, data from all volumes, britelechist.uoguelph.ca.
43. Williams, *History of the British Gas Industry*, pp. 68–9; Matthews, 'Laissez-Faire and the London Gas Industry', pp. 968–75.

44. Millward, *Private and Public Enterprise*, p. 36.
45. Roger Fouquet, 'The Demand for Environmental Quality in Driving Transitions to Low-Polluting Energy Sources', *Energy Policy* 50 (November 2021), pp. 138–49.
46. Williams, *History of the British Gas Industry*, pp. 68–9.
47. Roger Fouquet, National Infrastructure Commission Historic Energy Dataset, nic.org.uk.
48. Millward, *Private and Public Enterprise*, pp. 33–4, 78.
49. Georg Klingenberg, 'Electricity Supply of Large Cities', *Electrician* 72 (1914); Hughes, *Networks of Power*, pp. 197, 228, 258.
50. Hannah, *Electricity Before Nationalisation*, p. 39.
51. Hughes, *Networks of Power*, pp. 104–5.
52. Millward, *Private and Public Enterprise*, pp. 122–5.
53. Hughes, *Networks of Power*, pp. 214–17.
54. G. T. Bloomfield, 'London', British Electricity History, pp. 23–4, britelechist.uoguelph.ca; Hughes, *Networks of Power*, pp. 231–2, 258; Hannah, *Electricity Before Nationalisation*, pp. 45–50.
55. Tom McGovern and Tom McLean, 'The Genesis of the Electricity Supply Industry in Britain: A Case Study of NESCo from 1889 to 1914', *Business History* 59, no. 5 (2017), pp. 667–89; Hughes, *Networks of Power*, p. 250.
56. Hughes, *Networks of Power*, pp. 444–60.
57. McGovern and McLean, 'Genesis of the Electricity Supply Industry'.
58. Foreman-Peck and Millward, *Public and Private Ownership*: Williams, *History of the British Gas Industry*, pp. 19–27.
59. Hughes, *Networks of Power*, pp. 227–61.
60. G. T. Bloomfield, 'The East Midlands Electricity Board Area', British Electricity History, pp. 5–7, britelechist.uoguelph.ca.
61. Arnold Gridley and Arnold Human, 'Electric Power Supply During the Great War', *Journal of the Institution of Electrical Engineers* 57 (1919).
62. Hannah, *Electricity Before Nationalisation*, pp. 55–9.
63. Bloomfield, 'East Midlands'; G. T. Bloomfield, 'The South Western Electricity Board Area', British Electricity History, britelechist.uoguelph.ca; Julie Cohn, 'When the Grid Was the Grid: The History of North America's Brief Coast-to-Coast Interconnected Machine', *Proceedings of the IEEE* 107, no. 1 (January 2019), pp. 232–43.
64. Electric Power Supply Committee, *Report of the Committee Appointed by the Board of Trade to Consider the Question of Electric Power Supply* (HM Stationery Office, 1918).

65. Hughes, *Networks of Power*, p. 319.
66. Hannah, *Electricity Before Nationalisation*, p. 63.
67. Parsons, *Early Days of the Power Station Industry*, pp. 197–200.
68. Hannah, *Electricity Before Nationalisation*, pp. 71–3.

2. Rationalised Energy, 1920–1945

1. J. M. Keynes, *The Economic Consequences of the Peace* (Harcourt, Brace & Howe, 1920), pp. 253–4.
2. Leslie Hannah, 'A Pioneer of Public Enterprise: The Central Electricity Board and the National Grid, 1927–1940', in Barry Supple (ed.), *Essays in British Business History* (Clarendon, 1977); Robert Millward, *Private and Public Enterprise in Europe: Energy, Telecommunications and Transport, 1830–1990* (Cambridge University Press, 2005), p. 96.
3. Leslie Hannah, *Electricity Before Nationalisation: A Study of the Development of the Electricity Supply Industry in Britain to 1948* (Johns Hopkins University Press, 1979), p. 88; G. T. Bloomfield, British Electricity History, all volumes, britelechist.uoguelph.ca.
4. Ronald Coase, 'Review of *The British Gas Industry: An Economic Study*, by Philip Chandler', *Economic Journal* 48, no. 192 (1938), pp. 727–8; Trevor Williams, *A History of the British Gas Industry* (Oxford University Press, 1981), p. 69; Robert Millward and John Singleton (eds), *The Political Economy of Nationalisation in Britain, 1920–1950* (Cambridge University Press, 2010), p. 147.
5. Danny Lawrence and Helen Lawrence, *Growing Up with Gas: A History of the Gas Industry* (Brewin Books, 2023), p. 164; Williams, *History of the British Gas Industry*, p. 73; Coase, 'Review of *The British Gas Industry*', p. 728.
6. Millward and Singleton, *Political Economy of Nationalisation*, pp. 144–63.
7. Bloomfield, British Electricity History.
8. G. T. Bloomfield, 'London: Electricity Hub of Britain', British Electricity History, p. 15, britelechist.uoguelph.ca.
9. Hannah, *Electricity Before Nationalisation*, pp. 226–7.
10. Thomas Hughes, *Networks of Power: Electrification in Western Society, 1830–1930* (Johns Hopkins University Press, 1983), p. 402; Hannah, *Electricity Before Nationalisation*, p. 81; Political and Economic Planning, *Report on the Supply of Electricity in Great Britain* (PEP, 1936), pp. 140–1.
11. Hannah, *Electricity Before Nationalisation*, pp. 88–90.

12. Rob Cochrane, *Power to the People: The Story of the National Grid* (Littlehampton, 1985), p. 13.
13. Nicholas Crafts, *Forging Ahead, Falling Behind and Fighting Back: British Economic Growth from the Industrial Revolution to the Financial Crisis* (Cambridge University Press, 2018), pp. 37–40; Millward and Singleton, *Political Economy of Nationalisation*, p. 6.
14. Hughes, *Networks of Power*, pp. 350–62; Hannah, *Electricity Before Nationalisation*, p. 99.
15. John Sheail, *Power in Trust: Environmental History of the Central Electricity Generating Board* (Clarendon, 1991), pp. 10–15.
16. Ministry of Transport, *Report of the Committee Appointed to Review the National Problem of the Supply of Electrical Energy* (HM Stationery Office, 1926).
17. Hughes, *Networks of Power*; Hannah, *Electricity Before Nationalisation*; Cochrane, *Power to the People*.
18. Central Electricity Board (CEB), Annual Reports, 1927–1947, British Library, London.
19. James Foreman-Peck and Robert Millward, *Public and Private Ownership of British Industry 1820–1990* (Clarendon, 1994).
20. CEB Annual Report, 1947.
21. James Foreman-Peck and Michael Waterson, 'The Comparative Efficiency of Public and Private Enterprise in Britain: Electricity Generation Between the World Wars', *Economic Journal* 95 (1985), pp. 83–95; Foreman-Peck and Millward, *Public and Private Ownership*, pp. 204–19.
22. John Rowland, *Progress in Power: The Contribution of Charles Merz and His Associates to Sixty Years of Electrical Development, 1899–1959* (Newman Neame, 1960); Hughes, *Networks of Power*, pp. 350–3; CEB Annual Report, 1928, pp. 3–5; Bent Flyvbjerg and Dan Gardner, *How Big Things Get Done: The Surprising Factors That Determine the Fate of Every Project* (Macmillan Business, 2023).
23. CEB Annual Reports, 1927–1947.
24. Ibid.; Hannah, *Electricity Before Nationalisation*, pp. 118–19; Hughes, *Networks of Power*, p. 358.
25. CEB Annual Report, 1929, pp. 5–9; CEB Annual Report, 1932, p. 24.
26. CEB Annual Report, 1935, p. 6.
27. CEB Annual Report, 1937, p. 8.
28. Sheail, *Power in Trust*; Bill Luckin, *Questions of Power: Electricity and Environment in Inter-War Britain* (Manchester University

Press, 1990); G. T. Bloomfield, 'The Midlands Electricity Board Area', British Electricity History, pp. 19–20, britelechist.uoguelph.ca.
29. CEB Annual Report, 1929, p. 18.
30. CEB Annual Report, 1947, p. 8.
31. Simon Jack, 'Electricity Upgrade Plan Includes Miles of Pylons', BBC, 19 March 2024.
32. CEB Annual Report, 1934, pp. 12–13.
33. Hannah, *Electricity Before Nationalisation*, p. 122.
34. CEB Annual Report, 1936, pp. 19–20.
35. Cochrane, *Power to the People*, pp. 20–30.
36. Orren C. Hormell, 'Ownership and Regulation of Electric Utilities in Great Britain', *Annals of the American Academy of Political and Social Science* 159 (January 1932), p. 128; Hannah, *Electricity Before Nationalisation*, pp. 94–129; Cochrane, *Power to the People*, p. 13.
37. Robert Boothby et al., *Industry and the State: A Conservative View* (Macmillan, 1927).
38. Millward, *Private and Public Enterprise*, pp. 91–6; Sandeep Vaheesan, *Democracy in Power: A History of Electrification in the United States* (University of Chicago Press, 2024).
39. H. S. Burness, R. G. Cummings and Verne W. Loose, 'Scale Economies and Reliability in the Electric Power Industry', *Energy Journal* 6, no. 1 (January 1985), pp. 157–68; J. S. Highfield, 'The Supply of Electricity', *Journal of the Royal Society of Arts* 67, no. 3469 (16 May 1919), p. 415.
40. Millward and Singleton, *Political Economy of Nationalisation*, pp. 14–17.
41. Foreman-Peck and Millward, *Public and Private Ownership*, p. 281.
42. Hannah, *Electricity Before Nationalisation*, pp. 128, 432–3.
43. Roger Fouquet, National Infrastructure Commission Historic Energy Dataset, nic.org.uk (hereafter 'NIC Historic Energy Dataset').
44. Frank Trentmann and Anna Carlsson-Hyslop, 'The Evolution of Energy Demand in Britain: Politics, Daily Life and Public Housing, 1920s–1970s', *Historical Journal* 61, no. 3 (September 2018), p. 811.
45. R. Fouquet, 'Divergences in Long Run Trends in the Prices of Energy and Energy Services', *Review of Environmental Economics and Policy* 5, no. 2 (Summer 2011), pp. 196–218; W. D. Nordhaus, 'Do Real Output and Real Wage Measures Capture Reality? The History of Lighting Suggests Not', in T. F. Bresnahan and R. J.

Gordon (eds), *The Economics of New Goods* (University of Chicago Press, 1996).

46. Hannah, *Electricity Before Nationalisation*, p. 147.
47. Ibid., pp. 430–1.
48. Roger Fouquet, 'Long-Run Demand for Energy Services: Income and Price Elasticities over Two Hundred Years', *Review of Environmental Economics and Policy* 8, no. 2 (Summer 2014), pp. 186–207.
49. Hannah, *Electricity Before Nationalisation*, pp. 187–8.
50. Carroll Pursell, 'Domesticating Modernity: The Electrical Association for Women, 1924–86', *British Journal for the History of Science* 32, no. 1 (March 1999), pp. 47–67.
51. Hannah, *Electricity Before Nationalisation*, pp. 193–205, 430–1.
52. Political and Economic Planning, *Report on the Gas Industry in Great Britain: A Survey of the Current Trends and Problems of the Industry, with Proposals for Its Future Development* (PEP, 1939); Millward and Singleton, *Political Economy of Nationalisation*, p. 146; NIC Historic Energy Dataset; Williams, *History of the British Gas Industry*, p. 69; Roger Fouquet, 'The Demand for Environmental Quality in Driving Transitions to Low-Polluting Energy Sources', *Energy Policy* 50 (November 2021), pp. 138–49.
53. Trentmann and Carlson-Hyslop, 'Evolution of Energy Demand'.
54. Boyan Jovanovic and Peter Rousseau, 'General Purpose Technologies', NBER Working Paper 11093, January 2005.
55. Hannah, *Electricity Before Nationalisation*, p. 171.
56. G. T. Bloomfield, 'The East Midlands Electricity Board Area', British Electricity History, pp. 18–21, britelechist.uoguelph.ca.
57. Hannah, *Electricity Before Nationalisation*, pp. 181–2.
58. Cristiano Andrea Ristuccia and Solomos Solomou, 'Can General Purpose Technology Theory Explain Economic Growth? Electrical Power as a Case Study', *European Review of Economic History* 18, no. 3 (August 2014), pp. 227–47.
59. Steam only. Foreman-Peck and Millward, *Public and Private Ownership*, p. 261.
60. Crafts, *Forging Ahead*, pp. 63–4.
61. Julie Cohn, 'When the Grid Was the Grid: The History of North America's Brief Coast-to-Coast Interconnected Machine', *Proceedings of the IEEE* 107, no. 1 (January 2019), pp. 232–43.
62. I. P. Burdon, *Developments in UK Power Supply, 1947–2007* (IEEE, 2010), p. 7.
63. CEB Annual Reports, 1931–1947.

64. CEB Annual Report, 1944, p. 34.
65. CEB Annual Report, 1947, p. 4; CEB Annual Report, 1940, p. 14.
66. CEB Annual Report, 1944, p. 31.
67. CEB Annual Report, 1944, p. 33.
68. CEB Annual Report, 1947, p. 4.
69. Bloomfield, 'London: Electricity Hub', p. 28.
70. G. T. Bloomfield, 'The South East Scotland Electricity Board Area', British Electricity History, pp. 10–11, britelechist.uoguelph.ca; Bloomfield, 'Midlands', p. 16.
71. William A. Robson, *The Government and Misgovernment of London* (G. Allen & Unwin, 1939), pp. 241–2.
72. Bloomfield, British Electricity History; Millward and Singleton, *Political Economy of Nationalisation*, pp. 258–9.
73. Foreman-Peck and Millward, *Public and Private Ownership*, p. 283; Williams, *History of the British Gas Industry*, p. 96.
74. Ministry of Transport, *Report of the Committee on Electricity Distribution* (HM Stationery Office, 1936); Electricity Council, *Electricity Supply in the United Kingdom: A Chronology – From the Beginnings of the Industry to 31 December 1985*, 4th ed. (Electricity Council, 1987), p. 24; Millward and Singleton, *Political Economy of Nationalisation*, pp. 260–73.
75. Herbert Morrison, *Socialisation and Transport* (Constable, 1933), pp. 224–5.
76. Dieter Helm, 'British Utility Regulation: Theory, Practice, and Reform', *Oxford Review of Economic Policy* 10, no. 3 (Autumn 1994), pp. 17–39.
77. Millward and Singleton, *Political Economy of Nationalisation*, pp. 16–17.
78. Foreman-Peck and Millward, *Public and Private Ownership*, p. 282.
79. J. R. Beard and T. G. N. Haldane, 'The Design of City Distribution Systems, and the Problem of Standardization', *Journal of the Institution for Electrical Engineers* 65, no. 361 (1927); T. G. N. Haldane, 'The Heat Pump: An Economical Method of Producing Low-Grade Heat from Electricity', *Journal of the Institution for Electrical Engineers* 68, no. 402 (1930).
80. G. H., *The Socialization of the Electricity Supply Industry* (Victor Gollancz, 1934).
81. David Banks, 'Dr T. G. N. "Graeme" Haldane: Scottish Heat Pump Pioneer', *International Journal for the History of Engineering and Technology* 85, no. 2 (2015).

82. Hannah, *Electricity Before Nationalisation*, pp. 241–2.
83. Letter from T. G. N. Haldane to G. D. H. Cole on 6 August 1941, in ibid., p. 420.

3. Nationalised Energy, 1945–1979

1. Tom Nairn, 'The Nature of the Labour Party, Part II', *New Left Review* 1, no. 28 (November/December 1964), p. 52.
2. A. Carlsson-Hyslop and P. J. G. Pearson, 'How Did the Electrical Development Association Attempt to Mould Domestic Electricity Demand in Britain, 1945–1964?', Working Paper 2013/01 (2013), p. 3.
3. Leslie Hannah, *Engineers, Managers and Politicians: Electricity Supply Industry in Britain from 1948 to the Present* (Palgrave Macmillan, 1982), pp. 3, 139.
4. James Foreman-Peck and Robert Millward, *Public and Private Ownership of British Industry 1820–1990* (Clarendon, 1994).
5. Nicholas Crafts, *Forging Ahead, Falling Behind and Fighting Back: British Economic Growth from the Industrial Revolution to the Financial Crisis* (Cambridge University Press, 2018), pp. 79–90; David Newbery, *Privatization, Restructuring, and Regulation of Network Utilities* (MIT Press, 1999), p. 23.
6. R. H. Tawney, *The Radical Tradition: Twelve Essays on Politics, Education and Literature* (Pantheon, 1964).
7. Jim Tomlinson, 'A "Failed Experiment"? Public Ownership and the Narrative of Post-War Britain', *Labour History Review* 73, no. 2 (August 2008), pp. 228–43.
8. Massimo Florio, *The Great Divestiture: Evaluating the Welfare Impact of the British Privatizations, 1979–1997* (MIT Press, 2004), p. 17.
9. Ross McKibbin, *The Evolution of the Labour Party, 1910–1924* (Clarendon Press, 1984).
10. Robert Millward and John Singleton (eds), *The Political Economy of Nationalisation in Britain, 1920–1950* (Cambridge University Press, 2010), p. 19.
11. Robert Millward, 'The 1940s Nationalizations in Britain: Means to an End or the Means of Production?', *Economic History Review* 50, no. 2 (May 1997), pp. 209–34.
12. Millward and Singleton, *Political Economy of Nationalisation*, pp. 257–70.
13. Ibid., p. 272.

14. Trevor Williams, *A History of the British Gas Industry* (Oxford University Press, 1981), p. 98.
15. David Edgerton, *The Rise and Fall of the British Nation: A Twentieth-Century History* (Allen Lane, 2018).
16. Martin Chick, *Industrial Policy in Britain, 1945–1951* (Cambridge University Press, 1998), pp. 16–17, 43–5, 58.
17. Andrew Jenkins, 'Government Intervention in the British Gas Industry, 1948 to 1970', *Business History* 46, no. 1 (2004), pp. 57–78.
18. British Gas Corporation, *Annual Report, 1972–73* (British Gas Corporation, 1973), p. 12.
19. Foreman-Peck and Millward, *Public and Private Ownership*, pp. 297–8.
20. 'An Oral History of the Electricity Supply Industry, Final Report', National Life Stories and the British Library, 2017, p. 12.
21. Hannah, *Engineers, Managers and Politicians*, p. 63; Jenkins, 'Government Intervention', p. 61.
22. British Electricity Authority (BEA), *Electricity Supply: Historical Review, 1882–1948. Electricity Act 1947. The New Organisation* (BEA, 1948), pp. 11–15; Hannah, *Engineers, Managers and Politicians*, p. 17; 'Oral History of the Electricity Supply Industry', p. 13.
23. Chick, *Industrial Policy in Britain*, pp. 84–5.
24. Hannah, *Engineers, Managers and Politicians*, p. 18.
25. Christopher Hinton and William Holford, 'Power Production and Transmission in the Countryside: Preserving Amenities', *Journal of the Royal Society of Arts* 108, no. 5043 (February 1960), p. 206.
26. Central Electricity Generating Board (CEGB), *Annual Report, 1958–9* (HMSO, 1959), p. 2.
27. Edgerton, *Rise and Fall of the British Nation*, p. 131.
28. Harold Wilson, 'Labour and the Scientific Revolution', in *Report of the Sixty-Second Annual Conference of the Labour Party, Scarborough 1963* (Labour Party, 1963).
29. Edgerton, *Rise and Fall of the British Nation*, p. 330.
30. Dieter Helm, *Energy, the State, and the Market: British Energy Policy Since 1979* (Oxford University Press, 2003), pp. 14–34.
31. Hannah, *Engineers, Managers and Politicians*, pp. 12–15; BEA, *Electricity Supply*, p. 1.
32. Hannah, *Engineers, Managers and Politicians*, p. 197.
33. Foreman-Peck and Millward, *Public and Private Ownership*, p. 296.
34. Hannah, *Engineers, Managers and Politicians*, p. 53.

35. Williams, *History of the British Gas Industry*, pp. 231–3.
36. Helm, *Energy, the State, and the Market*, p. 25; Dieter Helm, 'Energy Network Regulation Failures and Net Zero', 5 January 2023, dieterhelm.co.uk.
37. Electricity Council, *Handbook of Electricity Supply Statistics* (Electricity Council, 1966–90), volumes for 1970–90, British Library, London.
38. Avner Offer, 'The Economy of Obligation: Incomplete Contracts and the Cost of the Welfare State', *Discussion Papers in Economic and Social History* 103 (August 2012).
39. Williams, *History of the British Gas Industry*, p. 106.
40. Hannah, *Engineers, Managers and Politicians*, p. 3.
41. Ibid., pp. 26–7.
42. John Sheail, *Power in Trust: Environmental History of the Central Electricity Generating Board* (Clarendon, 1991), pp. 30–44.
43. Hannah, *Engineers, Managers and Politicians*, pp. 68–70.
44. Ibid., pp. 73–5.
45. T. G. N. Haldane, 'Inaugural Address, 7 October 1948: Means and Ends', *Proceedings of the Institution of Electrical Engineers* 96, part 1 (1949).
46. Rob Burnett and James Watson, 'Seventy Years of the British 275-kV Supergrid', unpublished, 2024, p. 3; D. P. Sayers, J. S. Forrest and F. J. Lane, '275-kV Developments on the British Grid System', *Proceedings of the IEE* 99, no. 72 (1952); I. P. Burdon, *Developments in UK Power Supply, 1947–2007* (IEEE, 2010), p. 25; Rob Cochrane, *Power to the People: The Story of the National Grid* (Littlehampton, 1985), p. 42.
47. G. T. Bloomfield, 'The East Midlands Electricity Board Area', British Electricity History, pp. 24–5.
48. Burdon, *Developments in UK Power Supply*, p. 24; Hannah, *Engineers, Managers and Politicians*, pp. 102–3.
49. E. S. Booth et al., 'The 400 kV Grid System for England and Wales', *Proceedings of the IEE* 109, no. 48 (1962).
50. James Watson, 'Seventy Years of the British Supergrid', unpublished paper, 2024; CEGB Annual Report, 1971–2, pp. 28–9.
51. Department for Business, Energy and Industrial Strategy (BEIS), 'Appendix I: Electricity Networks Modelling', in *Electricity Networks Strategic Framework* (BEIS, 2022).
52. International Energy Agency (IEA), *Electricity Grids and Secure Energy Transitions* (IEA, 2023).
53. CEGB Annual Report, 1958–9, pp. 2–4.

54. Hannah, *Engineers, Managers and Politicians*, pp. 111–22.
55. G. T. Bloomfield, British Electricity History, all volumes, britelechist .uoguelph.ca.
56. Hannah, *Engineers, Managers and Politicians*, pp. 92–3.
57. Chick, *Industrial Policy in Britain*, pp. 142–3.
58. Sheail, *Power in Trust*, pp. 203–8; CEGB, *Dinorwig: Pumped Storage Power Station*, Institution of Engineering and Technology Archives, NAEST 253/13/14.
59. Jim Miller, *The Dam Builders: Power from the Glens* (Birlinn, 2002).
60. Martin Chick, *Electricity and Energy Policy in Britain, France and the United States Since 1945* (Edward Elgar, 2007), p. 93.
61. Peter L. Payne, *The Hydro: A Study of the Development of the Major Hydro-Electric Schemes Undertaken by the North of Scotland Hydro-Electric Board* (Pergamon, 1988); Hannah, *Engineers, Managers and Politicians*, pp. 152–3; Miller, *The Dam Builders*, p. 176.
62. Cochrane, *Power to the People*, p. 10; T. G. N. Haldane and P. L. Blackstone, 'Problems of Hydro-Electric Design in Mixed Thermal-Hydro-Electric Systems', *Proceedings of the Institution of Electrical Engineers* 102, no. 3 (1955).
63. Miller, *The Dam Builders*, pp. 236–7.
64. CEGB Annual Report, 1962–3, pp. 24–5.
65. Miller, *The Dam Builders*, pp. 190–203.
66. Chick, *Electricity and Energy Policy*, pp. 23, 73.
67. CEGB Annual Report, 1958–9, p. 5.
68. Keith Baker, 'Nuclear Power in Britain: A Series of Successful Failures', *International Review of Public Policy* 5, no. 1 (2023), pp. 293–313.
69. Helm, *Energy, the State, and the Market*, pp. 27–9.
70. Baker, 'Nuclear Power in Britain', pp. 31–2.
71. Hannah, *Engineers, Managers and Politicians*, pp. 229–34.
72. Baker, 'Nuclear Power in Britain'.
73. Vaclav Smil, *Energy Transitions: History, Requirements, Prospects* (Praeger, 2010), pp. 44–5.
74. Simon Taylor, *The Fall and Rise of Nuclear Power in Britain: A History* (Bloomsbury Sigma, 2016), p. 14.
75. David Edgerton, 'Don't Be Seduced by the Myths of the Economic Right', *New Statesman*, 8 October 2024.
76. Sheail, *Power in Trust*, p. 45; 'Lord Munster Comments in "Proposed New Super-Grid"', Parliamentary Debates, Lords, 31 July 1956, vol. 199, cols 487–513.

77. Cochrane, *Power to the People*, pp. 43–4.
78. Katrina Navickas, 'Conflicts of Power: Landscape and Amenity in Debates over the British Super Grid in the 1950s', *Rural History* 30, no. 1 (2019), pp. 87–103.
79. Sheail, *Power in Trust*, pp. 113–20; CEGB Annual Report, 1958–9, p. 6.
80. CEGB Annual Report, 1962–3, p. 5.
81. CEGB Annual Reports, 1958–9 and 1962–3.
82. Sheail, *Power in Trust*, p. 130.
83. CEGB Annual Report, 1974–5, p. 33.
84. Sheail, *Power in Trust*, pp. 167–84.
85. CEGB Annual Report, 1962–3, pp. 7–9.
86. Sheail, *Power in Trust*, pp. 195–7.
87. Hinton and Holford, 'Power Production and Transmission', p. 184.
88. Hannah, *Engineers, Managers and Politicians*, p. 252.
89. Sheail, *Power in Trust*, p. 129; Sylvia Crowe, 'The Landscape of Power', *Landscape Architecture Magazine* 49, no. 2 (1959), pp. 106–9.
90. CEGB Annual Report, 1962–3, p. 69.
91. Ibid., pp. 5–6.
92. *Country Life*, 8 December 1960 and 8 March 1962.
93. Maxustaxus, '"Count Your Blessings" CEGB, Electric Pylon Promo 1963 with Desmond Llewelyn of James Bond Fame F920', YouTube, 20 December 2023.
94. CEGB Annual Report, 1962–3, p. 42.
95. Williams, *History of the British Gas Industry*, p. 113.
96. Malcolm W. H. Peebles, *Evolution of the Gas Industry* (Macmillan, 1980), p. 26.
97. Williams, *History of the British Gas Industry*, p. 103.
98. Ibid., p. 116.
99. Danny Lawrence and Helen Lawrence, *Growing Up with Gas: A History of the Gas Industry* (Brewin Books, 2023), p. 249.
100. Williams, *History of the British Gas Industry*, pp. 116–17.
101. Ibid., pp. 121–33; Peebles, *Evolution of the Gas Industry*, pp. 27–8.
102. Stathis Arapostathis, Scott Laczay and Peter J. G. Pearson, 'Steering the "C-Day": Insights from the Rapid, Planned Transition of the UK's Natural Gas Conversion Programme', *Environmental Innovation and Societal Transitions* 32 (September 2019), p. 126.
103. Russell Thomas, *Lessons Learnt: Past Energy Transitions in the Gas Industry* (Wales & West Utilities, WSP and Northern Gas Networks, 2023).

104. Electricity Council, *Handbook of Electricity Supply Statistics* (1969).
105. Arapostathis, Laczay and Pearson, 'Steering the "C-Day"', p. 132; Williams, *History of the British Gas Industry*, pp. 133–7, 202–33; ephemeralfilm, 'Kitchen Magic – Fanny Cradock (1963) Gas Council Film NEW TRANSFER', YouTube, 21 July 2018.
106. Williams, *History of the British Gas Industry*; Leslie Minchin, *The Gas Industry: Today and Tomorrow* (Harrap, 1966), pp. 82–97; Peebles, *Evolution of the Gas Industry*, pp. 28–30.
107. Jeremy Paxman, *Black Gold: The History of How Coal Made Britain* (William Collins, 2021), p. 290.
108. Arapostathis, Laczay and Pearson, 'Steering the "C-Day"'; Peebles, *Evolution of the Gas Industry*, pp. 32–3.
109. Helm, *Energy, the State, and the Market*, p. 41.
110. Kenneth Hutchison, *High Speed Gas: An Autobiography* (Duckworth, 1987), pp. 260–70.
111. 'Gas and Electricity Bill', *Parliamentary Debates*, Commons, 22 May 1968, vol. 765, cols 543–660.
112. Arapostathis, Laczay and Pearson, 'Steering the "C-Day"'.
113. Charles Elliott, *The History of Natural Gas Conversion in Great Britain* (Burlington Press, 1980), p. 39.
114. Arapostathis, Laczay and Pearson, 'Steering the "C-Day"'.
115. Smil, *Energy Transitions*, p. 37.
116. National Infrastructure Commission, *The Second National Infrastructure Assessment* (2023), pp. 65–70; Arup, 'Future of Great Britain's Gas Networks: Report for the National Infrastructure Commission and Ofgem', October 2023, pp. 68–9.
117. Arapostathis, Laczay and Pearson, 'Steering the "C-Day"', p. 127.
118. Lawrence and Lawrence, *Growing Up with Gas*, pp. 261–2; Arapostathis, Laczay and Pearson, 'Steering the "C-Day"', p. 128; Peebles, *Evolution of the Gas Industry*, p. 39; British Gas Corporation, Annual Report, 1972–73, p. 8.
119. Thomas, *Lessons Learnt*, pp. 45, 53; Peebles, *Evolution of the Gas Industry*, pp. 35–8.
120. Peebles, *Evolution of the Gas Industry*, p. 42.
121. Thomas, *Lessons Learnt*; Williams, *History of the British Gas Industry*, pp. 180–90, 221–9.
122. British Gas Corporation, Annual Reports, 1970–80.
123. *British Gas Magazine*, 1978–9.
124. Carlsson-Hyslop and Pearson, 'How Did the Electrical Development Association', p. 14.

125. Hannah, *Engineers, Managers and Politicians*, p. 211.
126. Sue Bowden and Avner Offer, 'Household Appliances and the Use of Time: The United States and Britain Since the 1920s', *Economic History Review* 47, no. 4 (1994), pp. 725–48.
127. Roger Fouquet, National Infrastructure Commission Historic Energy Dataset, nic.org.uk.
128. Roger Fouquet, 'Divergences in Long Run Trends in the Prices of Energy and Energy Services', *Review of Environmental Economics and Policy* 5, no. 2 (Summer 2011), pp. 196–218; Roger Fouquet, 'Long-Run Demand for Energy Services: Income and Price Elasticities over Two Hundred Years', *Review of Environmental Economics and Policy* 8, no. 2 (Summer 2014), pp. 186–207.
129. Frank Trentmann and Anna Carlsson-Hyslop, 'The Evolution of Energy Demand in Britain: Politics, Daily Life and Public Housing, 1920s–1970s', *Historical Journal* 61, no. 3 (September 2018), pp. 810–21.
130. Hannah, *Engineers, Managers and Politicians*, p. 292; Anna Carlsson-Hyslop, 'Past Management of Energy Demand: Promotion and Adoption of Electric Heating in Britain 1945–1964', *Environment and History* 22, no. 1 (2016), pp. 75–102.
131. Martin Chick, 'The Changing Role of Space and Time in British Environmental Policy Since 1945', *Revue française d'histoire économique* 3 (2015), p. 74.
132. Lawrence and Lawrence, *Growing Up with Gas*, p. 257.
133. British Gas Corporation, Annual Report, 1979–80, p. 27.
134. Trentmann and Carlsson-Hyslop, 'The Evolution of Energy Demand', p. 826.
135. Chick, *Electricity and Energy Policy*, pp. 7–33.
136. Quoted in Mariana Mazzucato, *The Entrepreneurial State: Debunking Public vs. Private Sector Myths* (Anthem, 2013).
137. Miller, *The Dam Builders*.
138. Helm, *Energy, the State, and the Market*, p. 2.
139. Monopolies and Mergers Commission, *Central Electricity Generating Board: A Report on the Operation by the Board of Its System for the Generation and Supply of Electricity in Bulk*, HC 315 (HM Stationery Office, 1981).
140. Leslie Hannah, 'A Failed Experiment: The State Ownership of Industry', in Roderick Floud and Paul Johnson (eds), *The Cambridge Economic History of Modern Britain*, vol. 3 (Cambridge University Press, 2004), p. 94.
141. Jenkins, 'Government Intervention', p. 60.

142. Victor Ajayi et al., 'The Productivity Puzzle in Network Industries: Evidence from the Energy Sector', EPRD working paper 2021, July 2020.
143. Richard Molyneux and David Thompson, 'Nationalised Industry Performance: Still Third-Rate?', *Fiscal Studies* 8, no. 1 (February 1987), pp. 48–82.
144. Foreman-Peck and Millward, *Public and Private Ownership*, p. 312.
145. Robert Millward, *Private and Public Enterprise in Europe: Energy, Telecommunications and Transport, 1830–1990* (Cambridge University Press, 2005), p. 277.
146. Mazzucato, *The Entrepreneurial State*, p. 20.
147. Baker, 'Nuclear Power in Britain'.
148. CEGB Annual Report, 1958–59, p. 2.
149. Miller, *The Dam Builders*, p. 223.
150. Hannah, 'A Failed Experiment', p. 95.
151. Martin Chick, *Changing Times: Economics, Policies, and Resource Allocation in Britain Since 1951* (Oxford University Press, 2020), pp. 18–19, 34.
152. Avner Offer, *Understanding the Private-Public Divide: Markets, Governments, and Time Horizons* (Cambridge University Press, 2022), p. xi.
153. Martin Chick, 'The Power of Networks: Defining the Boundaries of the Natural Monopoly Network and the Implications for the Restructuring of Electricity Supply Industries', *Annales historiques de l'électricité* 2 (2004), p. 91; Chick, *Industrial Policy in Britain*, pp. 105–13; Chick, *Changing Times*, pp. 214–15.
154. Chick, 'The Power of Networks', p. 91.
155. Chick, *Electricity and Energy Policy*, pp. 66–8, 94–5; Martin Chick, 'The 3 Rs: Regulation, Risk and Responsibility in British Utilities Since 1945', *Business History* 53, no. 5 (2011), pp. 747–60; Chick, *Industrial Policy in Britain*, pp. 92–129, 213–14; Hannah, *Engineers, Managers and Politicians*, pp. 30–5.
156. I. M. D. Little, *The Price of Fuel* (Clarendon, 1953), p. 151.
157. Burdon, *Developments in UK Power Supply*, p. 11.
158. Hannah, *Engineers, Managers and Politicians*, p. 89; Carlsson-Hyslop, 'Past Management of Energy Demand'.
159. Chick, *Electricity and Energy Policy*, p. 75; Burdon, *Developments in UK Power Supply*, p. 18.
160. Millward, *Private and Public Enterprise*, p. 259; Paxman, *Black Gold*, p. 287.

161. Helm, *Energy, the State, and the Market*, pp. 42–3; Stephen Littlechild, 'Life Before Economic Regulation', presentation at the Conference on the Objectives of Economic Regulation, CCP UEA, Norwich, 16 September 2019.
162. Chick, *Electricity and Energy Policy*, pp. 66–71.
163. Foreman-Peck and Millward, *Public and Private Ownership*, pp. 297–9.
164. Martin Chick, 'Time, Water and Capital: The Unintended Contribution of the North of Scotland Hydro-Electric Board to the Application of Welfare Economics in Britain, 1943–1967', *Scottish Business and Industrial History* 25 (2009), pp. 29–55; Chick, *Electricity and Energy Policy*, pp. 93–4.
165. M. Chick and H. Viv Nelles, 'Nationalisation and Privatisation: Ownership, Markets and the Scope for Introducing Competition into the Electricity Supply Industry', *Revue économique* 58, no. 1 (2007), p. 283; Helm, *Energy, the State, and the Market*, p. 32; HM Treasury, *Accounting for Economic Costs and Changing Prices*, vol. 1, annex 1 (HM Stationery Office, 1988).
166. Helm, *Energy, the State, and the Market*, p. 16; Molyneux and Thompson, 'Nationalised Industry Performance', pp. 50–2.
167. Alex Henney, *Privatise Power: Restructuring the Electricity Supply Industry* (Centre for Policy Studies, 1987), pp. 7–37; Millward, *Private and Public Enterprise*, p. 277; Chick and Nelles, 'Nationalisation and Privatisation', p. 281.
168. Foreman-Peck and Millward, *Public and Private Ownership*, pp. 262–71; Molyneux and Thompson, 'Nationalised Industry Performance', p. 51; Peebles, *Evolution of the Gas Industry*, p. 48; Electricity Council, *Handbook of Electricity Supply Statistics*, (Electricity Council, 1980).
169. Florio, *The Great Divestiture*, pp. 18–24; Hannah, 'A Failed Experiment'.

4. Privatised Energy, 1979–2010

1. Massimo Florio, *The Great Divestiture: Evaluating the Welfare Impact of the British Privatizations, 1979–1997* (MIT Press, 2004), pp. 30, 341, 441; Brett Christophers, *The Price Is Wrong: Why Capitalism Won't Save the Planet* (Verso, 2024), p. 41.
2. David Parker, *The Official History of Privatisation*, vol. 1, *The Formative Years, 1970–1987* (Routledge, 2009), p. 166; Florio, *The Great Divestiture*, p. 33.

3. John Redwood, *Public Enterprises in Crisis: The Future of the Nationalised Industries* (Blackwell, 1980), pp. 16–20, 71–2; Aled Davies, Ben Jackson and Florence Sutcliffe-Braithwaite, *The Neoliberal Age? Britain Since the 1970s* (UCL Press, 2021), p. 5; Florio, *The Great Divestiture*, pp. 22–3.
4. Alan Watkins, *A Conservative Coup: The Fall of Margaret Thatcher* (Duckworth, 1992); James Foreman-Peck and Robert Millward, *Public and Private Ownership of British Industry 1820–1990* (Clarendon, 1994), pp. 331–9; Christopher Rhodes, David Hough and Louise Butcher, *Privatization*, House of Commons Research Paper 14/61, November 2014, pp. 3–5; Stephen Littlechild, *Privatization, Competition and Regulation in the British Electricity Industry*, ESM Report 226 (World Bank, 2000), pp. 4–5.
5. M. Chick and H. Viv Nelles, 'Nationalisation and Privatisation: Ownership, Markets and the Scope for Introducing Competition into the Electricity Supply Industry', *Revue économique* 58, no. 1 (2007), p. 283; James Meek, *Private Island: Why Britain Now Belongs to Someone Else* (Verso, 2015), pp. 10, 124; Conservative Party Policy Statement, *The Right Approach* (Conservative Party, 1976); *Conservative Manifesto, 1979* (Conservative Central Office, 1979); *The Conservative Manifesto, 1983* (Conservative Central Office, 1983); Florio, *The Great Divestiture*, pp. 27–8.
6. Dieter Helm, *Energy, the State, and the Market: British Energy Policy Since 1979* (Oxford University Press, 2003), pp. 48–50; Monopolies and Mergers Commission, *Central Electricity Generating Board* (HM Stationery Office, 1981).
7. S. C. Littlechild, 'Ten Steps to Denationalisation', *Economic Affairs* 2, no. 1 (October 1981), pp. 11–19; Stephen Littlechild, 'Life Before Economic Regulation', presentation at the Conference on the Objectives of Economic Regulation, CCP UEA, Norwich, 16 September 2019; Chick and Nelles, 'Nationalisation and Privatisation', p. 284.
8. Ben Jackson, 'The Think-Tank Archipelago: Thatcherism and Neo-Liberalism', in Ben Jackson and Robert Saunders (eds), *Making Thatcher's Britain* (Cambridge University Press, 2012), pp. 43–61.
9. Helm, *Energy, the State, and the Market*, pp. 57–8.
10. Florio, *The Great Divestiture*, pp. 29–30; Rhodes, Hough and Butcher, *Privatisation*, pp. 2–7.
11. Parker, *Official History of Privatisation*, vol. 1, p. 372; Mark Armstrong, Simon Cowan and John Vickers, *Regulatory Reform:*

Economic Analysis and British Experience (MIT Press, 1994), pp. 252–3; Martin Chick, *Changing Times: Economics, Policies, and Resource Allocation in Britain Since 1951* (Oxford University Press, 2020), p. 234.

12. E. M. Hammond, D. R. Helm and D. J. Thompson, 'British Gas: Options for Privatisation', *Fiscal Studies* 6, no. 4 (November 1985), pp. 1–20; Helm, *Energy, the State, and the Market*, pp. 114–15.
13. Alex Henney, *Privatise Power: Restructuring the Electricity Supply Industry* (Centre for Policy Studies, 1987), p. 5; Rhodes, Hough and Butcher, *Privatisation*, p. 15.
14. Littlechild, *Privatization, Competition and Regulation*, pp. 4, 18, 30–40; David Parker, *The Official History of Privatisation*, vol. 2, *Popular Capitalism, 1987–1997* (Routledge, 2012), pp. 514–15.
15. Parker, *Official History of Privatisation*, vol. 1, p. 447, and vol. 2, p. 254.
16. John Vickers and George Yarrow, *Privatization: An Economic Analysis* (MIT Press, 1988), pp. 39–43; Armstrong, Cowan and Vickers, *Regulatory Reform*, p. 8; David Newbery, *Privatization, Restructuring, and Regulation of Network Utilities* (MIT Press, 1999), p. 3.
17. Armstrong, Cowan and Vickers, *Regulatory Reform*, p. 283; Parker, *Official History of Privatisation*, vol. 2, p. 259.
18. Foreman-Peck and Millward, *Public and Private Ownership*, p. 322.
19. Newbery, *Privatization, Restructuring, and Regulation*, p. 176–87; Vickers and Yarrow, *Privatization: An Economic Analysis*, p. 429.
20. William Davies, *The Limits of Neoliberalism: Authority, Sovereignty and the Logic of Competition*, rev. ed. (Sage, 2016).
21. Helm, *Energy, the State, and the Market*, p. 141.
22. Armstrong, Cowan and Vickers, *Regulatory Reform*, p. 14.
23. 'An Oral History of the Electricity Supply Industry, Final Report', National Life Stories and the British Library, 2017, p. 8.
24. Monopolies and Mergers Commission, *Gas: A Report on the Matter of the Existence or Possible Existence of a Monopoly Situation in Relation to the Supply of Great Britain of Gas Through the Pipes to Persons Other than Tariff Customers*, Cm500 (HM Stationery Office, 1988); Monopolies and Mergers Commission, *Gas and British Gas plc*, Cm2317 (HM Stationery Office, 1993); Monopolies and Mergers Commission, *Gas: Reports Under the Fair Trading Act 1973 on the Supply Within Great Britain of Gas*

Through Pipes to Tariff and Non-Tariff Customers, Cm 2314 (HM Stationery Office, 1993).

25. Sandeep Vaheesan, *Democracy in Power: A History of Electrification in the United States* (University of Chicago Press, 2024), pp. 28–97; Martin Chick, 'The Power of Networks: Defining the Boundaries of the Natural Monopoly Network and the Implications for the Restructuring of Electricity Supply Industries', *Annales historiques de l'électricité* 2 (2004), p. 92.
26. Parker, *Official History of Privatisation*, vol. 2, p. 254; Harvey Averch and Leland Johnson, 'Behavior of the Firm Under Regulatory Constraint', *American Economic Review* 52, no. 5 (December 1962), pp. 1052–69.
27. Jon Stern, 'What the Littlechild Report Actually Said', Regulation Initiative Working Paper 55, London Business School, August 2003; Stephen C. Littlechild, *Regulation of British Telecommunications' Profitability* (Department of Industry, 1983).
28. Littlechild, *Regulation of British Telecommunications*, p. 36.
29. Albert O. Hirshman, *Exit, Voice, and Loyalty: Responses to Decline in Firms, Organizations, and States* (Harvard University Press, 1970); Armstrong, Cowan and Vickers, *Regulatory Reform*, pp. 80–90.
30. Newbery, *Privatization, Restructuring, and Regulation*, pp. 57–8, 405; Grahame Danby, *Regulating Energy Utilities*, House of Commons Research Paper 98/19 (February 1998), pp. 7–10; Littlechild, *Privatization, Competition and Regulation*, pp. 8–10.
31. Keith Baker, 'Nuclear Power in Britain: A Series of Successful Failures', *International Review of Public Policy* 5, no. 1 (2023), pp. 293–313; Simon Taylor, *The Fall and Rise of Nuclear Power in Britain: A History* (Bloomsbury Sigma, 2016), p. 22; World Nuclear Association, 'Nuclear Development in the United Kingdom', 12 June 2025, world-nuclear.org; Performance and Innovation Unit, *The Economics of Nuclear Power*, PIU Energy Review Working Paper (Cabinet Office, 2002).
32. Parker, *Official History of Privatisation*, vol. 2, pp. 285–92, 370; Chick, *Changing Times*, pp. 232–8.
33. Fergus McCullough, 'Why Did Nuclear Flop in Britain?', *Fitzwilliam*, Substack, 13 July 2023; Taylor, *Fall and Rise of Nuclear Power*, pp. 30–2.
34. World Nuclear Association, 'Nuclear Development'; Baker, 'Nuclear Power in Britain'; McCullough, 'Why Did Nuclear Flop?'.

35. David M. Newbery, 'The Impact of Sulphur Limits on Fuel Demand and Electricity Prices in Britain', *Energy Journal* 15, no. 3 (1994), pp. 19–41; Mark Winskel, 'When Systems Are Overthrown: The "Dash for Gas" in the British Electricity Supply Industry', *Social Studies of Science* 32, no. 4 (2002), pp. 563–98.
36. Winskel, 'When Systems Are Overthrown'; Helm, *Energy, the State, and the Market*, p. 144.
37. Chick and Nelles, 'Nationalisation and Privatisation', p. 291; 'Digest of UK Energy Statistics (DUKES)', gov.uk; Newbury, *Privatization, Restructuring, and Regulation*, p. 225.
38. Winskel, 'When Systems Are Overthrown'.
39. Dan Corry (ed.), *Profiting from the Utilities: New Thinking on Regulatory Reform* (IPPR, 1995), p. 7.
40. Derek Spooner, 'The "Dash for Gas" in Electricity Generation in the UK', *Geography* 80, no. 4 (1995), pp. 393–406.
41. Winskel, 'When Systems Are Overthrown'.
42. Newbery, *Privatization, Restructuring, and Regulation*, p. 227; Winskel, 'When Systems Are Overthrown'.
43. Anna Creti and Fulvio Fontini, *Economics of Electricity: Markets, Competition and Rules* (Cambridge University Press, 2019), pp. 98–102.
44. Martin Chick, 'The 3 Rs: Regulation, Risk and Responsibility in British Utilities Since 1945', *Business History* 53, no. 5 (2011), pp. 747–60; Parker, *Official History of Privatisation*, vol. 2, pp. 297–9.
45. Helm, *Energy, the State, and the Market*, p. 164; Parker, *Official History of Privatisation*, vol. 2, pp. 261–90; Chick, 'The Power of Networks'.
46. Chick, 'The Power of Networks', p. 97; Chick and Nelles, 'Nationalisation and Privatisation', p. 290; Littlechild, *Privatization, Competition and Regulation*, pp. 16–18; Helm, *Energy, the State, and the Market*, pp. 130–9, 162–4.
47. David Currie, 'The New Electricity Trading Arrangements in England and Wales', Institute of Economic Affairs, 10 October 2000, iea.org.uk; Ofgem, 'New Electricity Trading Arrangements (NETA) – One Year Review', July 2002, ofgem.gov.uk.
48. Helm, *Energy, the State, and the Market*, pp. 9, 319–25; Michael Grubb and David Newbery, *UK Electricity Market Reform and the Energy Transition: Emerging Lessons*, EPRG/CEEPR Working Paper 2018-004 (MIT, 2018); *The New Electricity Trading Arrangements in England and Wales: Report by the Comptroller and Auditor General*, HC 624 (HM Stationery Office, 2003).

49. Newbery, *Privatization, Restructuring, and Regulation*, p. 3; Vickers and Yarrow, *Privatization: An Economic Analysis.*
50. Paul Carpenter and Carlos Lapuerta, 'A Critique of Light-Handed Regulation: The Case of British Gas', *Northwestern Journal of International Law and Business* 19, no. 3 (1999), pp. 9–10; Helm, *Energy, the State, and the Market*, p. 205.
51. Steven Law, 'Assessing the Averch-Johnson-Wellisz Effect for Regulated Utilities', *International Journal of Economics and Finance* 6, no. 8 (2014).
52. Edward E. Zajac, 'Note on "Gold Plating" or "Rate Base Padding"', *Bell Journal of Economics and Management Science* 3, no. 1 (Spring 1972), pp. 311–15; Charles Needy, 'The Gold-Plating Controversy: A Reconciliation', *Southern Economic Journal* 45, no. 2 (1978), pp. 576–82.
53. Parker, *Official History of Privatisation*, vol. 2, pp. 308–9; Helm, *Energy, the State, and the Market*, pp. 211–16.
54. Corry, *Profiting from the Utilities*, p. 2.
55. Vickers and Yarrow, *Privatization: An Economic Analysis*; Carpenter and Lapuerta, 'Critique of Light-Handed Regulation', p. 17.
56. Dieter Helm, 'Energy Network Regulation Failures and Net Zero', DHELM, 5 January 2023, dieterhelm.co.uk.
57. Office of Electricity Regulation (Offer), *Review of Public Electricity Suppliers 1998–2000, Distribution Price Control Review: Consultation Paper* (Offer, May 1999), pp. 78–86; Dieter Helm, 'The Cost of Capital, the Regulatory Asset Base and Risk', DHELM, 26 September 2023, dieterhelm.co.uk.
58. Meek, *Private Island*, p. 131; Helm, *Energy, the State, and the Market*, pp. 204–6.
59. A. Ghobadian et al., 'The US Takeover of the UK Electricity Supply Industry', *Journal of General Management* 24, no. 3 (1999), pp. 53–76; Helm, *Energy, the State, and the Market*, pp. 221–3.
60. Dieter Helm, 'Utility Regulation, the RAB and the Cost of Capital', lecture to the Competition Commission, May 2009, ofgem.gov.uk; Helm, *Energy, the State, and the Market*, pp. 230–1; Council of European Energy Regulators (CEER), *Report on Regulatory Frameworks for European Energy Networks 2023*, Ref,: C23-IRB-70-03d (CEER, 2024); Armstrong, Cowan and Vickers, *Regulatory Reform*, p. 193.
61. Parker, *Official History of Privatisation*, vol. 2, pp. 271–5, 305–7, 507.

62. Littlechild, *Privatization, Competition and Regulation.*
63. Ofgas, *Annual Report, 1993* (HMSO, 1993), pp. 7–8, gov.uk.
64. For example, Ofgem, 'Proposed Merger of National Grid Group Plc and Lattice Group Plc to Create National Grid Transco Plc: A Consultation Paper', May 2002, ofgem.gov.uk; Helm, *Energy, the State, and the Market*, pp. 235–43.
65. Helm, *Energy, the State, and the Market*, pp. 222–37; Redwood, *Public Enterprises in Crisis*, p. 76.
66. Corry, *Profiting from the Utilities*, pp. 5–6; Newbery, *Privatisation, Restructuring, and Regulation*, p. 151.
67. Leslie Hannah, 'A Failed Experiment: The State Ownership of Industry', in Roderick Floud and Paul Johnson (eds), *The Cambridge Economic History of Modern Britain*, vol. 3 (Cambridge University Press, 2004), pp. 84–111; Mary O'Mahony, *Britain's Productivity Performance 1950–1996: An International Perspective* (National Institute of Economic and Social Research, 1999).
68. Giuliano Garavini, 'Thatcher's North Sea: The Return of Cheap Oil and the "Neo-Liberalisation" of European Energy', *Contemporary European History* 33, no. 1 (2024), pp. 37–52.
69. Victor Ajayi et al., 'The Productivity Puzzle in Network Industries: Evidence from the Energy Sector', EPRD Working Paper 2021, July 2020; Robert Millward, *Private and Public Enterprise in Europe: Energy, Telecommunications and Transport, 1830–1990* (Cambridge University Press, 2005), pp. 276–8.
70. Florio, *The Great Divestiture*; Massimo Florio, *Network Industries and Social Welfare: The Experiment That Reshuffled European Utilities* (Oxford University Press, 2013); David Parker, 'The UK's Privatisation Experiment: The Passage of Time Permits a Sober Assessment', CESifo Working Paper 1126, February 2004; Parker, *Official History of Privatisation*, vol. 2, pp. 523–6; Dieter Helm, 'Time to Pull the Plug on the Water Privatisation Model', DHELM, 12 May 2023, dieterhelm.co.uk.
71. Vickers and Yarrow, *Privatization: An Economic Analysis*, p. 40; Florio, *The Great Divestiture*, p. 362.
72. I thank Dieter Helm for the reference.
73. Littlechild, *Privatization, Competition and Regulation*, pp. 22–6, 32–5.
74. Roger Fouquet, National Infrastructure Commission Historic Energy Dataset, nic.org.uk.
75. Florio, *Network Industries and Social Welfare*, p. 330.
76. Corry, *Profiting from the Utilities*, p. 6.

77. Danby, *Regulating Energy Utilities*, pp. 20–1, 39; Helm, *Energy, the State, and the Market*, pp. 274–5.
78. Corry, *Profiting from the Utilities*, pp. 3–4, 58; Ofgas, *Annual Report 1993*, pp. 34–5.
79. Littlechild, *Privatization, Competition and Regulation*, pp. 8–10; Corry, *Profiting from the Utilities*, pp. 39, 60; Ofgas, *Annual Report 1993*, pp. 8–9.
80. Ofgem, *Annual Report and Accounts, 2011–12* (TSO, 2012), p. 71; Ofgas, *Annual Report, 1993*, p. 37; Littlechild, *Privatization, Competition and Regulation*, p. 10.
81. Michael Moran, *The British Regulatory State: High Modernism and Hyper-Innovation* (Oxford University Press, 2003); Littlechild, *Privatization, Competition and Regulation*, pp. 30–1.
82. Florio, *The Great Divestiture*; Mike Toms, 'The Thatcher Privatisation Legacy: Not Quite What She Planned?', *Oxera Agenda*, May 2013.
83. Parker, *Official History of Privatisation*, vol. 1, pp. 447–9, and vol. 2, pp. 510–22.
84. Parker, *Official History of Privatisation*, vol. 2; Florio, *The Great Divestiture*, pp. 346, 363, 197.
85. Ed Crooks, 'The Watchdog Who Should Have Barked Louder', *Financial Times*, 19 September 2008.
86. Meek, *Private Island*, pp. 135–9.
87. James Meek, 'Power from the People: What Privatisation Has Meant for Britain', *Financial Times*, 12 September 2014.
88. See the introduction.
89. Helm, *Energy, the State, and the Market*, p. 282.
90. Brett Christophers, *Our Lives in Their Portfolios: Why Asset Managers Own the World* (Verso, 2023), p. 241.
91. Parker, *Official History of Privatisation*, vol. 1, p. 448; Steve Thomas, 'Electricity Liberalisation: The Beginning of the End', research commissioned by Public Services International for the World Energy Council Congress, September 2004; Vivien Foster et al., 'Charting the Diffusion of Power Sector Reforms Across the Developing World', Policy Research Working Paper 8235, November 2017.

5. The Idea of an Energy Revolution, 1988–2010

1. Paul Warde, Libby Robin and Sverker Sörlin, *The Environment: A History of the Idea* (Johns Hopkins University Press, 2018), p. 115; Nathaniel Rich, *Losing Earth: The Decade We Could Have Stopped Climate Change* (Picador, 2020).

2. Margaret Thatcher, 'Speech to the Royal Society (Climate Change)', 27 September 1988, margaretthatcher.org; Dieter Helm, *Energy, the State, and the Market: British Energy Policy Since 1979* (Oxford University Press, 2003), p. 346.
3. Margaret Thatcher, 'Speech to United Nations General Assembly (Global Environment)', 8 November 1989, margaretthatcher.org.
4. Jean-Baptiste Fressoz, *More and More and More: An All-Consuming History of Energy* (Allen Lane, 2024), p. 211.
5. Helm, *Energy, the State, and the Market*, p. 277; Callum McCarthy, 'Lessons of Energy Regulation', *European Review of Energy Markets* 3, no. 3 (2009); David Parker, *The Official History of Privatisation*, vol. 2, *Popular Capitalism, 1987–1997* (Routledge, 2012), pp. 323–5.
6. Helm, *Energy, the State, and the Market*, pp. 350–3.
7. Dan Corry (ed.), *Profiting from the Utilities: New Thinking on Regulatory Reform* (IPPR, 1995), pp. 2–4.
8. Helm, *Energy, the State, and the Market*, pp. 355–63; Dieter Helm, *Net Zero: How We Stop Causing Climate Change* (William Collins, 2020), p. 71; Simon Taylor, *The Fall and Rise of Nuclear Power in Britain: A History* (Bloomsbury Sigma, 2016), p. 55.
9. McCarthy, 'Lessons of Energy Regulation'; Helm, *Energy, the State, and the Market*, p. 364.
10. DTI, *Our Energy Future: Creating a Low Carbon Economy*, Energy White Paper, Cm5761 (HM Stationery Office, 2003); Helm, *Energy, the State, and the Market*, pp. 400–21.
11. McCarthy, 'Lessons from Energy Regulation', pp. 3–4.
12. Helm, *Energy, the State, and the Market*, p. 280.
13. Helm, *Net Zero*, pp. x, 51, 74–5.
14. Martin Wolf, 'Market Forces Are Not Enough to Halt Climate Change', *Financial Times*, 2 July 2024.
15. Avner Offer, *Understanding the Private-Public Divide: Markets, Governments, and Time Horizons* (Cambridge University Press, 2022), pp. 147–8.
16. Andreas Malm and Wim Carton, *Overshoot: How the World Surrendered to Climate Breakdown* (Verso, 2024), pp. 56–7.
17. Fressoz, *More and More*, p. 187; Warde, Robin and Sörlin, *The Environment*, pp. 151–63.
18. Offer, *Understanding the Private-Public Divide*, p. 161.
19. Robert Pindyck, 'Climate Change Policy: What Do the Models Tell Us?', *Journal of Economic Literature* 51, no. 3 (2013), pp. 860–72.

20. Kevin Anderson, 'Climate-Policy Models Debates: Wrong Tools for the Job', *Nature* 573 (19 September 2019).
21. Offer, *Understanding the Private-Public Divide*, pp. 159–67.
22. Nicholas Stern and Joseph Stiglitz, 'Climate Change and Growth', *Industrial and Corporate Change* 32 (2023), p. 278.
23. Tyler Cowen and Derek Parfit, 'Against the Social Discount Rate', in Peter Laslett and James S. Fishkin (eds), *Justice Between Age Groups and Generations* (Yale University Press, 1992); Derek Parfit, 'Energy Policy and the Further Future: The Identity Problem', in Stephen M. Gardiner et al. (eds), *Climate Ethics: Essential Reading* (Oxford University Press, 2020), pp. 112–21.
24. Martin Chick, *Changing Times: Economics, Policies, and Resource Allocation in Britain Since 1951* (Oxford University Press, 2020), pp. 20–2.
25. Malm and Carton, *Overshoot*, pp. viii, 58–68, 83, 146; Fressoz, *More and More*, p. 206.
26. Robert Gross and Phil Heptonstall, 'Time to Stop Experimenting with UK Renewable Energy Policy', ICEPT Working Paper, October 2010.
27. Committee on Climate Change, *Building a Low-Carbon Economy: The UK's Contribution to Tackling Climate Change* (Stationery Office, 2008), pp. xiii, xv, 40–60; Taylor, *Fall and Rise of Nuclear Power*, p. 126.
28. Office of Gas and Electricity Markets (Ofgem), 'Plan and Budget: April 2000–March 2001', 16 March 2001, ofgem.gov.uk.
29. Ofgem, *Annual Report 2005–06* (TSO, 2006).
30. Ofgem, *Overview of Ofgem Annual Report 2010–11* (Ofgem, 2011).
31. Ofgem, 'Project Discovery: Options for Delivering Secure and Sustainable Energy Supplies', 3 February 2010, ofgem.gov.uk.
32. Nicholas Stern, *Why Are We Waiting?: The Logic, Urgency, and Promise of Tackling Climate Change* (MIT Press, 2015), pp. 33–6.
33. Jean-Baptiste Fressoz, 'In Tech We Trust: A History of Technophilia in the Intergovernmental Panel on Climate Change's (IPCC) Climate Mitigation Expertise', *Energy Research and Social Science* 127 (2025), p. 1.
34. Gross and Heptonstall, 'Time to Stop Experimenting', pp. 4–5.
35. Stern, *Why Are We Waiting?*, p. 33; Helm, *Net Zero*, p. 125.
36. *Building on Progress: Energy and the Environment*, HM Government Policy Review (2007).
37. Stern and Stiglitz, 'Climate Change and Growth', p. 297.
38. Stern, *Why Are We Waiting?*, p. 37.

39. Helm, *Net Zero*, p. 49.
40. Taylor, *Fall and Rise of Nuclear Power*, p. 104.
41. Malm and Carton, *Overshoot*, p. 47; Kevin Anderson and Jessica Jewell, 'Debating the Bedrock of Climate Change Mitigation Scenarios', *Nature*, 16 September 2019.
42. J.P. Morgan, 'Risky Business: The Climate and the Macroeconomy', Economic Research, Special Report, 14 January 2020.
43. Malm and Carton, *Overshoot*, pp. 47–8.
44. *Building on Progress*; Department of Energy and Climate Change (DECC), *Planning Our Electric Future: A White Paper for Secure, Affordable and Low-Carbon Electricity*, Cm8099 (Stationery Office, 2011).
45. Gross and Heptonstall, 'Time to Stop Experimenting'.
46. Stern, *Why Are We Waiting?*, pp. 67, 76, 82, 99.
47. Wolf, 'Market Forces Are Not Enough'; Stern and Stiglitz, 'Climate Change and Growth'.

6. Zombie Privatisation, 2010–2024

1. 'Britain's Overstretched Electricity Grid Is Delaying Housing Projects', *Economist*, 14 June 2022.
2. Energy System Operator (ESO), Future Energy Scenarios reports, 2022–24, available at neso.energy; NESO, Transmission Entry Capacity Register reports, 2020–25, available at neso.energy.
3. 'King's Speech 2023: Energy Security and Net Zero', House of Lords Library, 1 November 2023, lordslibrary.parliament.uk.
4. ESO, 'GB Connections Reform: Update on Implementation of Reformed Connections Processes', April 2024; George Anstey and Giovanni Raiteri, *Nothing More British than a Queue: NESO's Plan for Electricity Connections in Great Britain* (NERA, 2025).
5. Dieter Helm (ed.), *The New Energy Paradigm* (Oxford University Press, 2007), pp. 1–8, 9–35.
6. Andreas Goldthau, 'From State to the Market and Back: Policy Implications of Changing Energy Paradigms', *Global Policy* 3, no. 2 (2012), pp. 198–210.
7. Dominique Finon, 'Electricity: From a Market Regime to a Hybrid Regime', *Encyclopédie de l'énergie*, July 2021.
8. Emmanuelle Matthieu and Jose Maria Valenzuela, 'New Interventionism: The Re-Politicisation of Electricity Governance with Renewable Energy Policies in the UK, Mexico and Morocco', *Journal of European Public Policy* 32, no. 6 (2025).

9. Elizabeth Chatterjee, 'Underpowered: Electricity Policy and the State in India, 1991–2014', DPhil thesis (Oxford University, 2015).
10. Hannah Ritchie and Pablo Rosado, 'Electricity Mix', Our World in Data, 2020; Committee on Climate Change, *Building a Low-Carbon Economy: The UK's Contribution to Tackling Climate Change* (HM Stationery Office, 2008), pp. 195–6.
11. Department of Energy and Climate Change, *Planning Our Electric Future: A White Paper for Secure, Affordable and Low-Carbon Electricity*, Cm8099 (HM Stationery Office, 2011).
12. Department for Business, Energy and Industrial Strategy (BEIS), *Review of Electricity Market Arrangements: Consultation Document* (BEIS, 2022), p. 24.
13. Ibid., pp. 23–4.
14. Dieter Helm, 'The Systems Regulation Model', DHELM, 12 February 2019, dieterhelm.co.uk; Dieter Helm, *Cost of Energy Review* (2017), p. 90.
15. BVG Associates, 'After AR5, Where Next for the UK CfD?', 8 September 2023.
16. Emmanuelle Mathieu and Jose Maria Valenzuela, 'The Governance of Renewable Energy Auctions: A Multidimensional Comparative Policy Analysis', *Journal of Comparative Policy Analysis: Research and Practice* 27, no. 1 (2025), pp. 39–61; BEIS, *Review of Electricity Market Arrangements*, p. 14.
17. Adam Bell, 'The Ghost at the Feast', *Unbalancing Mechanism*, Substack, 5 September 2025.
18. Dieter Helm, 'Energy Network Regulation Failures and Net Zero', DHELM, 5 January 2023, dieterhelm.co.uk; Colin Robinson, 'Energy Policy: The Return of the Regulatory State', *Economic Affairs* 36, no. 1 (2016), pp. 33–47; Dieter Helm, *Net Zero: How We Stop Causing Climate Change* (William Collins, 2020), p. 219; Stephen Littlechild, '10/09/14 – Stephen Littlechild, Former Director General of Electricity Supply', presentation, All Party Parliamentary Group on Energy Costs, 10 September 2014, ecappg.org; Colin Robinson, 'Regno Unito: Il ritorno della pianificazione energetica', *Energia* 1 (2014).
19. SSE Renewables, 'Outcome of Danish Offshore Wind Project Tender', 1 December 2021, sserenewables.com; Simon Evans, 'Q&A: What Does "Subsidy-Free" Renewables Actually Mean?', *Carbon Brief*, 27 March 2018; Department of Energy and Climate Change, *Electricity Market Reform: Delivering UK Investment*, Cm8674 (HM Stationery Office, 2013), p. 9; Brett Christophers,

The Price Is Wrong: Why Capitalism Won't Save the Planet (Verso, 2024), p. 188.

20. BVG Associates, 'After AR5'.
21. Tracy London, 'Don't Let AR6 Trick You into Thinking Offshore Wind Is "Back on Track"', *Utility Week*, 24 October 2024.
22. Jan Emlemsvåg, 'Rethinking the "Levelized Cost of Energy": A Critical Review and Evaluation of the Concert', *Energy Research and Social Science* 119 (January 2025); Christophers, *The Price Is Wrong*, p. 141.
23. CEPA, 'Hurdle Rate Estimates for Electricity Sector Technologies, DESNZ, 30 July 2025', gov.uk; Christophers, *The Price Is Wrong*, p. 215.
24. Bain & Company, *Energy and Natural Resources Report 2023* (Bain & Company, 2023); Tom Brijs et al., *The Five Forces Transforming Power Markets* (Boston Consulting Group, 2024); International Energy Agency, *Renewables 2024: Analysis and Forecast to 2030* (IEA, 2024), p. 70.
25. Travis Bradford et al., *Financing Solar and Wind Power: Insights from Oil and Gas* (Center on Global Energy Policy, Columbia SIPA, 2017).
26. Department of Energy and Climate Change (DECC), 'Impact Assessment of the Transmission Constraint Licence Condition (TCLC)', IA No. DECC0045, December 2011; ESO, 'Balancing Costs: Annual Report and Future Projections, Technical Report', May 2024; FTI Consulting, 'Assessment of Likely Impacts of Proposed Reforms to the Balancing Mechanism Within a National Price Regime', Report for Octopus Energy, September 2024.
27. Thanks to Robin Hawkes for this analysis.
28. Florian Kern et al., 'From Laggard to Leader: Explaining Offshore Wind Developments in the UK', *Energy Policy* 69 (June 2014), pp. 635–46.
29. BEIS, *Review of Electricity Market Arrangements*, p. 43.
30. CCC, *Building a Low-Carbon Economy*, p. xix; Simon Taylor, *The Fall and Rise of Nuclear Power in Britain: A History* (Bloomsbury Sigma, 2016), p. 81.
31. 'EDF Acquires British Energy', *Financial Times*, 24 September 2008; 'Centrica Pulls Out of New UK Nuclear Projects', BBC, 4 February 2013; Tim Stone, 'Why Britain Does Not Have a Nuclear Fleet to Rival France', *Telegraph*, 27 September 2022; EDF, '2008 Results', 12 February 2009.

32. Stone, 'Why Britain Does Not Have a Nuclear Fleet'; Taylor, *Fall and Rise of Nuclear Power*, p. 129; HM Treasury and Infrastructure UK, 'National Infrastructure Plan 2010', October 2010.
33. M. V. Ramana, *Nuclear Is Not the Solution: The Folly of Atomic Power in the Age of Climate Change* (Verso, 2024), pp. 138–42; Taylor, *Fall and Rise of Nuclear Power*, pp. 160–73.
34. Ramana, *Nuclear Is Not the Solution*, p. 142; Taylor, *Fall and Rise of Nuclear Power*, pp. 2, 190.
35. Institute for Energy Economics and Financial Analysis, 'European Pressurized Reactors: Nuclear Power's Latest Costly and Delayed Disappointments', 2 February 2023; Adam Savage, 'Overbudget: Inside Britain's $57 Billion Nuclear Nightmare', *Bim*, 8 January 2025; Neil Gerrard, 'Hinkley Point C Nuclear Plant Costs Could Rise to £46 Billion, Delayed to End of Decade', *Construction Briefing*, 24 January 2024.
36. Ramana, *Nuclear Is Not the Solution*, pp. 131–3.
37. Stone, 'Why Britain Does Not Have a Nuclear Fleet'.
38. NESO, Future Energy Scenarios reports for 2011, 2016, 2024, available at neso.energy; Andrea Bacilieri, Richard Black and Rupert Way, 'Assessing the Relative Costs of High-CCS and Low-CCS Pathways to 1.5 Degrees', Oxford Smith School of Enterprise and the Environment Working Paper 23-08, 4 December 2023.
39. House of Commons, 'Science and Technology – First Report', Science and Technology Committee Publications, 2005–6, parliament.uk.
40. Michael Leibriech, 'Exploring Global Energy Transition Trends and Hydrogen', Energy Futures Lab Annual Lecture, Imperial College London, 13 June 2024.
41. Nicholas Earl, 'Shell Quits Major UK Carbon Capture Project – but Venture Insists Its Future Is Safe', *City AM*, 25 April 2023.
42. Amy Norman and Bertie Wnek, 'Fuelling Fairness: Five Years of the Energy Price Cap, Public First/Octopus Energy', February 2024; Stonehaven, 'Reinventing Retail Energy: Making the Energy Retail Market Fit for the Next Generation', Stonehaven, 28 September 2023.
43. Competition and Markets Authority, *Energy Market Investigation, Final Report* (CMA, 2016), p. 38.
44. Competition and Markets Authority, *Energy Market Investigation*; Stonehaven, 'Reinventing Retail Energy'; Norman and Wnek, 'Fuelling Fairness'.
45. Eileen C. Marshall and Colin Robinson, 'Ofgem Has Now Become a Creature of Government', *Financial Times*, 19 October 2012; 'Ex-Regulators' Letter to Nolan', *Utility Week*, 26 June 2017.

46. Norman and Wnek, 'Fuelling Fairness'.
47. Ibid., p. 36.
48. Dieter Helm, *Energy, the State, and the Market: British Energy Policy Since 1979* (Oxford University Press, 2003), pp. 330–44; Ofgem, 'RIIO: A New Way to Regulate Energy Networks', *Factsheet* 93, 4 October 2010.
49. National Grid Electricity Transmission, 'Network Asset Risk Metric (NARM) Methodology', November 2022; Western Power Distribution (WPD), *Our Business Plan 2023–2028, First Draft, January 2021* (WPD, 2021), pp. 82–4.
50. Ofgem, 'RIIO-ET1 Annual Report, 2020–21', 28 September 2022.
51. Common Wealth, 'Missing Money in UK Energy Networks', 6 May 2025.
52. Joe Perkins, 'The Future of Network Investment', Energy Policy Research Group Spring Seminar, University of Cambridge, 17 May 2024.
53. European Union Agency for the Cooperation of Energy Regulators (ACER) and Council of European Energy Regulators (CEER), *Energy Retail and Consumer Protection: 2023 Market Monitoring Report* (ACER-CEER, 2023).
54. Helm, 'Energy Network Regulation Failures'.
55. Office of Electricity Regulation (Offer), *Review of Public Electricity Suppliers 1998–2000, Distribution Price Control Review: Consultation Paper* (Offer, May 1999), p. 82.
56. Maxine Frerk, 'Understanding Asset Lives – Save Now, Pay Later? A Key Issue for Ofgem in the ED2 Business Plans', Grid Edge Policy, January 2022, ofgem.gov.uk; Energy Networks Association, 'ENA Response to Ofgem RIIO-ED3 Framework Consultation', 15 January 2025, pp. 25–9.
57. Martin Wolf, 'Britain's Utility Model Is Broken', *Financial Times*, 13 June 2008; Dieter Helm, James Wardlaw and Ben Caldecott, *Delivering a 21st Century Infrastructure for Britain* (Policy Exchange, 2009).
58. Vivien Foster et al., 'Charting the Diffusion of Power Sector Reforms Across the Developing World', Policy Research Working Paper 8235, November 2017.
59. Alban Kacher, 'TenneT Launches Potential Sale of German Grid Operation', Reuters, 11 March 2025.
60. Rebecca Willis et al., 'Getting Energy Governance Right: Lessons from IGov', Engineering and Physical Sciences Research Council, 12 September 2019, p. 2.

61. National Energy System Operator (NESO), 'ESO Announces the Name of the Forthcoming Future System Operator', 22 January 2024, neso.energy.
62. Christopher Hinton and William Holford, 'Power Production and Transmission in the Countryside: Preserving Amenities', *Journal of the Royal Society of Arts* 108, no. 5043 (February 1960).
63. Department for Business, Energy and Industrial Strategy and Ofgem, *Future System Operator: Government and Ofgem's Response to Consultation* (BEIS and Ofgem, 2022); italics mine.
64. Jose Maria Valenzuela and John Rhys, 'In Plain Sight: The Rise of State Coordination and Fall of Liberalised Markets in the United Kingdom Power Sector', *Energy Research and Social Science* 94 (December 2022).
65. Richard Lowes, 'GB Energy as a Vehicle to Coordinate the Energy Transition and Clean Up Heating', Dr Richard Lowes blog, 4 June 2024, richardlowes.com.
66. Rob Horgan, 'Ofgem Concerned by NESO's Overreliance on External Consultants', *Utility Week*, 9 September 2025.
67. Stonehaven, 'Rethinking Energy Network Regulation: Kickstarting a Debate on How We Deliver the Energy Infrastructure of the Future', Stonehaven, 2024.
68. Ofgem, 'Decision: Future of Local Energy Institutions and Governance', 15 November 2023; Maxine Frerk, 'ED3: Three Cheers and a Few Question Marks', *Utility Week*, 25 November 2024; James Wallin, 'RESPs Risk Creating "Parallel Universe" for Local Energy Planning', *Utility Week*, 4 July 2024.
69. Richard Howard, *Governing Power: Improving the Administration of the Energy Industry in Great Britain* (Policy Exchange, 2015); Helm, Wardlaw and Caldecott, *Delivering a 21st Century Infrastructure*.
70. Electricity System Provider, *Annual Report 2019/20* (National Grid ESO, 2020), p. 77; NESO, *Annual Report 2025* (NESO, 2025), p. 199; Ofgem, *Resource Accounts 2002–03 HC 789* (Stationery Office, 2003); Ofgem, *Annual Report and Accounts 2021–22 HC489* (HM Stationery Office, 2022); Tom Grimwood, 'ESO Sees Drop in Performance Scores', *Utility Week*, 3 September 2024.
71. Tom Grimwood, 'Shift to Central Planning Will Give Rise to "Lobbying Efforts" by Developers', *Utility Week*, 5 August 2025; Ofgem, 'Code Governance Review: Final Proposals', 31 March 2010, Ref.: 43/10; Ofgem, 'Grid Code GC0071: Code Governance

Review (Phase 2) – Significant Code Review', 18 October 2013; Howard, *Governing Power*, p. 14.

72. Ofgem, 'Access and Forward-Looking Charges Significant Code Review: Final Decision', 3 May 2022; Stonehaven, 'Rethinking Energy Network Regulation', p. 21; Ofgem, 'Consultation on Frameworks for Future Systems and Network Regulation: Enabling an Energy System for the Future', 10 March 2023.
73. Department for Energy Security and Net Zero (DESNZ), *Review of Electricity Market Arrangements: Options Assessment* (DESNZ, 2024).
74. Rob Horgan, 'Winser: Community Benefits Could Be Extended to Distribution Assets', *Utility Week*, 22 October 2024; David Blackman, 'Government Goes "Back to the Drawing Board" on Pounds for Pylons', *Utility Week*, 26 September 2024.
75. David Blackman, 'Moving Energy Levies on to Taxation Could Cost £5.9 Billion', *Utility Week*, 6 December 2024.
76. Willis et al., 'Getting Energy Governance Right'; Guy Newey, 'Governance for Net Zero: Boring, but Important', *Medium*, 24 June 2024.
77. Jillian Ambrose, 'Is Europe's Energy Crisis Over? Falling Gas Prices Conceal Wider Problems', *Guardian*, 4 April 2024.
78. Ofgem, 'Our Powers and Duties', 19 July 2013, ofgem.gov.uk; Michael G. Pollitt et al., 'Recommendations for a Future-Proof Electricity Market Design in Europe in Light of the 2021–2023 Energy Crisis', *Energy Policy* 188 (May 2024).
79. Alex Lawson, 'British Gas Owner Signs Deal with Norway Firm for Extra UK Supplies', *Guardian*, 16 June 2022.
80. 'Greg Jackson on BBC Radio 4 The Today Programme', Octopus Energy blog, 10 August 2022, octopus.energy.
81. National Gas Transmission, *Gas Winter Outlook, 2021/22* (National Grid House, 2021), p. 2.
82. *Guy Martin's Great British Power Trip*, episodes 1–3, Channel 4, 12 February 2023.
83. Becky Morton, 'Martin Lewis: Energy Bill Crisis on Scale of Pandemic', BBC, 10 August 2022.
84. Pollitt et al., 'Recommendations for a Future-Proof Electricity'.
85. 'UK Warned It Faces "Security Premium" for Long-Term Gas Supplies', *Financial Times*, 4 October 2022.
86. Pollitt et al., 'Recommendations for a Future-Proof Electricity'.
87. Christophers, *The Price Is Wrong*, p. 323.
88. DESNZ, 'UK Halfway to Net Zero', press release, 28 March 2024; Helm, *Net Zero*, p. 7.

89. Hannah Ritchie, 'How Do CO_2 Emissions Compare When We Adjust for Trade?', Our World in Data, 7 October 2019; Simon Evans and Verner Viisainen, 'Analysis: UK Electricity from Fossil Fuels Drops to Lowest Level Since 1957', Carbon Brief, 3 January 2024.
90. Ofgem, 'Large Legacy Suppliers: Domestic Dual Fuel Bill Breakdown over Time', Data Portal, ofgem.gov.uk.
91. Roger Fouquet, 'National Infrastructure Commission Historic Energy Dataset', nic.org.uk.
92. 'Is Britain's Net-Zero Push to Blame for Its High Energy Prices?', *Economist*, 31 July 2025.
93. Lauren Orso, Madeleine Gabriel and Elysia Lucas, 'For the First Time, UK Household Electricity Prices Rose to Levels Higher than Those in Any EU Country', Nesta blog, 20 June 2024; International Energy Agency, Energy Price package.
94. CCC, *Progress in Reducing Emissions: 2024 Report to Parliament* (Climate Change Committee, 2024).
95. Ibid.
96. Ibid.
97. Jonathan Marshall and Emily Fry, *Electric Dreams: How Can We Decarbonise Electricity Without Disadvantaging Poor Families?* (Resolution Foundation, 2024); Ana Barillas, 'Charging Ahead: The Grid Challenge in Europe's Pursuit of Net Zero', keynote address, Aurora Energy Spring Forum 2024.
98. See the introduction.
99. Adam John, 'Weekend Press', *Utility Week*, 13 January 2025.
100. Tom Grimwood, 'Weekend Press', *Utility Week*, 6 January 2025.
101. William Davies, *The Limits of Neoliberalism: Authority, Sovereignty and the Logic of Competition*, rev. ed. (Sage, 2016), p. 187; Mariana Mazzucato and Dani Rodrik, 'Industrial Policy with Conditionalities: A Taxonomy and Sample Cases', UCL Institute for Innovation and Public Purpose (IIPP) Working Paper 2023–07, 2023.
102. Abby Innes, *Late Soviet Britain: Why Materialist Utopias Fail* (Cambridge University Press, 2023), p. 116.
103. Daniel Bell, *The Cultural Contradictions of Capitalism* (Perseus, 1978), p. 25. Interpretation of this quotation in James Meek, *Private Island: Why Britain Now Belongs to Someone Else* (Verso, 2015), p. 13.
104. Christophers, *The Price Is Wrong*, p. 303.
105. Mike Cooley, *Delinquent Genius: The Strange Affair of Man and His Technology* (Spokesman Books, 2018).

7. The Future of British Energy

1. Danny Lawrence and Helen Lawrence, *Growing Up with Gas: A History of the Gas Industry* (Brewin Books, 2023), pp. 121–41, 270–2.
2. Brett Christophers, 'Author's Response', in 'Book Review Forum: Brett Christophers' "The Price Is Wrong: Why Capitalism Won't Save the Planet"', *Antipode*, 11 April 2025.
3. Ralph Miliband, *The State in Capitalist Society* (Basic Books, 1969).
4. Jamie Merchant, *Endgame: Economic Nationalism and Global Decline* (Reaktion Books, 2024); Michael Froman, 'China Has Already Remade the International System', *Foreign Affairs*, 25 March 2025.
5. Defined as Great Britain generating enough power to meet 95 per cent of total annual electricity demand from 'clean' sources (wind, solar, nuclear, biomass, etc.), with 5 per cent coming from unabated gas supply.
6. Aurora Energy Research, 'Pathways and Challenges to Decarbonise the GB Power Sector', Policy Exchange, March 2024, policyexchange.org.uk; UK Government, 'Clean Power 2030 Action Plan: A New Era of Clean Electricity', 13 December 2024.
7. National Energy System Operator (NESO), *Clean Power 2030: Advice on Achieving Clean Power for Great Britain by 2030* (NESO, 2024), pp. 63–7; NESO, 'Future Energy Scenarios: ESO Pathways to Net Zero', July 2024, ES07; National Infrastructure Commission, *The Second National Infrastructure Assessment* (2023), pp. 65–7.
8. Adam Bell, 'The New Electric Leviathan', *Politics Home*, 10 July 2024, politicshome.com.
9. Ofgem, 'Open Letter on the Reformed Regulatory Framework on Connections', 16 September 2024; Tom Grimwood, 'Zombie Projects Could Benefit from Connection Reforms', *Utility Week*, 10 December 2014.
10. See G. Fearn, 'The End of the Experiment? The Energy Crisis, Neoliberal Energy, and the Limits to a Socio-Ecological Fix', *Environment and Planning E: Nature and Space* 7, no. 1 (2023), pp. 212–33.
11. Kayleena Makortoff, 'I Was Frustrated: The Woman Who Told Labour It Didn't Need to Spend £28bn on Green Investment', *Guardian*, 27 August 2024.

12. 'BlackRock to Buy Global Infrastructure Partners for $12.5bn', *Financial Times*, 12 January 2024; Brett Christophers, *Our Lives in Their Portfolios: Why Asset Managers Own the World* (Verso, 2023), pp. 81–2, 125.
13. Jonathan Marshall and Emily Fry, *Electric Dreams: How Can We Decarbonise Electricity Without Disadvantaging Poor Families?* (Resolution Foundation, 2024).
14. Christophers, *Our Lives in Their Portfolios*, pp. 95–105; 'UK "Not Exciting" for Green Investors, Says Former Climate Adviser', *Financial Times*, 1 May 2024.
15. Ofgem, 'Onshore Competition in Electricity Transmission: Decision on the First Project to Be Competitively Tendered', 4 April 2025.
16. Ambrose Evans-Pritchard, 'Ed Miliband Shows Us How to Wreck Net Zero', *Telegraph*, 22 August 2025.
17. Gareth Fearns, 'Electricity Decarbonisation Targets and the Distribution Dilemma', *Energy Policy* 203 (2025), p. 6; David Blackman, 'Miliband's £22bn Carbon Capture Spree Is a Waste of Money, Warns Octopus Boss', *Utility Week*, 27 January 2025.
18. Department for Energy Security and Net Zero (DESNZ), 'Great British Energy Founding Statement', 25 July 2024.
19. Public First, *Great British Energy: From Pledge to Reality* (Public First, 2024); David Blackman, 'Narrow GBE Scope Will Limit Investment', *Utility Week*, 11 October 2024.
20. Christophers, *Our Lives in Their Portfolios*, p. 169; Ruth Williams, 'Losing Investors at PR24 Could Have Consequences Beyond Water', *Utility Week*, 12 September 2024; Ben Hargreaves and Rob Horgan, 'Overseas Investors Are "Spooked" by Thames Water Situation', *Utility Week*, 26 November 2024.
21. Daniela Gabor, 'The Wall Street Consensus', *Development and Change* 52 (2021), pp. 429–59; Daniel Driscoll and Mark Blyth, 'Decarbonising National Growth Models: Derisking, "Hobbled States", and the Decarbonisation Possibility Frontier', *Review of International Political Economy* 32, no. 3 (2025), pp. 617–42.
22. Michele Crepaz and Ben Worthy, 'Cleaning Up UK Politics: What Would Better Lobbying Regulation Look Like?', *Parliamentary Affairs* 77, no. 3 (2024), pp. 435–49.
23. David Blackman, 'Stark Backtracks on Feasibility of 2030 Target', *Utility Week*, 19 September 2024; Abby Innes, *Late Soviet Britain: Why Materialist Utopias Fail* (Cambridge University Press, 2023), p. 47; David Blackman, 'Power Play: Who Will Call the Shots in Energy?', *Utility Week*, 10 September 2024; Kit Million Ross,

'Energy Minister Updates CP30 Solar Capacities', *Solar Power Portal*, 8 April 2025.

24. NESO, *Clean Power 2030*; Tom Grimwood, 'NESO Warns Balancing Costs Will Spike to £8bn Unless Controversial Grid Upgrades Are Accelerated', *Utility Week*, 12 June 2025.
25. Baringa, *UK Renewables Deployment Supply Chain Readiness Study* (DESNZ, 2024); Raoul Ruparel et al., 'Uplift in Demand, Shortfall in Supply: Can the UK Deliver on Its Infrastructure Investment Ambitions?', Boston Consulting Group, 27 February 2025, bcg.com.
26. Ofgem, 'Consultation on the ASTI ODI Penalty Exemption Period Request for Eastern Green-link 1 – EGL1', 10 April 2025; Baringa, *UK Renewables Deployment*, p. 22; Adam John, 'Transmission Operators Need to Stop Viewing Each Other as Competitors', *Utility Week*, 22 January 2025.
27. Adam John, 'SSEN Outlines over £22bn in RIIO3 Transmission Spend', *Utility Week*, 10 December 2024; James Wallin, 'Cadent: Ofgem Is Pushing Up Bills by Paying Us Back Quicker', *Utility Week*, 18 December 2024.
28. Niamh O. Regen and Jamie Gollings, *Whose Energy Transition Is It Anyway? The Case of Clean Heat* (Social Market Foundation, 2024), smf.co.uk.
29. Barry Eichengreen, 'Explaining Britain's Economic Performance: A Critical Note', *Economic Journal* 106, no. 434 (1996), pp. 213–18.
30. Jose Maria Valenzuela and Nacxitl Calva, 'Beyond Derisking', *Economic Sociology* 26, no. 2 (2025).
31. Yuen Yuen Ang, *How China Escaped the Poverty Trap* (Cornell University Press, 2016).
32. Dan Davies, *The Unaccountability Machine: Why Big Systems Make Terrible Decisions – and How the World Lost Its Mind* (Profile, 2024).
33. Thomas Aubrey and Con Keating, 'A 10 Year Infrastructure Strategy? Or Financial Engineering to Reboot PFI/PPP with Limited Impact?', Long Finance, 4 July 2025, longfinance.net.
34. 'Vitol: The Secretive Trading Giant Minting Fortunes for Its Employees', *Financial Times*, 3 September 2025.
35. Adam Khan, Chris Heyes and Mathew Lawrence, 'Nationalise Gas to Lower Bills: How a Public Strategic Reserve Can Lower Costs and Enhance Energy Security', Common Wealth, 27 April 2025, common-wealth.org.

36. Jack Richardson, 'Britain's Gas Dependency: A Growing Vulnerability', Council on Geostrategy, April 2025, geostrategy.org.uk.
37. Donal Brown, Will Walker and Mathew Lawrence, 'A Local Power Plan That Works for Communities', Common Wealth, August 2025, common-wealth.org.
38. F. A. Hayek, 'The Use of Knowledge in Society', *American Economic Review* 35, no. 4 (1945), pp. 519–30.
39. Tom Brown, Fabian Neumann and Iegor Riepin, 'Price Formation Without Fuel Costs: The Interaction of Demand Elasticity with Storage Bidding', *Energy Economics* 147 (June 2025), pp. 1–15.